Antique Trader®
VINTAGE
MAGAZINES
PRICE GUIDE

Richard Russell and
Elaine Gross Russell

©2005 Richard Russell and Elaine Gross Russell
Published by

kp books
An Imprint of F+W Publications

700 East State Street • Iola, WI 54990-0001
715-445-2214 • 888-457-2873

Our toll-free number to place an order or obtain
a free catalog is (800) 258-0929.

Library of Congress Catalog Number: 2004098992

ISBN: 0-89689-156-9

Designed by Jon Stein
Edited by Dennis Thornton

Printed in Canada

Contents

Part Three: Magazine History and Price Guide

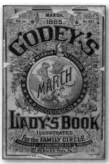

Dedication

To:
Heather, Laurel and Scott, who were always taught to reach for the stars.

Acknowledgments

We would like to thank the following experts for their contributions and scholarship:

Andreas Deja, Senior Animator, for the Walt Disney Feature Animation Studios (article on page 81). Deja is an expert on illustrator T.S. Sullivant. He has also graciously shared his personal collection of T.S. Sullivant's art. His work can be seen in such Disney classics as "Who Framed Roger Rabbit?" "The Lion King" and "Lilo & Stitch." He is currently working on a new Bambi feature.

William Stout, an Animalier who specializes in Pre-Historic and Fantasy Art, is an expert on the work of illustrator Joseph Clement Coll (page 59). The fantastic worlds of William Stout can be seen at: www.williamstout.com.

Dr. Harry Poe, President of the Poe Museum in Richmond, for his scholarly advice. The Poe Museum is located at 1914 East Main St., Richmond, VA 23223. The museum Web site is at: www.poemuseum.org.

W. Dale Horst for his entry on artist Frederick Stuart Church (page 57). Horst and his wife Rose Marie Horst have probably one of the most extensive collections of the illustration and print work of Frederick Stuart Church.

Peter Leeflang of the Berton Braley Cyber Museum, which is devoted to the works of Berton Braley (page 52). The Web address is: www.bertonbraley.com.

Susanne George Bloomfield, professor of English at the University of Nebraska at Kearney, is the author of three biography/collections of turn-of-the-century writers published by the University of Nebraska Press: *The Adventures of The Woman Homesteader: The Life and Letters of Elinore Pruitt Stewart (1993), Kate M. Cleary: A Literary Biography with Selected Works (1997),* and *Impertinences: Selected Writings of Elia W. Peattie, A Journalist in the Gilded Age (2005).* For more information: www.unk.edu/acad/english/faculty/bloomfields. (See articles on pages 57 and 73.)

Randall Stock has published in a number of Sherlockian periodicals including the **Baker Street Journal**. He has personally examined seven of the 27 recorded copies of **Beeton's Christmas Annual** 1887. His Web site with material on **Beeton's** and on Conan Doyle manuscripts is: http://members.aol.com/shbest

Karen Schwartz, a Reference Librarian in the Art Department of the Free Library of Philadelphia, for her guidance and help with the obscure and contradictory in the myriad world of vintage magazines.

Introduction

By Elaine Gross Russell

I started selling magazines from the stock of a disgruntled bookseller. He wanted to toss them. I won.

My fascination began with several boxes of **The Strand Magazine** more than 30 years ago. It wasn't just seeing the first appearance of Sherlock Holmes that got me hooked. Rather, it was seeing Victorian articles such as "Muzzles for Women" and other satirical commentary that I found fascinating. There was a wonderful British bookseller, Gaby Goldscheider, who was an expert on Sir Arthur Conan Doyle. About every six months, Gaby would issue a catalogue, which included **The Strand Magazine**. I remember calling and waking her up in England in the middle of the night worried that all the magazines had already been sold out of her catalogue.

The proliferation of the Internet has made collecting vintage magazines an instant worldwide phenomenon. Nowadays, a great magazine is only a mouse-click away. Magazines are sold online by the novice clearing out grandmother's attic as well as the seasoned booksellers trying to make space in their store. There are very few stores per se that specialize in vintage magazines, so one has to hunt creatively. Antique malls, flea markets, estate and yard sales all have magazines for sale. There are bargains to be had as well as rip-offs, especially on the various Internet venues. I have personally found that Antiquarian booksellers are the best sources. Magazines are difficult to handle in a store even when wrapped in a plastic sleeve. Therefore, a bookseller is grateful to see them go out the door.

The secrets of buying vintage magazines, however, are knowledge and research. The more I have learned, the easier it has been to spot a valuable magazine in the middle of a pile of old paper. If the writing of this book had occurred several years ago, I would have been rich from all of the great magazines I should have bought. (Although, admittedly a bookseller did simply give me a **Godey's** with Poe's "The Visionary" because he thought it was a worthless mess.) While there are several scholarly tomes on magazines in the local public library, there has been no comprehensive popular price guide to date. There are specific guides, especially on illustrators such as Norman Rockwell and Maxfield Parrish. But, for the most part, material such as all-important issue dates can only be found in various author/ illustrator bibliographies, many of which are privately printed, and on certain specialty Internet sites. Ultimately, the best source is the magazine itself, since a lot of information available can be erroneous or incomplete. Even the various experts who have graciously shared their knowledge for this book have been surprised by some previously unknown magazine appearances. Therefore, I have learned to only trust the magazine and, most importantly, make sure it is a complete copy. Even an incomplete copy of the most expensive magazine in the world, **Beeton's Christmas Annual** of 1887, has sold for more than $15,000. The last complete issue of it sold for $153,600 in fair condition; a fine copy today would be simply … priceless.

Now, if only some overcrowded bookseller would be kind enough to give me that issue….

By Rick Russell

It was all about a pile in the warehouse that was seemingly alive. Every time I'd look, it seemed to have grown a bit. It seems as a bookseller, you can't help but acquire magazines. Quite wonderful, fragile and, because they are often the first appearance of this, the first photo of that, and illustrated by … well, you get the idea. They get piled, somehow mate inside the pile and the pile keeps growing. They are difficult to deal with in a store, almost impossible for a scout, but nonetheless, fascinating and wonderful and nothing to put in a dumpster.

Well, fortunately, Elaine took an interest in my pile and started studying up on the market. In magazines, this proves to be a rather expensive proposition, however. Unlike books, for which several basic guides, numerous books of collecting lore and advice are available, vintage magazines have always lacked a simple popular guide. There are guides to artists, single titles, scholarly works that run to several volumes, but nothing basic, simple, in a nutshell. So, using my own book reference, *Antique Trader Book Collector's Price Guide*, as a guide, we set out to create a similar resource for vintage magazines. A dangerous little book actually. You could end up loving these little bits and pieces of disposable history, and that could become as obsessive and expensive as bibliomania. It has for us.

For those who may think that magazines are, somehow, below the scale of books as high ticket collectibles, I learned that on the weekend I finished up this book and started to pack it off to my editor a fair, and only fair, **Beeton's Annual** 1887 containing "Study In Scarlet" was auctioned at Sothebys for $153,600. The same sale also realized $63,000 for **Lippincott's Magazine** for February 1890 containing Conan Doyle's "Sign of the Four."

PART ONE:

Collecting Magazines

Why Magazines Are Collected

The disposable nature of magazines makes them a rarity. How many Maxfield Parrish covers have lined the bottom of birdcages or lit a warm fireplace? Unlike a book, there are a multitude of reasons to collect a vintage magazine: writer, illustrator and advertising.

For a lazy researcher, there is no controversy as to first edition. First appearances are in magazines, from Edgar Allan Poe to Jack London to Agatha Christie.

Most first appearances of the works of great authors were published in magazines. Many of these writers were also editors and publishers. Charles Dickens wrote and published **Household Words** with writer/editor Wilkie Collins in the 1850s. Edgar Allan Poe's first appearance in a magazine of national circulation was the anonymous publication of "The Visionary" in **Godey's Lady's Book** in January 1834. Poe was also an editor for **Graham's Magazine** where his first American detective story, "The Murders In The Rue Morgue," was published in April 1841. Poe's most famous poem, "The Raven," was published under the pseudonym of Quarles in **The American Review: A Whig Journal** in February 1845. Arguably, the world's most popular detective, Sherlock Holmes, made his first appearance in **Beeton's Christmas Annual** of 1887 in Arthur Conan Doyle's "A Study In Scarlet." However, it was the publication of "A Scandal in Bohemia" in **The Strand Magazine** in July of 1891 that made Sherlock Holmes a household name and boosted the circulation of **The Strand**. When Doyle "killed" off Holmes in "The Final Problem," **The Strand** and Doyle were besieged with upset and outraged readers. Doyle was "forced" to create the "return of Sherlock Holmes" in "The Empty House" and the rest is literary history.

Godey's Lady's Book was edited by Sarah J. Hale. Mrs. Hale was the original author of the poem "Mary Had A Little Lamb." She was one of the first women to actually make a living as a writer/editor. **Godey's** was the fashion and household bible for the American woman in the 1800s. Mrs. Hale was one of the earliest champions of women's rights. During the Civil War, it was one of the most sought after smuggling operations for the women in the South. They *had* to get their **Godey's** fashions and recipes. Mrs. Hale brought Edgar Allan Poe to the American public. Her son had known Poe at West Point. Each issue of **Godey's** contained hand-colored fashions for women that were, for the most part, hand-tinted by women. The fashions were copied and then removed for framing. It is sometimes difficult to find an early issue of **Godey's** with all of the illustrations intact. Today, however, they are still sought after for their content, whether it be writers such as Poe or Civil War reenactment enthusiasts.

At the turn of the century, American magazines, especially the Hearst-owned **Cosmopolitan**, attracted not only authors such as Jack London, but began to feature important illustrators on their covers. Hearst paid well, therefore, he got the best. Artists such as Harrison Fisher illustrated Hearst magazine covers exclusively under contract through the early 1930s until his death. The Fisher Girls rivaled the Gibson Girls created by artist Charles Dana Gibson. In 1886, Gibson sold his first drawing to John Ames Mitchell, the editor of the original **Life Magazine,** a weekly humor magazine, in January 1883. Gibson became the editor and publisher of **Life Magazine** after World War I. While well-known artists such as Maxfield Parrish, Coles Phillips and John Held Jr. illustrated **Life's** covers, a little-known artist, T.S. Sullivant, was drawing the cartoons. T.S. Sullivant (1854-1926) studied at the Pennsylvania Academy of Fine Arts. His mentor was A.B. Frost, who helped him connect with **Puck Magazine** and then onto **Judge** and **Life Magazine**. Out of all the aforementioned magazine artists/illustrators, Sullivant has probably had the most influence on our modern visual world. His cartoons of animals and cave people have been inspiring the animation artists of Disney and Warner since "Fantasia." The Disney Studio Library has Sullivant clippings that, in spite of computer-generated graphics, are still revered by Disney artists. If you or your children have seen "The Lion King," you have seen the heritage of T.S. Sullivant.

A German magazine called **Jugend** was the harbinger of art nouveau. Some of Aubrey Beardsley's earliest work was in **The Chap-Book**. **Vogue Magazine** featured the art deco illustrations of Helen Dryden, Georges Lepape and Erte.

The third area of magazines that collectors cultivate is advertising. Magazine specialists call these people "rippers," after Jack. These are the people who cull vintage magazines for Cream of Wheat ads, Packard, Ford and Ivory soap ads by artists such as Joseph Clement Coll, Jessie Willcox Smith, Coles Phillips, Maxfield Parrish (he did quite a few Colgate ads) and, of course, the king of ad collecting, Coca-Cola. Ad collectors are as stringent and exacting as author and illustrator collectors. If one page is missing from a magazine, it is returned, regardless of the fact that it does not have their coveted ad on that page.

Most of all, vintage magazines offer a wonderful opportunity for time travel. In the same day you can vicariously experience the San Francisco earthquake, follow the murderous trail of Jack the Ripper, cry for the children of the Donner Party or laugh at the wit of H.L. Mencken and Robert Benchley. You are on the scene in both words and pictures from a "now" point of view. The only thing you need to start your trip is the knowledge of what to collect.

Nuts and Bolts

The book is arranged in two sections: people and magazines. It is frankly impossible to produce a price guide that covers the field in any comprehensive way. Whole books are devoted to superficial surveys of a single magazine, even a single illustrator's association with a single magazine. So we were forced to look for some system that would allow us to bring a general price guide to the public.

It starts with the people whose contributions make magazines collectible. We divided them into two categories, based on the perception we get in buying them, as to which are well-known and which are relatively unknown to the general public. The "stars," people like L. Frank Baum, author of *The Wizard of Oz*, and F. Scott Fitzgerald are recognizable immediately as collectible contributors. Jack the Ripper is a prime collectible subject. Most people know them and, even in a flea market setting, they raise the prices of vintage magazines containing them. The "sleepers" are not so well known by the general public. However, they have the same effect as the "stars" on the collectible price of a vintage magazine. While most of the public would be aware that a vintage magazine with a story by Edgar Allan Poe, or a cover illustration by Maxfield Parrish, is going to be worth more than an unremarkable issue of the same magazine, most people would not attribute the same attributes to a vintage magazine with a story by Kate Cleary or a cover illustrated by Harrison Fisher.

The second section contains the magazines and prices, both of unremarkable issues and issues that are more desirable or collectible. It would be impossible to present all of the issues of a major magazine such as **The Saturday Evening Post.** This is true of most magazines outside of the very limited range of small literary magazines that were important, but short-lived, additions to our culture. Where possible, the entire run of a short-lived literary, "small" magazine, such as **The Wave** or **transition,** is given. With the larger magazines, a range of issues is given, and where possible, a conjecture, in the form of a contributor or contributors is given. As Elaine pointed out, there are numerous reasons to collect magazines and the "conjecture" is just that. The prominence of a single issue as a collectible can be determined by several factors. An issue with Agatha Christie AND an ad for Coca-Cola may be more collectible than Dame Agatha sans cola. However, you can get some indication and determine the value of your magazine accordingly.

To take an example, you found an old copy of **Good Housekeeping**. It was initially worth the unremarkable issue price of $10. Looking through it, you find an ad for Jantzen swimming suits in which the girl seems to fade away. If you have read the sleeper section, you know that you have one of the collectible "fade away girl" ads done by Coles Phillips, so on the strength of that alone, the magazine has jumped to $15. Looking more closely, you find a star, perhaps Agatha Christie, and the price jumps to $45. Or perhaps not, and $15 remains the tag.

Condition is a major feature of vintage magazine collecting. You can use the following scale to determine, roughly, the condition of a magazine. However, magazines have never been as well classified as books, so be sure to query before buying on the Internet or through mail order to be sure your grading scale is close to the one being used.

Fine: A magazine without paper loss of any kind and without stains or creases. Minor age toning only.

Very Good: Without paper loss, but with minor creasing and/or staining. Minor age toning.

Good: Minor paper loss (chipping, etc.) not affecting type and not obscuring the main body of art work. Some creasing and/or staining, as well as age toning which doesn't obscure type.

Fair: Complete, but with paper loss obscuring some type and or/artwork. Usually used for magazines that are intact, with a collectible feature in better condition than the magazine as a whole.

Poor: Fair, lacking pages.

Disbound: Pieces of a magazine without the binding.

Magazines are frequently "ripped," as Elaine mentioned. How do you think all those Norman Rockwell covers ended up framed at your local antique mall? So check each magazine carefully to be sure it is complete.

All of the prices in the book, with the exceptions of a couple noted auction records, have been determined by an average of at least three "fine" copies and are retail prices.

Happy hunting.

PART TWO:

Stars And Sleepers

L. (Lyman) Frank Baum (1856-1919) from Chittenango, N.Y., was the author of *The Wonderful Wizard of Oz,* which became one of the most popular children's book series ever written. He was a newspaper reporter, publisher and playwright. His first children's book, *Mother Goose in Prose* (1897) was illustrated by Maxfield Parrish (qv.). Collaborating with illustrator William Wallace Denslow (qv.), he produced the best selling *Father Goose, His Book* (1899), and the first successful Oz book, *The Wonderful World of Oz* (1900). Subsequent books in the Oz series were illustrated by John R. Neill. Baum also wrote children's stories for various magazines. His earliest known story publication was "The Extravagance of Dan" in **The National Magazine** issue of May 1897. "Animal Fairy Tales," a series of nine stories illustrated by Charles Livingston Bull, appeared in **The Delineator** January through September of 1905. Other appearances of Baum's fairy tale stories were in such publications as **St. Nicholas** magazine with "Juggerjook" (December 1910), "Aunt Phroney's Boy" (December 1912), and **The Lady's World** "The Man Fairy" (December 1910) and "The Tramp and the Baby" (October 1911). The Yellow Brick Road turns to gold when there is a magazine appearance of Baum's work.

Robert (Charles) Benchley (1889-1945) from Worcester, Mass., was a humorist, drama critic and film actor. Robert E. Sherwood enticed fellow Algonquin Round Table wits Dorothy Parker (qv.) and Benchley to work for the original **Life** magazine. Benchley became **Life's** drama critic from 1920-1929. He barely made the weekly deadline, since he was usually at the Algonquin Round Table. His scathing reviews of "Abie's Irish Rose" were notorious: "Opened in May 1922, and was immediately condemned by this department." Under the pseudonym "Guy Fawkes," from 1927-1939, he wrote "Wayward Press" (criticism) columns for **The New Yorker**. He became its regular drama critic from 1929-1940. He also published 12 books of short stories. The Benchley wit shaped the magazines of the era with such axioms as, "It took me 15 years to discover that I had no talent for writing,

but I couldn't give it up because by that time I was too famous."
His priceless wit has made some of his magazine appearances
priceless.

Ambrose Bierce (1842-1913?), an Ohio-born Civil
War soldier, traveled West to become one of the most witty
San Francisco columnists and editors of his time. Bierce's first
journalism job was with the *San Francisco News Letter* (1868-1872)
where he worked as editor, and wrote the Town Crier column. His
first short story, "The Haunted Valley," appeared in **The Overland
Monthly** (July 1871), edited by Bret Harte (qv.). As associate
editor of the **Argonaut** (March 1877), AGB wrote a column, "The
Prattler." That, along with his writing in the **San Francisco Wasp**
(March 1881-September 1886), became the basis for his most
famous book, *The Devil's Dictionary* (October 1906). Hired by
William Randolph Hearst in 1887 for the San Francisco *Examiner*,
Bierce began publishing his Civil War stories. In September of
1905 through 1908, he wrote columns for Hearst's **Cosmopolitan
Magazine** such as "The Passing Show" and "Small Contributions."
His comment on Hearst upon his resignation from **Cosmopolitan**
was, "Nobody but God loves him…" On Nov. 28, 1913, Bierce
crossed the International Bridge between El Paso and Ciudad
Juarez, Mexico, on horseback, reportedly to join Pancho Villa's
revolutionaries, and disappeared. His writing legacy remains highly
desirable.

Earl Derr Biggers (1884-1933), a Harvard graduate from
the "Wild West" of Warren, Ohio, was a newspaper columnist for
the *Boston Traveler*. Fired for his "offensive" drama reviews, he wrote
a successful novel, *Seven Keys to Baldpate,* which first appeared as
a serialization in the **Sunday Magazine** on Jan. 5, 1913. While
he was on vacation in Honolulu, a newspaper article about the
exploits of two Chinese detectives, Chang Apana and Lee Fook,
inspired Biggers to create a character that was unique to American
mystery readers in the 1920s: a Chinese detective. On Jan. 24,
1925, **The Saturday Evening Post** carried the first installment of
"The House Without a Key," thus introducing the world to Charlie
Chan. An instantaneous success, Biggers sold the movie rights and
moved to California. For the third Charlie Chan novel, *Behind
That Curtain,* **The Saturday Evening Post** paid Biggers $25,000
for the serialized version, which appeared in 1928. Subsequent
Chan novels were also serialized in the **Post**, making those issues a
fortune hunt for fans.

James M. Cain (1892-1977) was a journalist turned fiction
writer whose books became classics of film noir. H.L. Mencken
(qv.), a co-writer at the *Baltimore Sun*, talked Cain into his
first fiction pieces for **The American Mercury**, beginning with
"Pastoral" in March 1928. Cain continued to write both non-
fiction and fiction for magazines until the success of *The Postman
Always Rings Twice* (Knopf, 1934) and *Double Indemnity*, originally
a serial in **Liberty** (1936), brought him fame and became very

Agatha Christie was a frequent contributor to the Saturday Evening Post.

Wilkie Collins' Woman in White, considered the first detective novel, made its American debut in Harper's Weekly.

successful films. Along with Raymond Chandler and Dashiell Hammett (qv.), Cain is considered to be one of the founders of the "hard-boiled" school of crime writers. Film adaptations of his novels, notably *Double Indemnity* by Raymond Chandler, are credited with establishing film noir. Early Cain non-fiction and his early fiction enhance the values of **The American Mercury** dramatically. He is a plus for other magazines as well, but mostly for his fiction.

Agatha Christie (1890-1976) was a best-selling writer for

more than 50 years, creating ingenious mysteries and a large cast of detectives to solve them. More than half of her work originally appeared in magazines and all of her books were reprinted in magazine formats. Original appearances of Christie novels and short stories are highly prized collectibles. Reprints often enhance the value of the magazine in which they appear. Original appearances of Christie novels such as *Sad Cypress* (**Collier's**, Nov. 25, 1939 to Jan. 27, 1940) are valued at $500 or more. Original short stories, such as "The Mystery of the Baghdad Chest" in **The Strand** of January 1932, more than double the worth of unremarkable numbers of the same magazine. Christie's stories and serials in **The Saturday Evening Post**, originals, reprints and first American appearances have become classic collectibles and are highly sought after. American television showings of British television series, featuring Hercule Poirot and Jane Marple, have introduced her to a new generation.

Wilkie Collins (1824-1889), born in London, was the

eldest child of the British landscape painter, William Collins, R.A. In the early 1850s, Collins contributed to **Household Words**, a weekly periodical published by his friend, Charles Dickens. A prolific author, Collins' work consisted of 23 novels and 50 short stories. His highly popular novels, *The Woman in White* (1860) and *The Moonstone* (1868), are regarded as the first modern English detective novels. *The Woman in White* was serialized in 1859 in both Dickens' **Household Words** and the American **Harper's Weekly**. *The Moonstone* was in Dickens' **All The Year Round** from Jan. 4 to Aug. 8, 1868. *Armadale* was serialized in **The Cornhill Magazine** from November 1864 to June 1866. Perhaps one of his most controversial novels, *The Law and The Lady*, was serialized in **The Graphic** from Sept. 26, 1874 to March 13, 1875. Critics on both sides of the Atlantic panned the novel. They questioned whether Collins had reached a point of "mental decadence" and felt "obliged to fall back on monstrosities." Nevertheless, the work of Collins created a whole new genre of literature and is desirable today as a collectible.

Charles Dickens (1812-1870), born in Portsmouth,

England, started his writing career as a reporter and editor. His serialized novel, *The Pickwick Papers,* turned Dickens from an obscure reporter into a celebrity. *Oliver Twist*, the first of Dickens's novels

Gustave Dore's Biblical engravings made him the highest paid illustrator in France.

to be published as part of a magazine, was serialized in **Bentley's Miscellany** (Dickens was the editor) in 1838. Dickens later became half-owner and editor of **Household Words.** He handled every aspect of the magazine's production, from soliciting manuscripts to directing revisions to writing most of the articles. His good friend and fellow writer, Wilkie Collins, became a regular contributor to **Household Words,** although for the most part the writers were anonymous. After a dispute with the publishers, Dickens published the last issue of **Household Words** on May 28, 1859. He promptly began to publish **All The Year Round,** which served as another vehicle for his novel serializations, and it was turned over to his son prior to his death. His unfinished manuscript, "The Mystery of Edwin Drood," remains a mystery to this day. Dickens died when it was half-completed and only six parts were published in **All The Year Round** from April to September 1870.

Gustave Dore (1832-83) of Strasbourg was one of the most popular and prolific French illustrators of the 1800s. His output was remarkable both in the number of engravings (10,000+) and the number of editions (4,000+) that he produced. At the age of 16, Dore became the highest paid illustrator in France. He was the featured artist of publisher Charles Philipon's humor weekly, **Journal Pour Rire** (1847-1858). In 1861, Dore produced the folio for his now famous *Dante's Inferno,* which established him as a source for the horror genre. In December of 1865, Dore folios of the Bible, Milton and Tennyson were published in England by Cassell. With the introduction of electrotypes in the engraving process, Dore's illustrations gained an international following. In 1871, American publisher James Sutton began to feature the engravings of Dore in his monthly periodical **The Aldine, The Art Journal of America.** Claiming to be the "Handsomest Paper in the World," **The Aldine's** quality paper stock and large elephant folio size pages created the perfect venue for Dore's framable large engravings. Find an **Aldine** with Dore today, and it will look as if it came right off the press.

Arthur Conan Doyle's Sherlock Holmes was instrumental in putting The Strand at the top of the heap in British magazines at the turn of the century.

Arthur Conan Doyle (1859-1930) from Edinburgh,

Scotland, was an unsuccessful doctor who became a successful author. His first published story was "The Mystery of Sasassa Valley" in the October 1879 issue of **Chambers's Journal.** His biggest success was Sherlock Holmes, who was introduced in the 1887 **Beeton's Christmas Annual** with "A Study in Scarlet," and popularized with the publication of "A Scandal in Bohemia" in **The Strand Magazine** in July 1891. His other unique creation was Professor George E. Challenger in "The Lost World," a sci-fi/fantasy adventure. "The Lost World" captured the imagination of the American public in the **Sunday Magazine** from March 17-July 21, 1912, with illustrations by Joseph Clement Coll. Writing both fiction and non-fiction, Doyle's presence can be counted upon to enhance the value of any magazine. Alive or dead. "An Authentic Interview With Conan Doyle From Beyond," by Harry Price in **Cosmopolitan** magazine in January 1931 insured the issue as highly collectible.

Paul Laurence Dunbar (1872-1906) was one of

the most talented poets who ever lived. He had a natural ear and feeling for poetry in all forms, and could craft it in both conventional English and dialects, creating spellings as he went along. Despite an admirable record in high school, he began his career by self-publishing and working at menial jobs, selling his poetry to people who rode the elevator he operated. Despite his own lack of formal education, his obvious talent and self-education was evident in his writing. Dunbar's work was so impressive that exposure brought him many champions. One, W. D. Howells, wrote the introduction to his second book and, as editor of **Harper's Weekly,** brought him greater exposure, as did the regard of his high school classmates, Orville and Wilbur Wright. Dunbar published in **The Century**, the *Denver Post*, **Current Literature** and a number of other magazines and journals. His work usually more than doubles the worth of an average issue.

Thomas Alva Edison (1847-1931) was such an important inventor that he has been called "the most influential man of the modern age." As both a writer and a journalistic subject, Edison is a major part of collectible magazines. Edison's own writing on his inventions, as in his article in **Scientific American** Aug. 27, 1887; on other inventions such as the X-ray in **The Century**, May 1896, and other subjects like his article "Has Man an Immortal Soul" in **Forum**, November 1926, are all highly collectible and sought after. As a journalistic subject, each new Edison invention, even moving his laboratory, became the subject of several magazine articles, most of which have become collectible. From the 1880s on, Edison lived in a species of journalistic fishbowl. His work and his ideas were chronicled in American magazines. His stature can, perhaps, be glimpsed in the fact that even the ads for his inventions have become collectible features of many magazines.

T.S. Eliot (1888-1965), poet, critic and editor, was born Thomas Stearns Eliot in St. Louis, Mo., and spent most of his life in England. He became friends with Ezra Pound, who introduced him to Harriet Monroe, the editor of **Poetry** magazine. In 1915, **Poetry** published Eliot's first notable piece, "The Love Song of J. Alfred Prufrock." As assistant editor of Harriet Shaw Weavers' (qv.) avant-garde magazine the **Egoist**, Eliot proofread the serial publication of James Joyce's *Ulysses*. Eliot's poem "The Waste Land" was published in the November 1922 issue of **The Dial**. Consequently, he was awarded the magazine's annual prize of $2,000. Lady Rothermere, wife of the publisher of the *Daily Mail*, hired him to edit a high-profile literary journal in October 1922 called the **Criterion**. The **Criterion's** editorial voice placed Eliot at the center of London writing. It ceased publication in 1939 due to the impending war. Interestingly, the issue of **The Dial** containing "The Waste Land" is worth as much as Eliot's prize.

F. Scott Fitzgerald (1896-1940) from St. Paul, Minn., was the epitome of the Jazz Age. Having married Zelda Sayre, a Southern belle, the two partied together on both sides of the Atlantic. His first book, *This Side of Paradise,* made him a literary sensation, but his most significant tome was *The Great Gatsby*. Fitzgerald continually published magazine stories to afford his extravagant lifestyle with Zelda. He was a regular contributor to **The Smart Set, The Saturday Evening Post, Metropolitan Magazine, Hearst's International** and **Esquire** during the 1920s and '30s. Most of the stories he wrote were later collected in

F. Scott Fitzgerald's fiction is a major collectible in the Saturday Evening Post.

book form in *Tales of the Jazz Age, Taps at Reveille, Flappers and Philosophers,* and *The Price Was High.* In 1937, after Zelda's death in a fire in a mental institution, he won a contract to write for Metro-Goldwyn-Mayer in Hollywood and fell in love with English movie columnist Sheila Graham. Fitzgerald was a master of the English language and his magazine short stories were the perfect format for his unique gift.

Erle Stanley Gardner (1889-1970), a prolific and best-selling author, began his career in **Breezy Stories** with "The Police of the House" in June of 1921. Along with Dashiell Hammett (qv.), he became one of the mainstays of the pulp magazine **Black Mask**, starting with "The Shrieking Skeleton" under the pseudonym Charles M. Green in the Dec. 15 issue of 1923. As A.A. Fair, Carlton Kendrake, Charles G. Kenny and under his own name, he sent detectives such as Donald Lam and Bertha Cool, Lester Leith, Paul Prey, Doug Selby, Terry Clane, Gramps Wiggins and, of course, attorney Perry Mason against malefactors in pulps until the pulps began to fade in the early 1940s. From 1957 through 1966, the Perry Mason television show sparked an interest in Gardner and he turned to both fiction and non-fiction articles. Though his later, non-pulp production has yet to reach the worth or collectibility of his earlier pulp period, they might be looked on as a bargain.

Charles Dana Gibson (1867-1944) was a Roxbury, Mass., artist, editor and publisher. In the fall of 1886, Gibson sold a small drawing for $4 to John A. Mitchell for the satirical weekly **Life** magazine. His work began to appear in **The Century, Harper's Monthly** and **Weekly,** and **Harper's Bazaar** along with **Life.** In the 1890s, as the creator of America's sweetheart

Charles Dana Gibson's "Gibson Girl" defined American beauty for a generation.

"The Gibson Girl," he became an art superstar. His influential relationship with **Life** spanned 30 years. He built the **Life** home and offices in 1893 in New York City, which still exists today as the Herald Square Hotel. After the death of Mitchell, he became both the editor and publisher, contracting artists such as Maxfield Parrish, Coles Phillips and Norman Rockwell for its covers. John Held Jr.'s flapper girls on **Life's** covers symbolized the Roaring Twenties. Robert E. Sherwood, Robert Benchley and Dorothy Parker were the writers who satirized the era. The issues of the Gibson-produced **Life** magazine are the most sought after among collectors.

Johnny Gruelle's illustrations and his characters have been a part of the upbringing of American children for almost a century.

Johnny Gruelle (1880-1938) of Arcola, Ill., the son of a landscape artist, was the creator of the Raggedy Ann and Raggedy Andy books and rag dolls. In 1901, he started his artistic career as a newspaper cartoonist, working for such varied newspapers as the *Indianapolis Star,* the rival *Indianapolis Sentinel, Cleveland Press* and *The New York Herald.* While his early cartoons were geared to adults in such publications as **Cosmopolitan, Life, Judge** (which published his "Yapp's Crossing" series), **Physical Culture, Illustrated Sunday Magazine** and **College Humor,** his most important audience became children. Gruelle's illustrated juvenile features appeared in **John Martin's Book, McCall's Magazine, The Lady's World, Woman's World** and **Good Housekeeping.**

It was his illustrating work that led him to create a rag doll for his daughter, Marcella, named "Raggedy Ann." Initially, the Gruelle family hand-made small quantities of the rag doll, which Gruelle patented and trademarked in 1915. After the tragic death of his daughter, Marcella, from an infected vaccination, Gruelle continued his Raggedy Ann and Andy books (published by the P.F. Volland company) as a tribute. His magazine contributions are highly prized by collectors.

Zane Grey (1872-1939) began his career with *Betty Zane* (New York: Charles Francis Press, 1903), published with a vanity press. He parlayed its success into a career that, among other things, saw him become the best-selling author of Western fiction in the 20th century. Along with his Westerns, Grey published on fishing and travel, and wrote books for boys. Most of his work started in magazines, such as "Tales of the South Seas" in **Physical Culture,** August 1931. He had long associations with both **Country Gentleman** and **Field and Stream.** He published both original stories and reprints in most major magazines and pulps over his career. Grey was and is highly collectible as a magazine writer in all phases of his writing. A gauge to how closely he was tied to the magazine market is **Zane Grey's Western Magazine,** which reprinted abridged versions of his western stories as a very successful pulp magazine from 1946 through 1974.

H. (Henry) Rider Haggard (1856-1925), the son of a Norfolk, U.K., squire, spent six years in South Africa while still a young man. Haggard's interest in African tribal activity, landscape, wildlife and mysterious history influenced his writing career. His most famous and best-selling adventure novels *King Solomon's Mines* (1885), inspired by R.L Stevenson's *Treasure Island,* and *She* (1887), considered the first Lost Race story, were based on his African experiences. At the age of 34, Haggard had become a household name. He published one to three books a year, in which the setting ranged from Iceland to the South Seas to England and, of course, Africa. His output was extremely prolific, and he published more than 70 fiction and non-fiction books plus numerous articles and short stories. **The Pall Mall Magazine** and **The Windsor Magazine** serialized his novels and published his non-fiction, as did **The Strand Magazine, The Cornhill Magazine, Cassell's Magazine, Longman's Magazine, Macmillan's Magazine** and **The Queen.** In America, his work appeared in the **Sunday Magazine, Pearson's, Gunter's** and **Adventure,** to name a few. His magazine appearances are highly valuable including periodicals that negatively satirized him and reviewed his books, such as the American **Life** magazine and British **Punch, Or The London Chiavari.**

Dashiell Hammett (1894-1961), a Pinkerton detective, was discovered by H.L. Mencken, a high school classmate. He began his writing career in **The Smart Set** with "The Parthian Shot" (October 1922) and "The Great Lovers" (November 1922).

Switching to the Mencken/Nathan pulp **Black Mask** under the pseudonym Peter Collinson, and creating his first hard-boiled detective, the continental cop in "Arson Plus" (October 1923), Hammett became a mainstay of that pulp. He branched out to include **The New Pearson's Magazine, Sunset** and **Judge,** along with pulps **Argosy, True Detective, Brief Stories, Action Stories** and **Saucy Stories** in his resume before his first book, *Red Harvest* (New York: Alfred A. Knopf, 1929). Most of Hammett's work had its original appearance in a magazine, and most of it is highly collectible. Sam Spade from **American Magazine** (July 1932); and Nick Charles from **Redbook** (December 1933) are two major examples. One interesting and lucrative find for Hammett is "The Crusader" (**Smart Set**, August 1923), under the pseudonym Mary Jane Hammett.

Joel Chandler Harris (1848-1908) an Eatonton, Ga.,

journalist with the *Atlanta Constitution,* is still chiefly known for his stories of southern black folklore. His "Uncle Remus" tales with their wit, wisdom and sympathy, combined with his knowledge of southern black dialect and character, made his first book *Uncle Remus, His Songs and Sayings* (1881) a huge popular success. Unique among folk stories and distinctively American, his 40 books have been translated into 27 languages. Many of the Uncle Remus tales were featured in **The Saturday Evening Post.** **The Post** also serialized "A Little Union Scout," with illustrations by George Gibbs. Other periodicals such as **Collier's Weekly,** **The Century** and **St. Nicholas** featured his work. **Uncle Remus's Home Magazine** (1906-1909), founded by Harris and published by Sunny South Publishing in Atlanta, was flavored with his folksy humor. Don Marquis, creator of Archy and Mehitabel, was the associate editor. Contributors included writers like Jack London (qv.) and Frank Stanton, making this a very desirable publication for collectors.

Bret Harte reshaped American literature through his editing of the Overland Monthly.

(Francis) Bret Harte (1836-1902), born in Albany, N.Y.,

went west with his mother after the death of his father. In San Francisco, while writing for *The Californian,* he met and worked with Mark Twain. Harte became the first editor of **The Overland Monthly** in 1868. His stories, "The Luck of Roaring Camp" and "The Outcasts of Poker Flat," published in **The Overland Monthly,** brought him instant and wide fame. As the chronicler of frontier California, he was hailed during the 1860s as the "new prophet of American letters." Eastern magazines courted his work, since he had become a phenomenon in establishing the foundations of western American fiction. San Francisco critic Ambrose Bierce called his humor "incomparable." He moved to Boston to be a contributing editor for **Atlantic Monthly.** In 1877, he wrote the play "Ah Sin" with Twain. Eventually, he migrated to England, where his work was published in the great British periodicals such as **The Idler, The Strand, The Windsor, The London Magazine** and **The Pall Mall.** However, Harte's work in **The Overland Monthly** is as good as California gold.

John Held Jr.'s flappers were an icon of the Jazz Age.

John Held Jr. (1889-1958) of Salt Lake City, Utah, began his art career as a sports cartoonist for the *Salt Lake Tribune*. He sold his first drawing to **Life** magazine at the age of 15. After moving to New York City, he easily found work as a commercial artist. Along with his drawings and cover art for **Life** and **Judge,** he began to draw for the new Harold Ross magazine **The New Yorker** (1925). Held's flapper drawings of Betty Coed and Joe College took the place of the Gibson Girl in the public's mind during the Roaring Twenties. He was the artistic chronicler of the Jazz Age and the readers of **Harper's Bazaar, Redbook** and **Vanity Fair** couldn't get enough of Held. Fans would send him blank checks in the hopes of obtaining an illustration. The public's fascination and love affair with John Held Jr. remains to this day. Magazines with Held's cover art are snapped up by collectors, who are willing to pay a premium to own a piece of the Jazz Age.

Winslow Homer, as both a painter and illustrator, was a major influence on American magazines.

Winslow Homer (1836-1910) was born in Boston. The American naturalist painter was most famous for his American landscape paintings and his seascapes off the Maine coastline, where he lived the latter part of his life. Interestingly, he began the pursuit of his art career as an apprentice in the Boston lithographic firm of John Bufford. A self-taught artist, Winslow Homer started as an illustrator of magazines and became a regular contributor of engraved drawings to **Harper's Weekly** in the 1850s. Throughout the Civil War and afterwards, he did engravings for **Appletons' Journal, Frank Leslie's Illustrated Newspaper, Ballou's Monthly, The Galaxy** and **Harper's Bazar,** to name a few. Aside from his Civil War illustrations, his subject matter was usually rural farm scenes, children at play or fashionable women. He also did illustrations for **The Century** and the children's magazine **St. Nicholas.** The last magazine illustrations done by Winslow Homer can be found on page 664 of **St. Nicholas,** Volume VII May to October 1881.Winslow Homer's early magazine engravings are expensive, but they are at least obtainable to collectors.

PUNCH, OR THE LONDON CHARIVARI—September 29, 1888.

THE NEMESIS OF NEGLECT.

"THERE FLOATS A PHANTOM ON THE SLUM'S FOUL AIR,
SHAPING, TO EYES WHICH HAVE THE GIFT OF SEEING,
INTO THE SPECTRE OF THAT LOATHLY LAIR.
FACE IT—FOR VAIN IS FLEEING!
RED-HANDED, RUTHLESS, FURTIVE, UNERECT,
'TIS MURDEROUS CRIME—THE NEMESIS OF NEGLECT!"

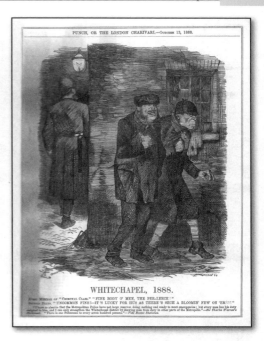

PUNCH, OR THE LONDON CHARIVARI—October 13, 1888.

WHITECHAPEL, 1888.

Jack the Ripper (August 1888-?), also known as the
"Whitechapel Murderer" and "Leather Apron," was a sexually-
oriented serial killer who murdered a number of prostitutes in
the East End of London in 1888. Jack the Ripper became a
"media event" in 1888, with his brutality and taunting messages
to the Metropolitan and City of London Police. He represented a
"cause celebre" for the press and political reformers upset with the
poverty-stricken conditions that prevailed in the Whitechapel area.
His exploits were chronicled daily in the London newspapers, along
with speculations as to the identity of the fiend, which eventually
became part of the "romance" of Jack the Ripper. There was not
even a consensus on how many women Jack murdered. It could
have been anywhere from five to nine or more, although there
were certainly five documented examples from August through
November 1888. There are several publications that Ripperologists
would kill to own, in addition to various newspaper accounts.
Punch, Or The London Chiavari satirized the Ripper murders in
six issues from 1888-1889, and the **Illustrated London News** on
Oct. 13, 1888, published an artist's sketch of a suspicious character
that many believe was the Ripper.

Jack the Ripper held England
spellbound in 1888.

Will James' influence on Western art, as well Western writing, is unquestioned.

Will James (1892-1942), the pseudonym of Canadian artist/writer Ernest Dufault, has been called "the pied piper of the West." As an illustrator and writer of both fiction and non-fiction, more than any other writer, James created the American mythology of the "cowboy." James began his publishing career as an illustrator for **Sunset** in January of 1920 with his drawing, "A One-Man Horse." In March 1923, he combined his drawing with an article for **Scribner's**, "Bucking Horses and Bucking-Horse Riders" that was so well received he became a regular contributor. Contributions to **Scribner's** and "Once A Cowboy," from **The Saturday Evening Post** in June 1924, made up his first book, *Cowboys North and South* (New York: Scribner's, 1924), followed the next year by another anthology of magazine pieces, *The Drifting Cowboy* (New York: Scribner's, 1925). During his career, James contributed to **Scribner's, The Saturday Evening Post, Sunset, Liberty, The Bookman** and **Southwest Review**, adding substantially to the value of those issues as collectibles.

Ring Lardner (1885-1933), humorist, satirist and charter member of the Algonquin Round Table, is perhaps most influential in the area of magazines for his view of sports. He began his career with the *South Bend Tribune* and worked his way up through the Chicago dailies to New York as a sports writer. Although remembered as a humorist for characters like Alibi Ike, his more serious pieces on sports, especially baseball, set a standard and a tone for sports journalism. He wrote such pieces as "TYRUS: The Greatest One Of 'Em All," in the June 1915 **American Magazine.** While most of his short stories saw print initially in magazines, it is his sports stories that remain at the top of the collectible heap from the early pieces in **The American** through the later pieces for **Esquire, Cosmopolitan** and **The Saturday Evening Post.** Original short stories are hardly throwaways and do have a collectible audience, but they not on the same level as collectibles or influences.

J.C. (Joseph Christian) Leyendecker (1874-1951) was born in Montabaur, Germany, and migrated to America when he was 8 years old. He studied at the Chicago Art Institute and the Academie Julian in Paris. His brother, Frank X. Leyendecker, was also an artist, but was overshadowed by Joseph. In 1896, Joseph won **The Century Magazine** cover competition, beating out a second place Maxfield Parrish. This led to cover assignments for 12 **Inland Printer** covers for 1897 and cover designs for the leading publications like **Life, The Century, Collier's** and **The Saturday Evening Post.** His first **Saturday Evening Post** cover was done in 1899, and he did more than 320 during the next 40 years. As a respected commercial artist, he received highly paid commissions for advertising illustrations. His advertising illustrations are as collectible in the magazines of the period as his covers. His Arrow Collar man was a debonair, handsome male, and women wrote thousands of love letters to him in care of Cluett, Peabody & Company. His illustrations for Hart, Schaffner & Marx were equally successful in promoting an image of suited elegance. J.C. Leyendecker is valuable to magazine collectors for covers, interiors and ads. He typified the "Golden Age of Illustration."

J.C. Leyendecker's unmistakable style was a favorite during the Golden Age of Illustration.

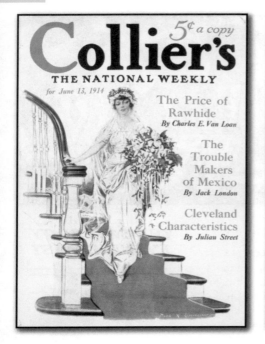

Jack London was a mainstay of a number of popular magazines in his heyday.

Jack London (1876-1916), from San Francisco and the waterfront dives of Oakland, Calif., became one of the highest paid novelists and short story writers of his day. His first commercial sale for $40 was "A Thousand Deaths" in **TheBlack Cat Magazine** May 1899. According to London, it was the "first money I ever received for a story." Other short stories appeared in **The Overland Monthly, Atlantic Monthly** and **McClure's Magazine.** Possibly his most famous novel, *The Call Of The Wild,* was first serialized in **The Saturday Evening Post** in five issues June 20 through July 18, 1903, illustrated by Charles Livingston Bull. **The Century Magazine** serialized *The Sea-Wolf* from January to November 1904. William Randolph Hearst serialized London's work in **Cosmopolitan:** "Moon Face and Other Stories" (1906), "The Voyage of the Snark" (1906), "Smoke Bellew" (1911), "The Valley of the Moon" (1913) and "The Little Lady of the Big House" (1915). London's Socialist leanings were expressed in **Collier's Magazine** in "The Trouble Makers of Mexico" June 13, 1914. Children's stories appeared in **St. Nicholas** and the **Youth's Companion**. Any magazine with Jack London's byline raises the value to an extraordinary level.

William Somerset Maugham (1874-1965), born in Paris at the British Embassy, was also a doctor who abandoned medicine for a lucrative career as a writer and playwright. His first novel, *Liza of Lambeth*, published in 1897, drew on his obstetric experiences in the London slums. By 1908, he had four plays running simultaneously in London. The semi-autobiographical novel *Of Human Bondage* (1915) is usually considered his outstanding achievement. *The Moon and The Sixpence* (1919), based on artist Paul Gauguin, was among the most popular of his novels. In the 1920s and 1930s, Maugham's short stories that appeared in American magazines made him more popular in America than England and very wealthy. **Hearst's International**, which later became **Cosmopolitan**, published his most memorable stories such as "The British Agent" in February 1928, "The Man Who Made His Mark" June 1929, "Marriage of Convenience" January 1930, "Virtue" February 1931, "Gigolo and Gigolette" July 1935, to name a few. Eventually, many of these stories became subjects for Hollywood films, which makes their magazine appearances even more valuable.

H.L. Mencken (1880-1956) was a newspaperman, author, and literary and social critic who was born and raised in Baltimore. During the 1920s, he was one of the most influential figures in the United States. His association with magazines began with **The Smart Set,** where he shared criticism and editing duties with George Jean Nathan (qv.) from 1908 through 1924. During this period, he co-founded, along with Nathan, the pulp magazines **Parisienne, Saucy Stories** and **Black Mask.** In 1924, Mencken launched **The American Mercury,** with Nathan as co-editor. He took over as sole editor after the fourth issue and continued in that post until 1933. Stories by and about H. L. Mencken add a factor of increased value to magazines beyond **The Smart Set** and **Mercury,** especially during the 1920s, the height of Mencken's popularity. Mencken's stature was such that stories about him, or arguing with him, have become as important, if not more important, than his own writing. His influence on American magazines was unquestionably one of the major factors in the evolution of modern publishing.

Alphonse Mucha (1860-1939), of Czech origin, made his fortune as an artist in Paris. As a pioneer of Art Nouveau in Paris and America, Mucha achieved immediate fame when, in December 1894, he accepted a commission to create a poster for the actress Sarah Bernhardt. The poster, "Gismonda," which appeared on Jan. 1, 1895, marked a sharp break with previous poster design because of its new unconventional style. Bernhardt loved it and so did the public. "Le style Mucha," as Art Nouveau was known in its earliest days, was born. The success of that first poster brought a six-year contract between Bernhardt and Mucha. In the following years, his work for her and others included costumes and stage decorations, designs for magazines and book covers,

Alphonse Mucha all but created Art Nouveau.

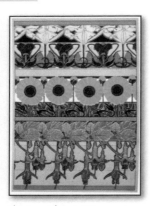

This is another Art Nouveau creation by Alphonse Mucha.

jewelry and furniture, and numerous posters. His unique art covers and advertising illustrations began to appear in French magazines such as **La Plume** in January 1899 and **Le Mois Letteraire Etpittoresque,** September 1906. In America, he produced a cover for **Burr-McIntosh Monthly,** December 1907. Mucha's magazine covers are worth a small king's ransom.

George Jean Nathan (1882–1958) was America's premier drama critic. He was one of the most influential magazine editors of the early 20th century. Along with H.L. Mencken (qv.), he edited **The Smart Set** and created the pulp magazines **Parisienne, Saucy Stories** and **Black Mask.** In 1924, he co-founded **The American Mercury,** again with Mencken, and in 1932 founded **The American Spectator,** which he edited until 1935. An early champion of such playwrights as August Strindberg and Eugene O'Neill, Nathan made magazine history by arranging that the first publication of the O'Neill play "All God's Chillun Got Wings" would appear in the third number of **The American Mercury.** Nathan is collected as a writer, critic and editor. While sometimes approached as a satellite of Mencken, Nathan's later work and his contributions to **Smart Set** often eclipse Mencken's writing of the same period. Nathan's self-effacing humor was not as strident as Mencken's, as evidenced by his characterization of a critic as "…a legless man who teaches running."

Dorothy Rothschild Parker (1893-1967) from New Jersey crossed the Hudson to become a writer and critic. Starting her career as **Vanity Fair's** drama critic (1917-1921), she was later fired for her iconoclastic wit. In 1919, she became the only female founding member of the legendary Algonquin Round Table. Her cohorts, Robert E. Sherwood and Robert Benchley, brought her to **Life** magazine. She was also given a free reign at **Ainslee's.** From the inception of **The New Yorker** in early 1925, Parker contributed drama reviews, poetry and book reviews under the column "The Constant Reader." In February 1929, her short story "The Big Blonde" won the O. Henry Award. Parker scripted films in Hollywood from 1933 to 1938, winning an Academy Award (1937) for her joint screenplay of "A Star is Born." Her socialist views clarified in 1937 covering the Spanish Civil War for **New Masses.** During the McCarthy era, she was brought before the House Un-American Activities Committee and pleaded in typical Parker-style the First, not the Fifth, Amendment. In 1957-1963, she worked as a book reviewer for **Esquire** magazine, which published her last piece in the November 1964 issue. Needless to say, her magazine pieces are priceless.

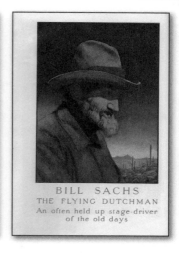

BILL SACHS
THE FLYING DUTCHMAN
An often held up stage-driver
of the old days

Maxfield Parrish remains one
of America's most collected and
respected artists.

Frederick Maxfield Parrish (1870-1966) was born
in Philadelphia and studied art at the Pennsylvania Academy of
Fine Arts. He was one of the most popular artists during America's
"Golden Age of Illustration," producing countless books, calendars,
art prints, advertisements and magazines (both covers and interior
illustrations). His first magazine cover was for the **Harper's Bazaar**
Easter 1895 issue, when he was 25 years old. Between 1895-1900,
his images graced the covers of **Harper's Bazaar, Harper's Weekly,
Harper's Monthly, Harper's Round Table** and **Harper's Young
People.** During the course of his long career, he also did covers and
interior illustrations for **Scribner's Magazine, McClure's, Success,
Collier's Weekly, Ladies' Home Journal, Life, Hearst's** and, of
course, **The Century.** In July 1896, Parrish won the second prize
of $75 from **The Century** for a poster advertising its Midsummer
Number. Other prized **Century** contributions by Parrish were
"L'Allegro" (1901), Ray Stannard Baker's "The Great Southwest"
(May 1902-April 1903) and his Edith Wharton collaboration

Here is an assortment of the artwork Maxfield Parrish contributed to magazines.

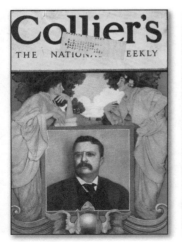

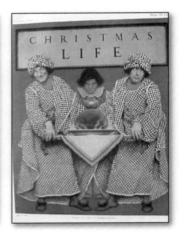

"Italian Villas and Their Gardens" (November 1903-November 1904). In the 1936 issue of **Time** magazine, Parrish was named one of the world's three most popular artists; the other two were Van Gogh and Cezanne. Parrish art in magazines is still one of the most highly sought after by collectors, and continues to appreciate.

Edgar Allan Poe (1809-1849) from Boston was a
controversial but brilliant American poet, critic, editor and writer. His first book, published as a pamphlet by "A Bostonian," was *Tamerlane And Other Poems* (1827) with perhaps 50 copies sold. His first appearance in a magazine of national circulation was the anonymous publication of "The Visionary" in **Godey's Lady's Book** in January 1834. Championed by editor Sarah Hale, Poe's work was continually published in **Godey's.** Throughout his brief career, he was an editor and writer for the **Southern Literary Messenger** (1836), **Burton's Gentleman's Magazine** *(*1839-1841), and eventually, **Graham's Magazine** (1841). During Poe's tenure, the circulation of **Graham's Magazine** increased from about 5,000 to nearly 37,000 subscribers. "The Murders In The Rue Morgue," considered to be the first modern detective story, was published in **Graham's** (April 1841). His most famous poem, "The Raven," for which he received $15, first appeared Jan. 29, 1845, in the *New York Evening Mirror.* Poe scholars, however, consider the accepted first version to have been published in **The American Review: A Whig Journal of Politics, Literature, Art and Science,** February 1845, under the pseudonym Quarles. Poe's magazine appearances to collectors are priceless.

Rustic (to beginner, who has charged the
edge). "It's no good, Sir. They things
won't jump!"

Arthur Rackham's illustrations, here and on the next page, are everyone's touchstone to childhood.

Arthur Rackham (1867-1939) of London, England, was the premier illustrator of children's book classics at the turn of the century. His first appearance in print was in **Scraps Magazine** in 1884. In 1900, he caught the imagination of the public with the publication of an illustrated edition of the *Grimm Brothers' Fairy Tales.* His illustrated *Rip van Winkle* (1905) introduced him to the American public and, one year later, *Peter Pan in Kensington Gardens* was published. His faeries and goblins could also be found in both black and white and color lithos in magazines of the era such as **Cassell's** (1896), **Little Folks** (1896), **Punch, Or The London Charivari** (1905), **Scribner's** (1906), **The Bookman** (1906) and **The Century** (1913-1914). He was commissioned to illustrate "The Nursery Rhymes of Mother Goose" for **St. Nicholas** in 1912 through 1914. In addition to his magazine story illustrations, Rackham also did a series of colorful ads for Cashmere Bouquet Soap that appeared in **Ladies' Home Journal, Pictorial Review, Vogue, Asia** and **Good Housekeeping** (1923-1925), which are of interest to collectors.

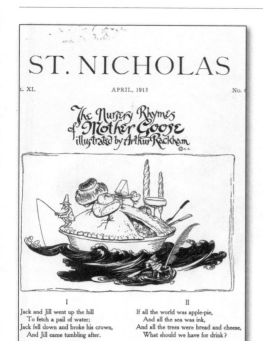

ST. NICHOLAS

L. XL   APRIL, 1913   No.

The Nursery Rhymes of Mother Goose illustrated by Arthur Rackham

I

Jack and Jill went up the hill
  To fetch a pail of water;
Jack fell down and broke his crown,
  And Jill came tumbling after.

II

If all the world was apple-pie,
  And all the sea was ink,
And all the trees were bread and cheese,
  What should we have for drink?

VOL. XL.—61–62.
481

ST. NICHOLAS

VOL. XL   JUNE, 1913   No.

The Nursery Rhymes of Mother Goose illustrated by Arthur Rackham

I

As I was going to St. Ives,
I met a Man with seven Wives.
Each Wife had seven Sacks,
Each Sack had seven Cats,
Each Cat had seven Kits.

Kits, Cats, Sacks, and Wives,
How many were going to St. Ives?

II

Two legs sat upon three legs,
With one leg in his lap;
In comes four legs,
And runs away with one leg:
Up jumps two legs,
Catches up three legs,
Throws it after four legs,
And makes him bring back one leg.

VOL. XL.—85.
673

Frederic Remington remains the epitome of the art of the American frontier. Examples are shown here and the following page.

Frederic Remington (1861-1909) of Canton, N.Y., was
one of the great illustrators of the American West. He attended Yale College of Art, but became more involved in playing football. **Harper's Weekly** published his first cartoon in 1882. After a trip to the Arizona Territory in 1885, which he spent with the U.S. cavalry chasing the Apaches of Geronimo, Remington returned to the East with a portfolio of drawings. Beginning in January 1866, **Harper's Weekly** published his work on a consistent basis, including his beloved subjects of horses, Indians, soldiers and cowboys. **The Century Magazine** (1888) serialized Teddy Roosevelt's *Ranch Life and the Hunting Trail*. Remington illustrated the series and became a life-long friend of Roosevelt. During the Spanish-American War in 1898, William Randolph Hearst sent Remington to Cuba to illustrate the "atrocities." Unhappy with the situation, Remington sent a message to Hearst: "There is no War. Request to be recalled." Typically, Hearst replied: "Please remain. You furnish the pictures, I'll furnish the War." Even though Remington devoted his energies to sculpture in later years, he still continued his Western illustrations for **Collier's Weekly** (1906) and other publications. His magazine illustrations are still coveted by collectors of Western Americana.

Eugene Manlove Rhodes (1869-1934) was born in
Nebraska and raised in New Mexico. Until his emergence as a popular writer, he was a cowboy and his writing reflects the authenticity of his background. Rhodes began his publishing career in **Out West** (later **Sunset**) in January of 1902 with the story "The Hour and the Man." In November of 1907, he began his long and

fruitful association with **The Saturday Evening Post. Post** serials, *Good Men and True* Jan. 8 and 15, 1910, and *The Little Eohippus* Nov. 30, Dec. 7, 14, 21 and 28, 1912, were his first novels to see print and established him as one of the major writers of Western fiction. During his career, Rhodes was published in **Sunset, McClure's, Redbook** and **Cosmopolitan** as well as the **Post.** Rhodes' stories add a good deal to a magazine, in some cases more than doubling the average issue value. Rhodes' best-known story is "Paso Por Aqui," published in the **Post** Feb. 20 and 27, 1926.

Jacob Riis (1849-1914) migrated from Denmark to New York City to become America's first journalist-photographer. Riis was a turn of the century muckraker known as the "Emancipator of the Slums." As one of the top New York City investigative reporters, he began working for the *New York Tribune* as a police reporter. His beat was police headquarters, Mulberry Street, infamous for the city's worst slums and tenement buildings. In 1890, his landmark work, *How The Other Half Lives,* was published. His friend, Theodore Roosevelt, would go with him on his nighttime excursions into tenement streets while he photographed the poverty and depredation. Riis' shocking exposes of the tenements on New York City's Lower East Side appeared primarily in **The Century Magazine** in "The Making of Thieves in New York" (November 1894), "Merry Christmas In The Tenements" (December 1897), "Feast-Day In Little Italy" (August 1899), "The Last of the Mulberry Street Barons" (1899) and "A Story of Bleecker Street (1901). The magazine work of Riis is as important for its artistic significance as for its incredible insight into the human condition.

Norman Rockwell and his vision of Americans is indelibly linked in the American mind to his covers for The Saturday Evening Post.

Norman Rockwell (1894-1978) landed his first commission with **The Saturday Evening Post** in 1916. He did illustrations and even covers for **The American Magazine, Boy's Life, Judge, Good Housekeeping, Look, McCall's, St. Nicholas, Woman's Home Companion** and **Literary Digest;** advertisements for Edison Mazda Lamp Works, Encyclopedia Britannica, Fisk Tire, Interwoven Socks, Maxwell House Coffee, Overland Cars, Parker Pens, Coca-Cola, Brown & Bigelow, the Boy Scouts, Ford, Hallmark; and book illustrations, notably Mark Twain illustrations for LEC and Heritage Press. But the **Post** and Rockwell remain linked in the public imagination. In the collectible market, however, the reverse can be true. More often than not, it is the obscure ad or early children's illustration from **St. Nicholas,** circa 1917-1918, that draws collectible interest. Rockwell has been popular for so long that much of his early work has been ripped and framed. This makes complete early magazine work by Rockwell correspondingly scarcer and more sought after.

Sax Rohmer (1883-1959), the pseudonym of Arthur Henry Sarsfield Ward, has been characterized as "the master of villainy" for his creation of Fu Manchu and other master villains. He began his career with "The Mysterious Mummy" in **Pearson's Magazine** (November 1903) and "The Leopard-Couch" in **Chambers's Journal** (Jan. 30, 1904), followed by three more titles in **Pearson's Magazine:** "The Green Spider" in October 1904, "The Mystery of Marsh Hole" in April 1905 and "The M'Villin" in December

1906. All five ran with the byline of "A. Sarsfield Ward." From 1908 through 1913, he used variations of his real name, such as Sarsfield Ward as well as the pseudonym Sax Rohmer. The success of *The Mystery of Dr. Fu Manchu* (London: Methuen, 1913) apparently decided that the pseudonym would be used henceforth. Rohmer was a frequent contributor to magazines of both original and reprint material, and his presence, even in a pulp reprint, often enhances the value of a magazine.

Jessie Willcox Smith

Jessie Willcox Smith (1863-1933) was born in Philadelphia and studied art at the Pennsylvania Academy of Fine Arts with the great Thomas Eakins. She also went to the Drexel Institute of Arts and Sciences, where she studied with the illustrator Howard Pyle along with Elizabeth Shippen Green and Violet Oakley. The three women illustrators became roommates and life-long friends. Although her earliest work appeared in **St. Nicholas,** it was "The Last of the Fairy Wands" in the December issue of **Scribner's Magazine** (1901) that had an impact on her future. The focus of her work was children. To this end, her illustrations appeared in **Century, Collier's Weekly, Leslie's, Harper's, McClure's, Scribner's** and **The Ladies' Home Journal.** However, it was her paintings on the covers of **Good Housekeeping** that made her a popular success, as people became familiar with her art. For more than 15 years, from December of 1917 through March of 1933, a new Jessie Willcox Smith painting was on the newsstands and in countless homes. Today, those covers of children are just as sought after by collectors.

Jessie Willcox Smith covers of children endear her to collectors.

Nero Wolfe and his creator, Rex Stout, debuted in The American Magazine.

Rex Stout (1886-1975) of Noblesville, Ind., wrote more than 70 detective novels, 46 of them featuring one of the most unique creations in detective literature, Nero Wolfe. Wolfe was an eccentric, gourmet and overweight sleuth who raised orchids and never left his venerable Manhattan brownstone. Archie Goodwin was his wisecracking aide and companion, who served as Wolfe's eyes, ears and legs. The first appearance of the two was in **The American Magazine** in November 1934 in "Point Of Death," with color illustrations of Archie and Wolfe done by illustrator Fred Ludekens. The story was later expanded to become Rex Stout's first book, *Fer de Lance.* Although some Rex Stout material appeared in **The Saturday Evening Post,** many of the Nero Wolfe novels and stories were serialized in **The American Magazine.** "The Red Box" appeared in December 1936, and "Two Many Cooks," which featured the illustrations of Rico Tomaso, was serialized from March 1938 to July 1938. Readers were invited to send in a stamped self-addressed envelope to request the recipes for the dishes that appeared in "Too Many Cooks." The "free" recipe boxes and recipes, along with the magazine issues, are worth a small fortune today.

HARPER'S WEEKLY
JOURNAL OF CIVILIZATION

Vol. XXXV.—No. 1814.
Copyright, 1891, by Harper & Brothers.
All rights Reserved.

NEW YORK, SATURDAY, SEPTEMBER 26, 1891.

TEN CENTS A COPY.
FOUR DOLLARS A YEAR.

SAMUEL L. CLEMENS (MARK TWAIN).—From the Painting by J. Carroll Beckwith.—(See Page 734.)

Mark Twain is a collectible feature as a writer and a journalistic subject.

Mark Twain (1835-1910), pseudonym for Samuel Langhorne Clemens, was an American writer, journalist and humorist who was born in Florida, Mo. As a licensed Mississippi riverboat pilot (1857-1861), he adopted his name from the call ("mark twain!" meaning by the mark of two fathoms). Some of his earliest writing appeared in **The Galaxy** 1868-1871. Twain wrote a column "Memoranda" on such topics as The Noble Red Man, Unburlesquable Things and Mark Twain's hand-drawn Map of Paris with satirical commentary by Twain. According to Twain, Napoleon said of his map: "It is very nice, large print." Other magazines he contributed to were **Harper's, The Atlantic Monthly** and **North American Review.** However, the author of *Tom Sawyer* had his most controversial book, *Huckleberry Finn,* excerpted for **The Century Magazine** (December 1884, January and February 1885). Huck Finn created an immediate sensation. It was banned by the Concord Library Committee, which thought that Huck Finn was unsuitable for their shelves and viewed it as "trashy and vicious." The *New York Times* reported that Huck "disfigured **The Century Magazine**." The readers of **The Century** loved it. They made Twain and the book a success. Twain, in fact, eventually serialized many of his novels in **The Century,** although none became more valuable than Huck Finn.

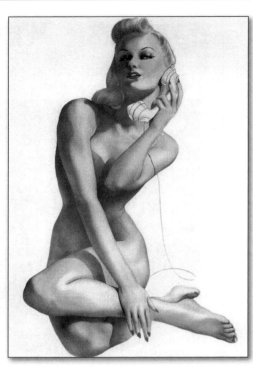

The Varga Girl in Esquire and Playboy fueled many an adolescent fantasy.

Alberto Vargas (1896-1982) was born in Peru in 1896. He studied in Switzerland and was heavily influenced by Raphael Kirchner, a premier artist for **La Vie Parisienne.** Moving to New York City, he became the official painter for the Ziegfeld Follies. In 1940, he shared space in **Esquire** with pinup artist George Petty until Petty left to pursue advertising work in 1942. **Esquire** suggested he drop the "s" in his name and the "Varga Girl" entered the American scene. He created watercolor and airbrush pinups for **Esquire** from 1940 until 1947, and the Varga Girl became a species of icon in wartime America. Appearing on the noses of aircraft, submarines and torpedoes, as well as in calendars, playing cards and in **Esquire** magazine, she held her own with photos of movie stars and the girls of the **Police Gazette** (qv.). Vargas created his first pinup for **Playboy Magazine** in 1957 and appeared regularly in **Playboy** from 1960 until his retirement in 1978.

H.G. Wells (1866-1946), novelist, journalist, sociologist, scientist and historian, began his writing career with a textbook, *Text Book of Biology* (London: University Correspondence College Press, 1893). His science fiction novels were extremely popular and elevated him to a position of free-lance intellectual/futurist. His journalism was as frequent in magazines as his fiction, such as his investigation of the new technology of tank warfare, "The Land Ironclads" (**The Strand**, December 1903). Wells' science fiction, both as original publications and pulp reprints, is highly collectible, and, in many cases becomes a two-fer being published with another highly collectible author. **The Strand,** 1901-1902, for example,

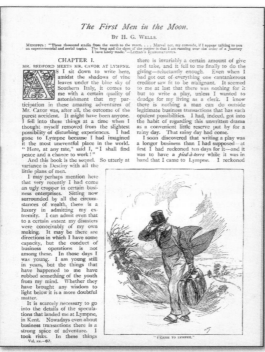

H. G. Wells was, for half a century, the world's most recognizable futurist.

carried both the original publications of Arthur Conan Doyle's (qv.) *Hound of the Baskervilles* and Wells' *First Men in the Moon*. A complete run featuring both has sold for as much as $1,500. Wells adds a collectible feature to almost all magazines he appeared in, and enhances the collectible value of issues where he appears beside other collectible writers.

Ella Wheeler Wilcox (1850-1919), who seems rather

tame today, was once quite a scandal. Books such as *Poems of Passion* (Chicago: Belford & Clarke, 1883) and *An Erring Woman's Love* (Chicago: W.B. Conkey, 1892) brought an undercurrent of sensuality to romantic poetry that was revolutionary in a woman poetess of the time. No less scandalous, in the framework of the times, was her free thinking, embracing the New Thought movement, occultism and spiritualism. In many ways, she was a modern woman in a Victorian world. Her poems and writings on New Thought were widely circulated in **The Century, Munsey's, Cosmopolitan, The Smart Set, Woman's Home Companion, St. Nicholas, Ladies' Home Journal** and successfully jumped the Atlantic to appear in **Windsor, Nash's** and **Pall Mall**. Today, she still has a large following of collectors and her magazine appearances are reasonably well sought after. As a poetess, she often appeared with other collectible authors in highly collectible issues of such magazines as **Century.**

Thomas Wolfe (1900-1938), born in Asheville, N.C.,

studied at Harvard University and went on to teach at New York University. Although his career was brief, it was mercurial. In 1925, he met Aline Bernstein, a successful New York theater set and costume designer. She was married and 20 years older. Their turbulent affair ended in 1930. Wolfe's first novel, *Look Homeward, Angel,* was published in 1929 by Scribner's. His editor was Maxwell Perkins, who also edited F. Scott Fitzgerald and Ernest Hemingway. *The Web and the Rock, You Can't Go Home Again* and *The Hills Beyond* were published posthumously. Wolfe published short stories in all the leading literary magazines of the day, including **The American Mercury, The Atlantic Monthly, New Republic, Scribner's, Harper's, Redbook Magazine, The Saturday Evening Post** and **Esquire. The New Yorker** issue of June 15, 1935, published "Only The Dead Know Brooklyn," which was written in dialect: "Maybe he's found out by now dat he'll neveh live long enough to know duh whole of Brooklyn. It'd take a guy a lifetime to know Brooklyn t'roo an' t'roo. An' even den, yuh wouldn't know it all." Priceless.

N.C. (Newell Convers) Wyeth (1882-1945) of

Needham, Mass., was one of the Brandywine School of Artists who had studied under Howard Pyle. He made his home in Chadds Ford, Pa. During his lifetime, he produced more than 3,000 illustrations along with 25 books. He was paid $50 for his first published work, a Bronco Buster, which appeared on the cover of **The Saturday Evening Post** (February 1903). He traveled west to work as a ranch hand in Colorado and rode mail routes in New Mexico and Arizona. Back East, the results were a series of magazine illustrations, "A Day with the Round-Up" in **Scribner's** (1906) and "The Indian in His Solitude" in **Outing** (1907). Other Western illustrations were for "Arizona Nights" by Stewart Edward White and the original "Hopalong Cassidy" stories by Clarence Mulford. In 1911, he was contracted by Charles Scribner & Sons to illustrate a new edition of R.L. Stevenson's *Treasure Island.* As the demand for his work increased, Wyeth became a regular contributor to **Harper's, McClure's, Scribner's, The Saturday Evening Post, Success Magazine, Collier's, The Century, Outing** and **The Ladies' Home Journal.** His illustrations are collected whether in black and white or color.

Advertising was only one string to the bow of the versatile N.C. Wyeth.

Sleepers

Rolf Armstrong virtually created the pin-up.

Rolf Armstrong (1889-1960) has often been characterized

as "the father of the American pin-up girl." After graduating from the Art Institute of Chicago, Armstrong moved to New York, where his early illustrations concentrated on "macho" types such as sailors, boxers and cowboys. In 1912, an assignment for the cover of **Judge** changed his focus to young women. Throughout the 1920s, Armstrong created illustrations that would become known as pin-up art, adapting it to advertising for the agency Brown and Bigelow, and to calendars, sheet music and greeting cards. His magazine covers for **Life, Shrine, College Humor, Puck** and **Photoplay,** among others, are sought-after collectibles as is his advertising work, notably his ads for Oneida silverware. Armstrong's style was imitated by such artists as Billy De Vorss, Earl Morand and Zoe Mozert, and was a major influence on later pin-up illustrators such as Petty (qv.) and Vargas (qv.) His most notable and collectible work is pre-World War II, though he would continue to be active in illustration into the 1950s.

T.S. (Timothy Shay) Arthur (1809-1885) of

Newburg, N.Y., moved to Philadelphia, where he became a successful author, editor, publisher and temperance crusader. During the 1840s, **Godey's Lady's Book** published 60 of Arthur's tales and sketches on topics ranging from marital and family relations, to temperance to women's rights. Sarah Hale, **Godey's** editor, regretted his departure from the magazine in 1850, when he

began a weekly titled **Arthur's Home Gazette.** In 1853, it became a monthly **Arthur's Home Magazine,** which was similar to **Godey's,** but with a distinct Christian moralistic and temperance bent. "Ten Nights in a Bar-Room and What I Saw There" (1854) is the temperance tract for which he achieved lasting fame. He became the literary patron saint of the American temperance movement and, interestingly, a practitioner of the Swedenborg religion. During the decade preceding the Civil War, he was outsold in American fiction only by Harriet Beecher Stowe's *Uncle Tom's Cabin.* In January 1867, Arthur's juvenile periodical, the **Children's Hour,** was a major contribution to the literature of youth in the period. It was eventually absorbed by **St. Nicholas** magazine in 1874. Arthur's influence during his lifetime contributes to his collectibility today.

Boris Artzybasheff's visual imagination astounded magazine readers for half a century.

Boris Artzybasheff (1899-1965) was born in Russia,

the son of novelist Mikhail Artzybasheff. He came to the United States after fighting with the White Army during the Russian Revolution. He began his career as an engraver in New York City, designing ornamental borders and some lettering. He was paid $15 per week. Eventually he was able to get work as a free-lance artist through his connections with the Russian exile community. As a free-lance commercial artist, he combined fantasy with whimsical human qualities in his renderings of machines. He illustrated 50 books, including *As I See* (1954), which he wrote and illustrated.

Here's another example of
Boris Artzybasheff's artwork.

He also designed restaurants and theatrical stage sets. Eventually, his cartoons and covers appeared in **Life** (the original and the Luce version), **Fortune, Collier's** and **Esquire.** But it was **Time Magazine,** for which he produced 200-plus covers between 1941 and 1965, that gave him the most public exposure and collectibility. He also created advertising for companies as varied as Xerox, Shell Oil, Pan Am, Casco Power Tools, Alcoa Steamship lines, Parke Davis, Avco Manufacturing, Scotch Tape, Wickwire Spencer Steele, Vultee Aircraft, World Airways and Parker Pens. His magazine art and advertising is in high demand.

Ray Stannard Baker (1870-1946), along with Ida Tarbell, Lincoln Steffens, William Allen White and Upton Sinclair, was one of the journalists labeled "muckrakers." Baker's coverage of the Pullman strike for the *Chicago News-Record* introduced him to the public and, beginning with **McClure's** in 1896, his exposes of corruption in high finance and railroads kept him in the public eye. In 1906, Baker, together with Lincoln Steffens and Ida Tarbell, founded **The American Magazine.** Baker wrote some fiction, notably for **Youth's Companion,** and authored the "Adventures" series of books under the pseudonym David Grayson. Baker's support for Woodrow Wilson in 1912 began a relationship that saw Baker appointed press secretary for the Versailles conference. Baker was a prolific magazine journalist and most major magazines of the period carried now-collectible pieces by him. Most sought after are his articles on race relations originally published in **McClure's**

and **the American**, and collected into the book *Following the Color Line* (New York: Doubleday, Page & Company, 1908). His autobiography, *American Chronicle* (New York: Scribner's, 1945), won the Pulitzer for biography.

John Kendrick Bangs (1862-1922) was a uniquely American humorist/satirist whose sometimes savage humor was extremely popular in the late 19th and early 20th centuries. His fantasies *Houseboat on the River Styx* and *Pursuit of the Houseboat* were very influential, and the sub-genre they spawned from Thorne Smith's Topper to Philip Jose Farmer's Riverboat books is termed Bangsian fantasy. Bangs' short stories were a common feature of many magazines through the last two decades of the 19th century, most often in **Harper's Monthly** and **Scribner's.** Bangs edited a number of magazines; notably he was the initial editor of **Munsey's.** He edited **Harper's** and headed **Puck** in 1905-1906. He appeared in **The Saturday Evening Post, The Smart Set, Cosmopolitan, Ladies' Home Journal** and **St. Nicholas,** among others, along with his frequent contributions to **Harper's** and **Scribner's.** Both as an editor and a writer, Bangs was a major influence on American magazines and his work is currently a bargain in the collector's market.

Eustace Robert Barton (1854-1943) was a mystery man who had a major impact on mystery. Dr. Eustace Robert Barton wrote (or rather collaborated) under the name Robert Eustace. Beginning in the **Harmsworth Magazine** as the collaborator of Mrs. L.T. Meade on "The Arrest of Captain Vandaleur" (July 1894), and ending his career in collaboration with Dorothy L. Sayers on *The Documents in the Case* (London: Ernest Benn, 1930), he had a long and impressive career in the creation of scientific detection stories. Between collaborations with the ladies, he collaborated with Edgar Jepson in both **The Strand** and **The Windsor.** While it has generally been assumed that he supplied scientific facts to writers, some collectors claim to have noticed a consistent stylistic change in the authors he is known to have worked with. This has, in turn, set off a hunt for other authors who might have worked with him. So, not only are the collaborations of Robert Eustace collectible, but all similar British scientific detective stories, between 1894 and 1943 benefit in collectibility, based on the possibility Dr. Barton had a hand in them.

Philip Boileau (1864-1917) was born in Quebec to a career diplomat and Susan Taylor Benton, the daughter of U.S. Sen. Thomas Hart Benton. He emigrated to Philadelphia where he met his wife and super model, Emily Gilbert. "The Boileau Girls" were considered to be the successor to the "Gibson Girls." Between 1907 and 1917, the "Boileau Girls" appeared on 34 covers of **The Saturday Evening Post**. Boileau's work also appeared on the covers of **The Sunday Magazine** (Jan. 5, 1905, was his first cover design*),* **Collier's, The Delineator, Every Week, Holland's, The Housewife, Ladies' Home Journal, Lady's World, McCall's,**

Philip Boileau's conception of American beauty captivated turn of the century America.

People's Home Journal, Pictorial Review, Southern Magazine, Success, War Cry (the Salvation Army Magazine) and Woman's Home Companion. Most of the Post and Sunday Magazines covers appeared on postcards issued by Reinthal and Newman. Interestingly, in a 1915 art competition sponsored by Pictorial Review Magazine, readers voted for their favorite artist as "Artist of the Year." Boileau came in second, earning a $500 prize. First place prize went to childhood and infant artist Bessie Pease Gutmann. Magazine covers with the Boileau Girls and Boys are highly prized by collectors.

Philip Boileau's artwork was a highlight of many magazines in the early 1900s.

Berton Braley (1882-1966), the leading American poet of his time, was once published in virtually every national newspaper and magazine. He created more than 10,000 poems, all in the classical craftsman tradition of telling a condensed musical story with help of rhyme and meter. Braley called himself modestly a "versifier." The poet's subject choice would always be universal, romantic and often humorous. He would talk on love, marriage, philosophy, politics, work, business, war, friendships, family and sports. Braley admired man and his achievements, as can be read in his most popular poem "The Thinker" and in "Enchanted Machines." For the World Series of 1914, he wrote a series of poems, syndicated by United Press, where he praised baseball star Christy Mathewson. Braley's experiences as a journalist and a miner in Butte, Mont., resulted in verses for "Mining Camp Ballads" and "Songs Of The Workaday World." In 1910, at **Puck** magazine he briefly worked as the editor, and at **Life** he contributed more than 15 years with versified book reviews and poems. As a foreign correspondent during World War I, Berton wrote humorous poetry about comradeship and horror in the battlefield, published later

Harrison Cady was an accomplished painter as well as children's illustrator.

in his 1918-1919 books *In Camp And Trench* and *Buddy Ballads.* Altogether, Braley published more than 22 books. Some called Berton Braley the American Kipling, others the O. Henry of poetry. Like those authors, Braley was a craftsman who inspired common men to believe that anything is possible if you work hard enough and take inconveniences along the road with humor so they never become too important.

(Walter) Harrison Cady (1877-1970) of Gardner,

Mass., had no formal art training. He moved to Brooklyn, N.Y., where he obtained a steady job on the *Brooklyn Eagle* as an illustrator for $10 a week. His cartoons of fantastic and friendly animals living in magical worlds caught the attention of **Life** magazine editor John Ames Mitchell. Mitchell offered Cady a job as a staff artist and cartoonist with a salary to match.

Throughout the publishing history of the original **Life** magazine, Cady contributed numerous covers, centerfolds and cartoons of a whimsical nature, mostly revolving around animal themes. In 1913, he began a collaboration with Thornton W. Burgess, illustrating stories and cartoons for children, that lasted until the death of Burgess. This successful team worked together not only on books and comic strips, but in the **People's Home Journal.** In 1920, Cady created his best-known comic strip for the *Herald-Tribune,* "Peter Rabbit." His work also appeared frequently in **Boy's Life, Child Life, Country Gentleman, St. Nicholas, Saturday Evening Post, Ladies' Home Journal** and **Good Housekeeping.** Today, Cady has an intense following among collectors.

Robert W. Chambers (1865-1933) began his career as

an illustrator, although he would eventually become a well-known writer. Chambers studied art at the Art Student's League in New York. In 1893, Chambers began illustrating for **Vogue, Truth** and was recruited for **Life** by his schoolmate at the Art Student's League, Charles Dana Gibson (qv.). He turned to writing in 1894 and never returned to illustration. His best-known book, *The King in Yellow* (Chicago: F. Tennyson Neely, 1895), a collection of short stories, was widely reprinted in horror pulps. Though primarily a writer of popular romances, Chambers also wrote historical fiction and science fiction, most of which was serialized as an original appearance in magazines such as **Cosmopolitan, The Saturday Evening Post** and **The Century.** Chambers is uneven as a collectible magazine author. His romances draw much less interest than the anomalies such as the science fiction tale "The Green Mouse," which was originally published in **The Saturday Evening Post** in a landmark issue Nov. 12, 1904, with Part Two of Florence Maybrick's (qv.) "A Travesty of Justice" and Part Two of Agnes and Edgerton Castle's "Rose of the World" illustrated by Harrison Fisher (qv.).

Howard Chandler Christy (1873-1952) began his

career at 22 with a commission from **The Century** for four images for the story "The Tragedy of the Comedy" by Chester Bailey Fernald (November 1895). All pictured women, and the "Christy Girl" was born. In 1898, **Scribner's** sent Christy, along with fellow artist F. C. Yohn, to cover the Spanish American War in Cuba. Christie's drawings of the Rough Riders, paired with the articles of Richard Harding Davis, and his only attempt at journalism, "An Artist at El Poso" (**Scribner's,** October 1898), made his reputation. Christy contributed regularly to magazines and was one of the most popular and visible illustrators in America through World War I. His illustrations appeared in most major magazines such as **Harper's, Scribner's, The Century, McClure's** and **Ladies' Home Journal**. He had two books of his own, *American Girl* and *Christy Girl*. Christy remains today as one of the most frequently ripped illustrators. Single, framed Christy illustrations are an antique mall staple, which has, unlike Norman Rockwell, hurt his collectibility in vintage magazines.

Howard Chandler Christy defined an "American girl" with his illustrations.

F.S. Church defined a world of fantasy in his illustrations.

THE BOY IN THE MOON.

By Clara L. Burnham.

A WEE baby boy sitting up in his cradle,
With fleecy cloud-curtains draped high o'er his head.—
He blinks at the "dipper," that big starry ladle,
Nor fears that the "great bear" will tread on his bed.
But night after night, as he sails through the heavens,
His cradle is changed to a golden balloon,
And baby, grown older, leans out and looks earthward,
Where children hail gayly the Man in the Moon.

F.S. (Frederick Stuart) Church (1842-1924) was

born in Grand Rapids, Mich. He showed an early penchant for
hard work and sketching. As a child, he studied with Grand Rapids
artist Marinus Harding. In 1855 at the age of 13, Church moved,
alone, to Chicago where he worked for the American Express
Company and continued informal art training. After the Civil
War, Church returned to Chicago and, while working again for
the express company, studied art with Walter Shirlaw. In 1870, he
moved to New York City to be a full time artist/illustrator, where
he remained until his death. Church's early published illustrations
were advertising materials for Elgin Watches and Valentine
Varnish. Late in 1872, Church began a long association with the
Harper publishing firm. Over the next two decades, hundreds of
his illustrations appeared in the **Harper's** periodicals, where he
was frequently honored by having his pictures appear on covers
or special holiday outer wraps. His illustrations for children also
appeared in **St. Nicholas, Wide Awake** and **Our Little Ones.** Later
his pictures appeared in the **Outlook, The Ladies' Home Journal,
Cosmopolitan, Frank Leslie's Weekly, McClure's Magazine,** and
Woman's Home Companion. Church's illustrations frequently
included animals, children and/or attractive young girls. His
pictures are endowed with a gentle nature and a vivid imagination.
They continue to charm and amuse today.

Kate Cleary (1862-1905), the daughter of Irish immigrants,

was born in New Brunswick. After her father's death, the family
moved to Ireland, Philadelphia and then Chicago. Cleary began
publishing stories and poems in **Saturday Night** at age 14, and
later in the *Chicago Tribune*. At first Cleary wrote under various
names and pseudonyms: K. Temple More, Kate McPhelim, Mrs.
Kate Chrystal (*The Lady of Lynhurst*, 1884) and Mrs. Sumner
Hayden (*Vella Vernel, or an Amazing Marriage*, 1887). After her
marriage to Michael Cleary and their move to Hubbell, Neb.,
in 1884, she also began signing her works "Kate M. Cleary" or
"K.M.C." Although some of her stories and sketches are bleakly
naturalistic, much of her best writing offers a humorous look at
Western society. Her mystery novel, *Like a Gallant Lady*, 1897,
created controversy in Nebraska over its depiction of the state and
its people. The family returned to Chicago in 1898 where they
struggled to survive; thus, many of her later stories are potboilers.
When Cleary died in 1905, Chicago newspapers named her "one
of the best-known magazine writers in the country." A complete
bibliography of her known works can be found in *Kate M. Cleary:
A Literary Biography with Selected Works* (1993), by Susanne K.
George.

Joseph Clement Coll was the unquestioned master of pen and ink. His illustrations are shown here and on the next page.

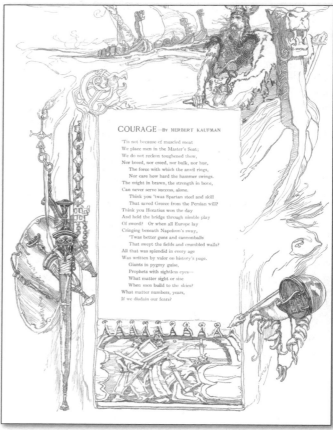

Joseph Clement Coll (1881-1921) of Philadelphia,
Pa., perhaps the greatest pen illustrator who ever lived, joined the
Philadelphia North American in 1901 after working for the *New
York American* and *Chicago American*. Coll had no formal art
training; his relentless and varied daily newspaper drawings were
his art school. Although mentored by William Glackens, Coll's
distinctive style was influenced by Daniel Vierge, Edwin Austin
Abbey, Howard Pyle and Mariano Fortuny. **Sunday Magazine**
(later **Every Week**) art director J. Thomson Willing recognized
Coll's potential, assigning him Sunday newspaper fiction to
illustrate. Willing's confidence was repaid by Coll's illustrations
for Arthur Conan Doyle's *Sir Nigel* (serialized 1905-1906). Coll
continued at **Sunday Magazine** through at least 1918 (highlights:
the *Galloping Dick* series, *The Garden of Fate* and Conan Doyle's
The Lost World). Coll's Fu Manchu pictures exemplify his **Collier's
Weekly** (1910-1922) work. **Appleton's** (1907), **Hampton's** (1910),
Everybody's Magazine (1907-1921; includes *King of the Khyber
Rifles* and *Messiah of The Cylinder*), **Pictorial Review** (1919-1921),
Ladies' Home Journal (1916-1921), **The Delineator** (1918),
The New Red Cross Magazine (1919), **Hearst's International**
(1922), **Cosmopolitan** and **The Red Book** (both 1921) have Coll
drawings. Two fine Coll collections by John Fleskes are available:
Joseph Clement Coll – The Art of Adventure and *Joseph Clement Coll
– A Legacy in Line*.

W.W. Denslow brought legends and nursery rhymes to life.

W.W. (William Wallace) Denslow (1856-1915)

was born in Philadelphia and studied art at New York's Cooper Union. In 1882, he opened a studio in New York where he drew magazine illustrations and designed theater costumes. He also worked with Elbert Hubbard for the Roycrofters in East Aurora, providing cartoons of humor and social commentary to **The Philistine** magazine. Denslow's trademark signature included a stylized rendering of a seahorse. Hubbard eventually adapted it to many Roycrofters logos, including the cover of **The Philistine** magazine itself, and watermarks in the paper for many Roycrofters books. After moving to Chicago and meeting writer L. Frank Baum, the two published *Father Goose, His Book* (1899). It was an instant success, becoming the best-selling children's book of 1900. The most important collaboration between Baum and Denslow, however, was the best seller *The Wonderful Wizard of Oz* (1900). Denslow's magazine appearances in addition to **The Philistine,** included the **Sunday Magazine** (1908) and **St. Nicholas** magazine (1909). His work in any form is worth mega bucks.

Dick Donovan/J.E.P. Muddock (1842-1934) were

one and the same. "Dick Donovan" was the pseudonym and the hero used by Joyce Emmerson Preston Muddock. Donovan was so popular that, even today, a detective is referred to as a "Dick." As Dick Donovan, Muddock wrote at least 278 short stories and 12 true crime articles, most of which were originally published in magazines, four in **The Strand** (July, August, September, October 1892), to fill a gap in A.C. Doyle's (qv.) *Adventures of Sherlock Holmes.* Muddock was a journalist and edited the *Savage Club Papers.* Dick Donovan was a mainstay of the British version of

Maud Tousey Fangel defined a generation of children.

pulp magazines, known as "penny dreadfuls," though he did show up from time to time in the slick magazines of the era, as did Muddock writing both fiction, and non-fiction. Due perhaps to the fragility of the penny dreadful, Muddock is very sought after in original stories both as himself and as Dick Donovan. First American appearances and reprints in such magazines as **The Armchair Detective** are also collectible.

Theodore Dreiser (1871-1945) was faced with censorship

throughout his early career, and made ends meet as a journalist and magazine editor. He was the managing editor of **Broadway Magazine** from 1906 to 1907 and was the editor in chief of the Butterick women's magazines from 1907 to 1910. Dreiser's journalism appeared consistently from about 1900 on in such publications as **The Munsey** and **Puritan** magazines. A personal friend of H. L. Mencken (qv.), Dreiser was a regular contributor to **The American Mercury** throughout the 1920s. Dreiser's effect on a magazine's value is not that great except for the more obscure magazines he appeared in, such as **Puritan.** However, both as an editor and a writer, his influence on American magazines was profound and increasingly recognized. Currently, his magazine work is a bargain, though it should be assumed that his stock will rise, as his recognition in the field rises to meet his literary reputation.

Maud Tousey Fangel (1881-1968) was born in Boston

and studied at Boston's School of Fine Arts before going to New York City on a scholarship to study at Cooper Union. After presenting a portfolio of her work to the art director of **Good**

Harrison Fisher had an eye for beauty and elegance.

Housekeeping, Guy Fangel, she not only got her first commercial assignments, but later a marriage proposal. The birth of their son, Lloyd, began Fangel's fascination with drawing babies. She did more than 1,500 pictures of him before he was 3 years old. Her magazine covers during the 1930s, 1940s and 1950s included publications such as the **Modern Priscilla, Ladies' Home Journal, Woman's Home Companion** and **Needlecraft Magazine.** She also did magazine advertising for Colgate's Talc Powder, Cream of Wheat and Squibb's Cod Liver Oil. She used her son's face for the boy on the famous Cracker Jack Box. Her book, *Babies,* with verses by Alice Higgins, was published in 1933 by Whitman Publishing, featuring 16 large color illustrations. Her magazine covers and advertising are usually framed by collectors.

Harrison Fisher (1875-1934) was born in Brooklyn and

moved to San Francisco where he studied at the Mark Hopkins Institute of Art. At 16, Fisher had begun to make drawings for the *San Francisco Call* and later for the Hearst-owned *San Francisco Examiner.* After moving East, he took a staff illustrator job at **Puck** magazine. He became noted for his ability to draw beautiful women, and his Fisher Girls became rivals to those of the "Gibson Girls" and the "Christy Girls." The American Girl was a favorite theme for magazines at the turn of the century, and Fisher did cover illustrations for most of them. Hearst signed him to an exclusive contract through the early 1930s until his death for the covers of **Cosmopolitan.** His beautiful women also appeared on covers and inside in illustrations for **The Saturday Evening Post, McClure's** and **Ladies' Home Journal.** Interestingly, the "Fisher Girls" are considered more valuable by collectors today than either of their former rivals.

James Montgomery Flagg (1877-1960) was a child

prodigy, making his first professional sale to **St. Nicholas** in 1890 at the age of 12. At 15, he was on the staff of both **Life** and **Judge.** His early career was divided between magazine and book illustration, adding **Harper's** to his list before World War I. After

Child prodigy James Montgomery Flagg worked as an illustrator into the 1950s.

the war, Flagg expanded his magazine work to include **Photoplay, McClure's, Cosmopolitan, The Saturday Evening Post, Redbook, Hearst's International, Liberty, Collier's, Woman's Home Companion, Ladies' Home Journal** and **The American Magazine.** It was Flagg, who, with **Cosmopolitan,** created the visual touchstone for P.G. Wodehouse's Jeeves and Bertie Wooster, much as Joseph Clement Coll (qv.) created a visualization of Sax Rohmer's (qv.) Fu Manchu. Flagg continued to draw and sell his work into the 1950s, notably his caricatures of film stars for **Photoplay.** Flagg's caricatures, such as a striking black and white of Carole Lombard with red lipstick from **Photoplay** (November 1936) are very sought after; his early work tends to be less in demand.

Philip Goodwin illustrated London's Call of the Wild and was a premier wildlife artist.

Jacques Futrelle (1875-1912) was a journalist, theatrical manager and mystery writer born in Pike County, Ga., who was the descendant of French Huguenots. In 1895, he married fellow writer Lily May Peel. His "Thinking Machine" character Professor Van Dusen, who solved impossible crimes, first appeared in a serialized version of "The Problem of Cell 13" in the *Boston American* (1905). Most of his stories such as "The Chase of the Golden Plate" (1906), "The Simple Case of Susan" (1908), "The King of Diamonds" (1908-1909) and "The High Hand" (1910) were serialized in **The Saturday Evening Post**. His work also appeared in **Everybody's Magazine** (1905) and **The Popular Magazine** (1912). Unfortunately, in 1912, Futrelle was returning with his wife to New York on the Titanic. After the ship had collided with the iceberg, he escorted her to lifeboat 9, which was filled almost to capacity. When Mrs. Futrelle hesitated, an officer forced her into the boat and she survived the disaster. Jacques Futrelle and several of his stories, which he had written during his stay in England, went down with the ship. Due to his untimely demise, his work is in demand even in Japan.

Philip Goodwin (1882-1935) of Norwich, Conn., studied at the Rhode Island School of Design, the Art Student's League in New York and Howard Pyle's Brandywine School in Pennsylvania. Amazingly, he sold his first illustrations at the age of 11 to **Collier's Weekly.** At 22, along with Charles Livingston Bull, he illustrated Jack London's "The Call of the Wild" (1903) and the following year Stewart Edward White's "The Silent Places" (1904). An avid sportsman and outdoorsman, he was friends with Charles Russell, N.C. Wyeth, Carl Rungius, Theodore Roosevelt, Will Rogers and Ernest Seton Thompson. Rungius taught Goodwin an appreciation

for hunting, which gave him closer insight to his wildlife subjects. His friendship with Roosevelt led to his illustrations for "African Game Trails." His magazine illustrations and covers included such periodicals as **McClure's Magazine** (March 1905), **The Saturday Evening Post** (May 18, 1907), **Scribner's** (1910), **Outdoor Life** and **Everybody's Magazine.** Goodwin also did advertising, posters and a series of calendars for **Bristol.** Collectors search for magazines with his wildlife illustrations in order to frame the prints.

Bessie Pease Gutmann was one of the first "investigative artists."

Bessie Pease Gutmann (1876-1960) is best known for

her heartwarming art prints featuring innocent children during the early part of the 20th century, and is highly collectible for her magazine and advertising work. The popularity of her art prints has led to the ripping of her work in magazines for purposes of framing as "original" which, in her case, is not always accurate, an art print having preceded the magazine publication. A highly collectible feature of her magazine work was as an "investigative artist," typified by her illustrations for "The Lost Children of Greater New York" (Robert Sloss and Annette Austin, **Pearson's,** October 1905) and its follow-up, "The Foundlings of New York City" (Robert Sloss and Annette Austin, **Pearson's,** February 1906). Her commercial art is also collectible, and much of it is not credited. Ads for Hygrade Pajamas, R & G Corsets, Ralston's Clothing Patterns and Lanita's (predecessor of Kellogg's) Corn Flakes are highly collectible features of **Pearson's, Cosmopolitan, The Delineator, Woman's Home Companion, Pictorial Review, St. Nicholas** and **Everybody's.**

Sarah Josepha Hale (1788-1879) of New Hampshire, without any formal education, was one of the first women to make a living as a writer/editor. Mrs. Hale was the author of the poem "Mary Had A Little Lamb" in **Juvenile Miscellany** (September 1830) and the editor of **Ladies' Magazine** (1828–1837), which eventually became **Godey's Lady's Book** (1837–1877). **Godey's Lady's Book** was the fashion and household bible for the American woman in the 1800s. Mrs. Hale, one of the earliest champions of women's rights, also promoted exercise for women. She Americanized the hand-colored Paris fashions and included many paid advertisements in the monthly book, including the first advertisement for the first washing machine. She helped organize the first ladies' college, Vassar College, and persuaded President Lincoln to sign the Thanksgiving Day proclamation. She brought the writing of Edgar Allan Poe to the American public, as her son had known Poe at West Point. During the Civil War, **Godey's** was one of the most sought after smuggling operations for the women in the South, who had to get their fashions and recipes. Today, the legacy of Sarah Hale is valued by re-enactment buffs as well as literary scholars.

Marietta Holley (Josiah Allen's wife) (1836-1926) was considered "the female Mark Twain" for her creation of Samantha Allen, and her humorous commentaries in dialect. In an understated, humorous manner, she was an early champion of women's rights. Samantha, for example, could not understand why men were trying so hard to protect women from the effort it takes to slip a piece of paper into a box at a polling place. She had noticed that these same attitudes did not apply to churning butter, baking bread and washing clothes, which took a good deal more effort. Samantha had her original appearances in magazines, notably **Pearson's, Ladies' Home Journal** and **People's Home Journal.** Her original articles and stories in magazine form often eclipse her books in the collectible market, as is true with many early feminist writers. Holley's opinions, shifted through Samantha's gentle humor, were an important feature of late 19th and early 20th century American social history.

(Robert) Bruce Horsfall (1869-1948) of Clinton, Iowa, studied art at the Cincinnati Art Academy and in Munich and Paris. Upon returning to the U.S., he worked as a decorator for Rookwood Pottery from 1893 to 1895. In 1903-1906, he focused on painting birds, and from then on, he devoted his life to the design of plates for books and magazines. His paintings of wildlife brought him international recognition. He painted backgrounds for many of the exhibits for the Rutgers University Geological Museum. He was a researcher and artist for the Smithsonian

Institution, American Museum of Natural History, the Peabody Museum of Natural History, the United States National Museum, and was affiliated with the Paleontology Department at Princeton University. He also painted the American eagle in front of the Chicago Museum of Fine Arts. He was director of arts, an illustrator and cover artist for **Nature Magazine**, along with his wife, Carra. He also did many animal illustrations for the children's periodical **St. Nicholas** magazine.

(James) Langston Hughes (1902-1967) a poet, author

and journalist, was quietly a champion of civil rights before it became a popular cause. His essay, "The Negro Artist and the Racial Mountain" (**The Nation,** June 23, 1926), set a tone for young African-American writers that continues to the present time. Hughes fulfilled his own words with the innovative jazz-based poetry of *Weary Blues* (New York, Alfred A. Knopf, 1926). His work was a cornerstone of the Harlem Renaissance. Hughes was, with the possible exception of Richard Wright, the black writer most identified with the Communist Left during the 1930s and he was a frequent contributor to **New Masses.** In 1943, Hughes turned to gentle, satirical humor to make his points by creating Jesse B. Semple, known as "Simple" for, first, *The Chicago Defender* and then the *New York Post*. Hughes' magazine appearances, for magazines such as **Esquire,** are highly sought after, and his more radical pieces for **New Masses** and smaller magazines are very collectible.

Eugene Jolas (1894-1952) of Union Hill, N.J., was a

journalist who in the 1920s took a position with *The Chicago Tribune* Paris edition. Through his column "Rambles Through Literary Paris," he met the artistic and literary expatriate community as well as the leading French artists of the period. In 1927, he began one of the most important avant-garde literary reviews, **transition,** with the assistance of co-editor Elliot Paul. **transition,** over a period of 11 years, published such luminaries as Gertrude Stein, Andre Breton, Man Ray, Andre Masson, Henri Matisse, Joan Miro, Hart Crane, William Carlos Williams, Marcel Duchamp and Henry Miller. But it was Jolas' acquaintance with James Joyce that had the most impact on the magazine and literature. Joyce's "Work in Progress," which was later published as *Finnegans Wake,* appeared in the first issues of **transition.** The association became such that Jolas eventually acted as an unofficial editor of much of Joyce's new writings as well as his friend. In 1938, Jolas was one of the founders of another new literary monthly, **Volontes,** which also involved writer Raymond Queneau. The Jolas publications are literary and collector's treasures. They are truly scarce because the paper quality was so poor.

Heinrich Kley, whose work is on this page and the facing page, was a major influence on Disney animation.

Heinrich Kley (1863-1945) was born in Karlsruhe, Germany, and studied art in Munich. His pen and ink drawings satirized Germany, often using humans and anthropomorphic animals as metaphors. The drawings appeared in the German magazines **Simplizissimus** and **Jugend**, and brought him instant fame. Kley was first introduced to the American audience by the then new **Coronet Magazine** in three consecutive issues in 1937. A few of his satirical line drawings were reproduced. In its introduction to Kley, **Coronet** said that he had "died in a mad house a few years back." However, Kley still had eight years to live and he had never been in a mental institution. Kley, along with T.S. Sullivant, has been studied by Disney animators. The influence of Kley's humanized animals can be seen in Walt Disney's "The Dance of the Hours" sequence from "Fantasia." His drawings have been used as illustrations in magazines such as **Atlas** and **Motive.** Even The Fillmore West Auditorium of San Francisco used his art in a poster.

HEINRICH KLEY

In this issue CORONET again presents the drawings of Heinrich Kley, this time confining the selection to his sur-human studies of elephants. You will find eleven of these delectable pages interspersed throughout the text pages. The January issue also contained eleven Kley drawings.

CORONET
15

THE TRIP

THE TIP

IN FLAGRANTE . . .

. . . DELICTO

Rose Wilder Lane (1886–1968) was born in the Dakota Territory to author Laura Ingalls Wilder. She lived in Missouri, Louisiana, Kansas City and New York, and became a world traveler and political activist. Rose was already a noted writer and journalist before her mother was published and is considered the influence that got Laura started writing her "Little House" books. In 1915, Rose began writing serial stories and columns for the *San Francisco Bulletin*. During the next three decades, she wrote numerous short stories and articles for major magazines, including **The American Magazine, Good Housekeeping, Harper's, Sunset, Life and London** (1917), **The Ladies' Home Journal, Harper's Monthly, Asia** magazine, **Travel Magazine, Country Gentleman** and **The Saturday Evening Post.** In 1918, she became involved in radical politics, meeting John Reed, Max Eastman and Floyd Dell, editor of **New Masses,** while living in New York City. She also wrote a biography of Herbert Hoover, which was serialized in **Sunset Magazine** (1919). She edited the "Little House" books for her mother, Laura.

Florence Maybrick (1862-1941) was born in Mobile, Ala., the daughter of a wealthy American family. She became the first American woman convicted of murder in England. Florence Maybrick was accused of poisoning her husband, James, a Liverpool cotton merchant and confirmed arsenic-eater. Her trial was an international sensation in the press, especially when she was convicted and was sentenced to be hanged. Public and private pressure got her a reprieve with a 15-year sentence in an English prison. The Maybrick case shook England's criminal justice system to the core. The facts presented a compelling reason to establish a court of appeals. Upon her release from prison, Mrs. Maybrick had her story "A Travesty of Justice, The Story of Fifteen Lost Years" serialized in **The Saturday Evening Post** (1904), and became a fixture on the American lecture circuit. In the early 1990s, a diary purportedly written by James Maybrick, indicating he was Jack The Ripper and describing the Whitechapel murders in detail, was found, creating even more speculation about Florence.

Neysa McMein (1888-1949) from Quincy, Ill., attended the Art Institute of Chicago before moving to New York City in 1913. In 1914, she sold her first drawing to the *Boston Star*. The next year, she sold a cover to **The Saturday Evening Post**. By 1916, she became the "house" cover artist for **McClure's Magazine.** As a regular member of the Algonquin Round Table set, she hosted nightly salons in her New York studio with Dorothy Parker, Robert Benchley, George Gershwin, Cole Porter, Noel Coward, Walt Disney, Edna Ferber, Charlie Chaplin, Helen Hayes and Harpo Marx. Her specialty as a portrait artist was featured from 1923 through March 1938 on all of the covers for **McCall's Magazine.** She also supplied work to **McClure's, Liberty, Woman's Home Companion, Collier's, The Saturday Evening Post** and **Photoplay.** McMein ads for Palmolive, Coca-Cola, Cadillac, Wallace Silver and Wamsutta are also in demand. She created the domestic design for the original Betty Crocker character.

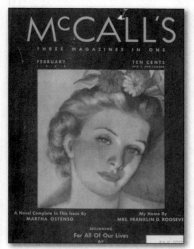

Neysa McMein's feminine concept of American beauty was widely copied.

Arthur Morrison (1863-1945) wrote both fiction and journalism for several British magazines in the late 19th and early 20th centuries. His "private inquiry agent," Martin Hewitt, debuted in **The Strand** with "The Lenton Croft Robberies" (January 1894) as the replacement for Sherlock Holmes. In 1895, Hewitt moved his cases to **The Windsor** with "The Ivy Cottage Mystery" (January). Morrison created somewhat of a sensation with his best seller *Tales of Mean Streets* (London: Methuen, 1894), a collection of magazine pieces originally appearing in the **National Observer.** Morrison was a reliable and frequent contributor to **National Observer, Macmillan's Magazine, The Strand, The Windsor, Metropolitan** and **Tit-Bits.** In the 1920s and '30s, he became a mainstay of the British version of **Argosy**, contributing both original stories and reprints of earlier short stories. Original Hewitt stories, and the sketches comprising *Tales of Mean Streets* are much sought after in the collector's market, as are various other pieces similar in character to the *Mean Street* sketches.

John R. Neill provided the visual touchstones for the Oz stories.

John R.(ea) Neill (1877-1943), a Philadelphia newspaper illustrator, was best known for his illustrations of L. Frank Baum's Oz books. Although W.W. Denslow illustrated the initial Oz book, publisher Reilly & Britton persuaded Neill to illustrate all the Oz books that Baum wrote, starting with *The Marvelous Land of Oz* (1904). Neill's two nieces, Marie (5) and Roberta (3), were used as the models for the illustrations of Ozma and Dorothy in this Oz book, which is the second in the series. After Baum's death, Neill continued with all the Ruth Plumly Thompson Oz books, and then wrote and illustrated three of his own in the 1940s. Neill was a prolific magazine illustrator for such publications as **Argosy, Boy's Life, The Century Magazine, Collier's, The Delineator, Ladies' Home Journal, People's Home Journal, Pictorial Review, The Saturday Evening Post, Physical Culture** and **Today's Housewife.** His illustrations ran the gamut from covers to stories, and his work now commands prices on the high end.

Elia Wilkinson Peattie (1862-1935), novelist, poet, dramatist, short story writer, literary critic, historian and journalist, was a consummate professional in a prolific writing career that spanned more than 50 years. Described as "tall, dignified and kindly, and possessing a wicked sense of humor," she published writings in diverse magazines and newspapers that ranged from romanticized and pastoral children's stories, sentimental fiction, realistic local color tales and naturalistic depictions of lower-class society's struggles to logically argued political and social editorials. Except for the years between 1888 and 1896 when she lived in Omaha, Neb., and wrote for the *Omaha World Herald,*

George Petty's pin-ups captivated postwar American men.

she lived most of her professional life in Chicago. In addition to publishing in countless newspapers and magazines, her work was accepted by prestigious periodicals such as **Harper's Weekly, Cosmopolitan, Atlantic Monthly, Lippincott's, St. Nicholas** and **Youth's Companion**. She published approximately 40 books, but *A Mountain Woman* (1896), a collection of short stories about the West, and *The Precipice* (1914), a novel about settlement houses and workers, are considered her best works. A biography and bibliography of her known works can be found in *Impertinences: Selected Writings by Elia Peattie, A Journalist in the Gilded Age* (2005) by Susanne George Bloomfield.

George Petty (1894-1975) is best remembered as the creator

of "The Petty Girl," his own take on pin-up art. Originally based on Petty's wife and his daughter, the Petty Girl evolved from a combination of the best features from a variety of models. He also drew the head a touch smaller in proportion to elongated torso and legs, which gave his creation an immediately recognizable look. Autumn issue of **Esquire** magazine in 1933 was the initial debut of the Petty Girl, and almost instantly Petty was a success, as commissions poured in for advertisements, calendars and film posters featuring the Petty Girl. Petty continued to contribute to **Esquire** until 1942, when the pressures of his advertising work and the presence of Alberto Vargas' (qv.) pin-ups saw him leave **Esquire** to concentrate on advertising work. He worked into the 1970s with advertising commissions from companies like American Motors, the Ice Capades and the Rigid Tool Company, making the Petty Girl a fairly standard fixture in magazines from the war years through the early 1970s.

Coles Phillips was the master of the "fadeaway girl."

Coles Phillips (1880-1927) of Springfield, Ohio, moved to New York in 1904 to seek a career in art illustration. J.A. Mitchell, the publisher of **Life** magazine, was impressed with his work, and was interested in hiring him. He never went to the interview and instead enrolled in art classes. Finally, in 1907, he took Mitchell up on his offer. At 26, Coles Phillips had arrived and the association with **Life** magazine would last throughout his life. In 1908, Phillips created a cover that would become his trademark: the "fadeaway girl." The first **Life** appearance was in May 1908, and public demand was so great that he produced print and calendar versions of them as well. Phillips was a star within a year with the fadeaway "Phillips Girl." **Good Housekeeping** lured him away from **Life** with a lucrative, five-year contract to produce every cover for **Good Housekeeping** (1912-1917). Although competing magazines paid other artists (such as Valentine Sandberg) to produce fadeaways, none could match Phillips. He also produced collectible ads for Luxite Hosiery and Overland Auto Liberty, Good Housekeeping, Vogue, Collier's Holeproof Hosiery, Willy's Overland, Vitralite Paint, Scranton Lace, National Mazda Lamps, Jantzen Swimsuits, Oneida Community Silver and Palmolive featuring his "fadeaway girls."

Samuel Roth (1893-1974) was called "the dirtiest pig in the world" and "the louse of Lewisburg." Roth was one of the most influential, resourceful and daring erotica publishers America ever produced. His career started in the early 1920s, and by 1931 he had already served three jail terms. He indignantly defended his right to publish pornography before Sen. Estes Kefauver's 1955 investigating committee, and defiantly served out jail terms that saw him behind bars as often as not. Roth published Joyce's *Finnegans Wake,* which he pirated, in his magazine **Two Worlds,** along with a piracy of *Ulysses.* Between prison stretches, he published **Two Worlds, The Beau Book, Casanova** and **American Aphrodite,** all of which are prized by collectors. Roth was a major factor in later decisions on obscenity and he lived to see himself, in many cases, vindicated. He is collected for both literary value and as a champion of publishing freedom.

(Alfred) Damon Runyon (1884-1946) of Manhattan, Kansas, became a legendary Broadway reporter, short-story writer and humorist. In 1910, he went to New York City to work for Hearst's *New York American.* He gained fame with his tales of the gambling, racing and criminal world. His cronies on Broadway were Al Capone, Jack Dempsey, Babe Ruth, Arnold Rothstein and Walter Winchell, and their daily meetings made Lindy's Restaurant a household name. His column "As I See It" was syndicated in the Hearst newspapers across the country. At the peak of his career, Runyon had a daily readership of more than 10 million and was considered America's premier journalist. His characters, Lemon Drop Kid, Dave the Dude, Harry the Horse, Dream Street Rose and Izzy Cheesecake reflected the colorful side of the city's underworld life. His stories appeared in magazines such as Hearst's **Cosmopolitan, The Saturday Evening Post, Munsey's, The Popular Magazine** and **Collier's Weekly. Collier's** published three of his most memorable stories, "The Snatching of Bookie Bob" (1931), "The Three Wise Guys" (1933), and "The Idyll of Miss Sarah Brown" (1933), which became the basis for the Broadway play and movie "Guys and Dolls." Runyon's magazine stories remain a colorful tribute to a bygone era.

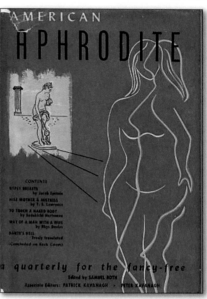

Samuel Roth's magazine came with the scandals attached.

Sidney Sime all but invented fantasy illustration.

Sydney H. Sime (1867-1941) of Manchester, England, studied art at the Liverpool School of Art. His fantasy-style and humorous illustrations were first published in the humor magazine **Pick-Me-Up** in 1895. As his work found an audience, he was published continually in **The Idler** and **The Pall Mall Magazine.** His most successful artistic partnership was with the 26-year-old Lord Dunsany. Dunsany sought him out to illustrate *The Gods of Pegana.* This was the start of a 15-year collaboration, which led to Dunsany actually writing stories around Sime's illustrations. Other than two frontispieces for a pair of Arthur Machen books, Dunsany's were the only books he illustrated. In 1898, Sime's uncle died and bequeathed the bulk of his estate to the artist. He used a portion of his inheritance to purchase **The Idler**, which he co-edited with Arthur Lawrence (May 1899-January 1901). Other periodicals that featured Sime's fantasy/fantastic art included **The Graphic, The Illustrated London News, The Tatler, The Strand Magazine** and **Punch.** His creativity also extended to costume design, including a 1909 production of "The Blue Bird" by Maeterlinck and a trio of original operas by Howard de Walden based on the Welsh legends of The Mabinogian.

Frank Spearman (1859-1950) has been called the "dean of America's railroad writers." That alone makes him a very desirable and collectible magazine writer. Spearman's magazine writing was very prolific and spanned most major publications in the first two decades of the 20th century. The Whispering Smith stories, originating in **McClure's,** became a popular motion picture, starring Alan Ladd. And it seemed, in the 1900s, that **The Saturday Evening Post** was, somehow, incomplete without a Spearman railroad story or article. Spearman wrote for children and published in **St. Nicholas,** as well as contributed his railroad fiction and non-fiction to **Munsey's, Harper's, McClure's** and **Everybody's.** Spearman is collected both in his own right and in conjunction with collections of railroadiana. The Whispering Smith stories, both in **McClure's** and **The Saturday Evening Post,**

As a painter, illustrator, architect and film director, Penryhn Stanlaws was a true renaissance man.

bring premiums from collectors. A further field in which Spearman figures for the collector is the collection of objectivist literature. Ayn Rand collected Spearman and he is considered a major influence on Rand and her philosophy.

Penrhyn Stanlaws (1877-1957), born in Dundee,

Scotland, was the younger brother of illustrator Sydney Adamson. He changed his name to avoid a confusion of identity, although their styles were completely different. Stanlaws studied art in Paris, and worked both in New York City and Hollywood. His focus as a magazine illustrator and painter was beautiful women. The "Stanlaws Girl" became as famous as the Gibson Girl. Interestingly, the original Stanlaws Girl was movie star Anna Q. Nilsson. In 1915, Olive Thomas, another movie star, was the model for his famous nude painting "Between Poses." Stanlaws' illustrations

G.E. Studdy's canine friend Bonzo was among the first neon signs in Piccadilly Circus.

appeared on covers and inside the pages of **The American Magazine, Life, Judge, Collier's Weekly, The Saturday Evening Post, Associated Sunday Magazine, Hearst's International** and **The Metropolitan Magazine.** Interestingly, his construction of the Hotel des Artistes, at 1 West 67th St. in New York City, is now a famous landmark for having housed so many prominent artists over the intervening years. He also wrote plays and movies, directing such Hollywood films as "Pink Gods" and "The House That Jazz Built."

G.E. (George Ernest) Studdy (1878-1948) of

Devonport, England, studied at Heatherley's Art School in London. He also attended Calderon's Animal School to study animal anatomy as well as drawing. **Comic Cuts** was the first publication to regularly buy Studdy's work. By 1903, his work was appearing consistently in **The Boy's Own Paper, The Graphic, The Tatler, Illustrated London News** and **The Windsor Magazine.** In 1912, he produced a weekly full-page cartoon for **The Sketch**, a weekly periodical published by *The Illustrated London News.* The first "Studdy Dog" appeared in 1921. The no-name dog was to become Britain's pet. Finally, on Nov. 8, 1922, **The Sketch** announced the name of what was to become Studdy's most famous cartoon creation: the little dog called "Bonzo." Other publishers fought for a stake in Bonzo in books and ads, where Bonzo was selling everything from tobacco, cars, soap and polish to confectionery and pickles. Bonzo was also among the first neon signs put up in London's Piccadilly Circus in 1924. Producer William A. Ward collaborated with George Studdy to produce the first of 26 short films featuring Bonzo. The craze for anything Bonzo continues with today's collectors.

J. Allen St. John provided the first visual image of Tarzan.

J. Allen St. John (1872-1957) of Chicago, Ill., traveled with his artist mother to Paris and consequently decided to study at the Art Students' League in New York. In 1898, he worked for the *New York Herald*. Early illustrations appeared in **Harper's Monthly** (1898) and **The Delineator** (1901). After a move to Chicago, he illustrated magazine covers for **Woman's World** (1912). In 1915, McClurg hired him to provide small black and white chapter headings for the second novel in a new series "The Return of Tarzan" by a then little-known author named Edgar Rice Burroughs. A tremendous success, the next Burroughs novel, *The Beasts of Tarzan,* was a complete St. John product, including the colored dust jacket and interior illustrations. For two decades, all of the Burroughs material published by McClurg featured St. John art. Additionally, St. John did cover art and illustrations for **Blue Book, The Green Book** and **The Red Book** magazines. The late 1930s found his work in **The Boy's World** and **Child Life** although the majority of his work appeared in pulps like **Amazing Stories** and **Fantastic Adventures.**

Though a relative unknown, T.S. Sullivant's later influence was as great or greater than any of his contemporaries. Samples of his artwork are on this and the facing page.

T.S. (Thomas Starling) Sullivant (1854-1926) of

Columbus, Ohio, was possibly the most influential artist on the
"magic" that is Disney animation. He studied academic drawing
and painting at the Pennsylvania Academy of Fine Arts. He sold
his first drawings for publication when he was in his late 20s. His
early works were mildly humorous, but drawn in a rather accurate
and realistic style, nicely executed, but typical of so many other
illustrators at the time. Sullivant was influenced by Arthur Burdett
Frost (1851-1928), whose work clearly stood out as the illustrator
for *Br'er Rabbit* and *Uncle Remus*. Sullivant was so impressed by
Frost's loose, yet insightful caricatures that he sought him out for
some professional advice. Frost evidently liked what he saw in
Sullivant and recommended him to **Puck** magazine (1886) for
what would become Sullivant's big break. However, it was the
astute J.A. Mitchell, the publisher and editor of **Life** magazine,
who put Sullivant in the spotlight, where his drawings became
a prominent regular feature (from 1888-1926). In 1896, he
collaborated on a **Life** series with writer/artist H.W. Phillips called
"Fables For The Times," which eventually was published in book
form (1896). Other publications that Sullivant contributed to were
Punch, Or The London Charivari, Judge and **The Ladies' Home
Journal** (May 1925). He was a master at giving his characters a
sense of movement, which required the skill to draw from very
difficult angles. With an extraordinary sense of anatomy and
humor, his characters were quirky and unique, but at the same time
believable and very appealing. The legendary Disney animators
have in the past and still today study Sullivant's work in the
archives of Disney's extensive library. They have found inspiration
for the hippos in "Fantasia's" "Dance of the Hours" and, in my own
case, "Scar" from "The Lion King."

Albert Payson Terhune's dog stories have been beloved by several generations.

Albert Payson Terhune (1872-1942), born in Newark,
N.J., was the son of novelist Mary Virginia Terhune. Terhune was a novelist who wrote books about dogs, and collies in particular. Beginning in 1915, he sold stories about his collie dogs to **Red Book Magazine.** He became a popular and financial success after the 1919 publication of *Lad: A Dog,* which was a collection of his magazine stories. He also wrote about Sunnybank, the estate he shared with his wife and with Lad, Bruce, Grey Dawn and all the other collies he raised and trained. Although he wrote about many different topics including boxing and religion, his magazine stories about dogs and dog-related material were and are the most sought after by collectors. Between 1914 and 1942, his work was published in such varied publications as **Ainslee's, All-Story, The American Boy, The American Magazine, The Argosy, The Blue Book Magazine, Collier's, Cosmopolitan, Country Gentleman, The Delineator, The Green Book Magazine, Red Book, Ladies' Home Journal, Nature, The Popular Magazine, AKC Gazette, The Saturday Evening Post** and even **The Smart Set.**

Nikola Tesla (1856-1943) of Smiljan, Croatia, was a brilliant,
eccentric electrical engineer, who emigrated to the United States in 1884 where he worked for Thomas Edison. While Edison was developing direct current (DC), Tesla discovered a way to transmit power over long distances. He developed the alternating current system (AC), which we use today. Tesla sold the patent rights to his system of alternating-current dynamos, transformers and motors to George Westinghouse. Westinghouse made it the basis of the Westinghouse power system, which still defines the modern electrical power industry. In 1891, Tesla invented the Tesla coil, an induction coil widely used in radio technology. Tesla also worked with radio-frequency electromagnetic waves and, despite the claims made by Marconi, actually did invent the idea of radio. In fact, the Supreme Court eventually made a decision that overruled the Marconi patent, awarding it to Tesla. Tesla demonstrated the wireless transmission of power in 1899 and wrote the "Blueprint" for his concepts in "The Problem of Increasing Human Energy," which appeared in the June 1900 issue of **The Century Magazine.** He also wrote for Hugo Gernsback's **Electrical Experimenter Magazine** and **Technical World Magazine.**

Anthony Trollope (1815-1882) was born in London. His
mother, Frances, became a writer to support the family after her husband died. A civil servant, Trollope worked with the British Post Office, which provided him the opportunity for travel to Ireland, Egypt, the West Indies and the United States. He began to write and his first book based in Ireland, *The Macdermots of Ballycloran,* was published in 1847. He eventually wrote 47 novels, various short stories and articles. Most of his novels appeared in serialized form in both British and American periodicals. The new **The Cornhill Magazine** (qv.) edited by Thackeray serialized "Framley Parsonage" (1860), which established his reputation. In 1861, he declined the editorship of **Temple Bar**, although he was

a consistent contributor with such serializations as "The American Senator" (1877). **Blackwood's Magazine** serialized "Nina Balatka" anonymously (1866-1867). For a short period, he assumed the editorship of **St. Paul's Magazine** (1867). His work continually appeared in publications such as **Pall Mall, Good Words, Harper's New Monthly Magazine, The Galaxy** and **Appletons' Journal.** Although Trollope is "out of fashion" as a literary star, his work is appreciated by a fervent group of collectors and readers who have "found" his work.

Jim Tully (1888-1947) has been accused of making writing a "blood sport," and the gritty, realistic style that characterized his work tend to make this an apt description. A former hobo and professional boxer, Tully's grasp of the "low-life" came through his writing to impress such editors as H.L. Mencken, who published Tully's stories and articles in both **The Smart Set** and **The American Mercury**. Tully wrote both fiction and non-fiction in the same gritty style. "A California Holiday" (**The American Mercury**, January 1928), where Tully reported on a San Quentin execution, is still used in arguments against capital punishment. Tully published interviews with Hollywood figures and even worked for a while as a publicist for Charlie Chaplin. From 1924 until his death, he published regularly in both major slick magazines and pulps. His style has made him an almost underground favorite of magazine collectors and his contributions nearly always add value to a magazine.

Harriet Weaver (1876-1961) edited 58 issues of **Egoist,** from July 1914 to December 1919. During that rather brief period, she managed to popularize Ezra Pound, and jump start the literary careers of both T. S. Eliot and James Joyce. Every issue of **Egoist** is a collectible, and the magazine stories about Harriet Weaver are, likewise, collectible. T.S. Eliot served as the assistant editor of **Egoist** from 1917 to 1919 and even the association of a literary giant hasn't made the earlier **Egotists** worth any less. The backbone was Harriet Weaver. Her literary judgments, her decision to support James Joyce, as well as to publish *Ulysses* in Britain despite the atmosphere of censorship, has elevated her work at the **Egoist** to a very collectible and expensive property. With only 58 issues, the cachet of collectibility due to Harriet Weaver has extended to her as a journalistic subject, and to the previous incarnation of **Egoist**, a feminist journal edited by Dora Marsden, and originally titled **The New Freewoman.**

PART THREE:

MAGAZINES AND VALUES

Modern Magazines

Luce (Time 1923-present and Life 1936-2000)

Time was founded by Henry Luce and Briton Hadden in 1923, with the concept of a news magazine of short, concise summaries of events. The first issue was published on March 3, 1923, with Haddon as editor and Luce as the business manager. The death of Haddon in 1929 elevated Luce to the position of editor, which he held until 1964. **Time** did well enough for Luce to acquire **Life** in 1936.

The Maxwell family sold **Life** (qv.) magazine to Henry Luce in 1936. The first issue of the new **Life** appeared Nov. 23, 1936. The old **Life** had been a sophisticated humor magazine with a decidedly New York slant and attitude. The new **Life** became the innovator, if not the originator, of the photo essay. As a weekly from 1936 through 1971, and a monthly from 1971 through 2000, **Life** had a profound effect on journalism. Cover photos of Marilyn Monroe (Aug. 17, 1962) and The Beatles (Aug. 28, 1964) are among the many collectibles in the history of the later incarnation of **Life**.

The Luce magazine empire also established **Fortune** and **Sports Illustrated**. It is, perhaps, a tribute to the circulation and the acumen of Henry Luce in creating that success, that his publications are rarely counted among the most expensive collectibles.

Life

Single unremarkable issue	**$3**	May 1, 1939 (Joe DiMaggio)	**$100**
May 8, 1950 (Jackie Robinson)	**$100**	April 20, 1959 (Marilyn Monroe)	**$75**
Aug. 17, 1962 (Marilyn Monroe)	**$50**	Sept. 13, 1968 (The Beatles)	**$100**

Time

Single unremarkable issue	**$3**	April 12, 1937 (Virginia Woolf/Man Ray)	**$65**
May 9, 1938 (Orson Welles)	**$75**	Dec. 27, 1954 (Walt Disney)	**$75**
Sept. 15, 1961 (J. D. Salinger)	**$100**	Sept. 22, 1967 (The Beatles)	**$75**

Playboy (1953-present) and its imitators

In 1953, **Child Life** staffer Hugh Hefner created **Playboy,** an on-the-edge publication crafted from parts of **Esquire** (qv.), **Snappy** (qv.) and **Captain Billy's Whiz Bang** (qv.). The nudity and jokes pioneered by **Whiz Bang** and the glamArt magazines in the 1930s were added to the sophisticated pretensions of **Esquire** to produce a literary/erotic magazine that bordered on pornography. Hefner cobbled together his first issue in December of 1953, leaving it undated. Featuring Marilyn Monroe, it was an immediate success, and it has become a much sought after collectible. Hefner featured tastefully done nudes, reminiscent of the art photos of such 1930s and 1940s magazines as **Snappy** and **Paris Nights**. **Playboy,** despite the carping of critics and moralists, carried some of the best magazine writing of its era, including original pieces by such writers as John Steinbeck, Ernest Hemingway, Ian Fleming, Jack Kerouac, Alex Haley, Stephen King, Kurt Vonnegut, Ray Bradbury and many more. Of course, this spawned the joke, " Should children read **Playboy**?" The answer was: "No, they should just look at the pictures like the rest of us."

First Bob Guccione with **Penthouse,** which debuted in Britain in 1965, and then Larry Flynt with **Hustler** in 1974, ratcheted up the pornographic content of the over the counter men's magazines, forcing an even more pornographic approach in **Playboy**. As the pornography increased, the market became increasingly fragmented and overall began to drop. Few, if any, of the Guccione/Flynt magazines are collectible, and their influence dramatically reduced the collectibility of the later issues of **Playboy.**

Playboy

Single unremarkable issue	$5	Undated (1953) Monroe issue	$1,500
February 1954	$650	April 1954	$250
August 1954	$300	September 1954	$150
November 1954	$150	December 1954	$300
January 1955	$500	May 1955	$80
September 1955	$250	January 1956	$75
March 1960	$100	August 1960	$150

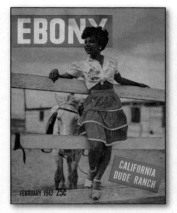

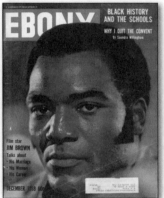

Ebony (1945-present)/Jet (1951-present)

While African-American media have a much longer history and such newspapers as the *Chicago Defender* and *The Abolitionist* have had significant effects on American social history, the advent of **Ebony** in 1945 and **Jet** in 1951 brought African-American magazines to a mass audience. A fact that seems to slip by many social historians, but not past collectors, is the ads that pioneered in these two magazines. For almost a century, the image of the African-American in magazine ads was typified by Cream of Wheat or Aunt Jemima. The success of **Ebony** and **Jet** in terms of circulation brought home to the advertising industry the neglected market of an emerging African-American middle class. For the first time, African-Americans were featured sipping a popular soft drink, dressed in the latest fashions or driving a new car.

Both **Ebony** and **Jet** played a significant role in the civil rights movement. Collectible issues focus on both the historical aspect of their civil rights articles and the socially significant effect of their advertisements.

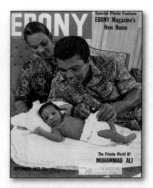

Ebony

November 1948 (Langston Hughes)	$75	August 1968 (Black soldier)	$45
June 1969 (Betty Shabazz)	$30	April 1970 (Martin Luther King)	$25
January 1971 (Muhammad Ali)	$20		

Jet

April 18, 1965 (Martin Luther King) $70		May 4, 1978 (Reggie Jackson)	$45
July 27, 1978 (Muhammad Ali)	$45	Jan. 31, 1980 (Smokey Robinson)	$50
March 19, 1981 (Joe Frazier)	$50		

Eros (1962)

Eros Magazine hit the stands in early 1962 and the U.S. government, apparently, wasn't ready for it. Accompanying the magazine was a newsletter and a book. **Eros** is so tame by modern standards that it is hard to believe that less than 50 years ago, the publisher was jailed for the act of publishing it. It was a classy, hardcover magazine, with some serious discussion as well as a few nicely done photographs, including, in Issue Three, the last studio portraits of Marilyn Monroe.

Eros lasted four issues, despite its overwhelming success with the public. Ralph Ginzburg and other members of the **Eros** team were hounded through the courts, all the way to the top. In 1966, the Supreme Court upheld Ginzburg's conviction on obscenity charges, as well as his five-year prison term. Despite its short life, **Eros** was the beginning of a new type of thought about sex in the U.S. Barney Rossett and Grove Press had begun to reprint the Olympia Press titles of Henry Miller and Pauline Reage, Hugh Hefner's **Playboy** was hitting new heights and the film *I am Curious (Yellow)* was driving the last nail into the coffin of the Hayes Office. The government was playing the role of the old lady, trying to sweep back the sea. Unfortunately for Ginzburg, he was the broom.

Eros is collected both as a significant piece of art and literature as well as a cornerstone of collections of banned and censored material.

Single issue except issue 3	$30	Issue 3	$75
Set of four	$175		

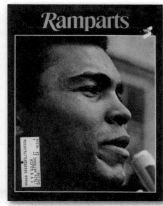

Ramparts (1962-present)

Ramparts Magazine was a hippy, New Left, glossy intrusion into American middle class existence that broke numerous important stories and never made money. All of which has made it extremely attractive in the collector's market.

Founded in 1962 as a Catholic literary quarterly in San Francisco by wealthy convert Ed Keating, it became almost a bible in the new Left community, questioning the church's support of the corrupt South Vietnamese regime and taking up left wing causes. It jumped from 5,000 circulation to 400,000 in its first year.

Ramparts, aside from opposing the Vietnam War, published the first conspiracy theory concerning the Kennedy assassination, revealed the undercover presence of the CIA in radical movements, published Che Guevara's diaries and printed Eldridge Cleaver's diaries (later to become *Soul on Ice* [New York: McGraw-Hill, 1968]). It featured notables such as Susan Sontag, Noam Chomsky, Seymour Hersh, James Ridgeway, Pete Hamill, Abbie Hoffman, Stanley Scheinbaum, **Rolling Stone** publisher Jann Wenner and **Mother Jones** founder Adam Hochschild. **Ramparts** has become a sought after collectible.

October 1965 (Beatles)	$25	February 1967 (Jack Ruby)	$40
October 1967 (John Lennon)	$65	January 1968 (Che Guevara)	$45
March 1968 (Che Guevara)	$30	August 1969 (Jules Feiffer)	$40
December 1969 (Jerry Rubin)	$40	October 1969 (Eldridge Cleaver)	$45
June 1970 (Jean Genet)	$75	February 1971 (Eldridge Cleaver)	$70

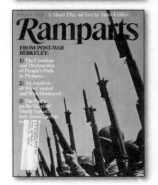

Vintage Price Guide

1924: A Magazine of the Arts (1924)

Published in Woodstock, N.Y., and edited by Edwin Seaver and A. Vera Bass, there were only four issues of this literary periodical published from July through December 1924. The December issue invited subscriptions to the forthcoming continuation, 1925, which never appeared. Nevertheless, this was an important literary periodical which, during its short run, included contributions by Hart Crane ("Sunday Morning Apples," "Interludium" and "Voyages"), Edwin Seaver, Gorham Munson, Ezra Pound ("A Communication"), William Carlos Williams, Malcolm Cowley, Waldo Frank ("Seriousness and Dada"), illustrations by William Gropper, Isidor Schneider ("A Marriage of Venus") and others. Edwin Seaver, the editor, became an influential writer, critic and editor. He was part of the literary Left during the 1930s and apparently embraced a radical viewpoint. As an editor and critic, he championed the writings of black authors Langston Hughes and Richard Wright. In the 1950s, he was forced to give testimony during Sen. Eugene McCarthy's hearings for the House Un-American Activities Committee as an accused Communist sympathizer, along with fellow writers Dashiell Hammett and Hughes. During his testimony, he spoke of himself as the Hollywood ghostwriter of the movie *Four Jills And A Jeep* (the AFI catalogue also speaks of the book as ghost-written by Seaver). The book became a very patriotic musical movie about a USO tour during World War II.

1924: A Magazine of the Arts Issue No. 3 (November)	**$50**
1924: A Magazine of the Arts Issue No. 1 (July)	**$150**
All four issues	**$400**

The Adelphi (1923-1955)

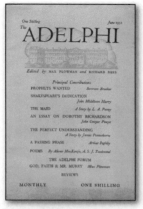

The magazine was founded in London in June 1923 by John Middleton Murry. Although Max Plowman and Richard Rees were listed as editors, **The Adelphi** was the platform for the political and literary ideas of Murry and his friend, D.H. Lawrence. The idea of the magazine had been developed in conversations and correspondence between Murry and Lawrence. It was notable for the first publication of much of Lawrence's critical prose. It was published from 1923 to 1955 in three sequences: monthly from 1923 to 1927; the second entitled **The New Adelphi,** published quarterly from 1927 to 1930; and the third monthly until 1955.

Murry was the central figure from the start until 1948. In the first incarnation, he wrote at least once in each issue, often twice or more. In the 1930s, he wrote a short important literary series entitled "Reminiscences of D.H. Lawrence." Murry's political emphasis was pacifism. The Adelphi Centre (1934-1943) was founded as a tribute to the magazine's political ideals. Jack Common, friend and correspondent of George Orwell, began working for **The Adelphi** magazine in 1928 as the circulation manager and eventually, the acting editor, against the wishes of his father. A collection of his articles "The Freedom of the Streets," which appeared in **The Adelphi** in 1938, had a tremendous influence on Orwell's works. In 1931, W.H. Auden sent a set of 23 poems, entitled "Case-Histories" and written on the theme of Sigmund Freud's psychology, to **The Adelphi** for publication. Murry rejected all but two of the poems, which were published in the June 1931 issue. Apparently, Murry wrote comments such as "unprintable" and "no" next to the rejected poems, which were handwritten and per Auden's instructions kept by Murry. Auden's rejected poems were auctioned in 2001 for a hefty sum, thus guaranteeing **The Adelphi** an extremely collectible status.

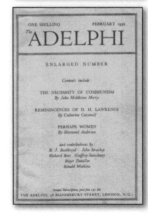

The Adelphi average unremarkable issue **$10-$15**		June 1923 (D.H. Lawrence)	**$50**
August 1923 (H.G. Wells)	**$50**	September 1924 (Robert Graves)	**$25**
June 1930 (D.H. Lawrence)	**$50**	July 1930 (D.H. Lawrence)	**$50**
August 1930 (D.H. Lawrence)	**$50**	December 1930 (John Middleton Murry)	**$25**
June 1931 (W.H. Auden)	**$50**	February 1932 (Murry)	**$25**

Ainslee's (1898-1926, 1934-1938)

Founded in February 1898, **Ainslee's** was originally a general magazine. It adopted an all-fiction policy in Fall 1902. Authors included Stanley J. Weyman, Bret Harte, Anthony Hope, Stephen Crane, Jack London, some of the earliest stories by O. Henry, Albert Payson Terhune, I.A.R. Wylie and E. Phillips Oppenheim. It switched to pulp in 1920 and returned some general features, employing Dorothy Parker as a critic. It ceased publication in 1926, but was revived as **Ainslee's Smart Love Stories** by Street and Smith from December 1934 to August 1938.

Ainslee's unremarkable single issue	$15	Ainslee's Smart Love Stories unremarkable single issue	$10
June 1912	$20	May 1926	$65
June 1926 (H. G. Wells, Gautier)	$75	Single six-month volumes, publisher's consecutive numbers	$50

Ainsworth's Magazine (1842-1854)

Founded and edited by popular "pot-boiler" (Rookwood) novelist William H. Ainsworth, **Ainsworth's Magazine** was "A Monthly Miscellany of Romance, General Literature and Art." The novels and tales were mainly romantic tales such as "Windsor Castle" and "The Miser's Daughter" by Ainsworth, and also short pieces by Thackeray and other "romance" writers of the Victorian era. Part of the magazine's success was due to Ainsworth's feel for Victorian taste and his use of illustrations for the periodical. In fact, popular illustrator George Cruikshank was a major participant in the early issues of the venture. Cruikshank illustrated the first six volumes. Other important illustrators included Tony Johannot, W. Alfred Delamotte and Hablot Knight Browne, better known as "Phiz." In 1843, Ainsworth sold the magazine, but remained as editor until 1845 in between editorial stints with **Bentley's Miscellany** and the **New Monthly.** He eventually repurchased the magazine and reissued a series of his own previously published novels such as "The Lancashire Witches" and "Guy Fawkes."

Rarely found as single issues in collectible condition	
Bound volumes in six-month publisher's consecutive numbers	$105

The Aldine (1868-1879)

In August 1868, a firm of printers headed by James Sutton produced a four-page paper called **The Aldine Press,** which they circulated gratuitously in the wholesale business section of New York City. The paper derived its name from Aldus Manutius, who in 1490 established his press, the Aldine Editions, in Venice, Italy. The first issue of **The Aldine, The Art Journal of America** had only one illustration, a map of Central Park, accompanying an article by Calvart Vaux. It was 14 by 20 inches, on heavy, expensive paper. The second and third issues focused on a high-class type of woodcut, which became **The Aldine's** trademark of success. In January of 1869, the size of **The Aldine** was increased to eight pages, and in May the number of pages increased to 12. In 1871, with 16 pages, **The Aldine** began national circulation and, according to the publisher, had a circulation of 70,000 copies per month by January of 1872. The publisher claimed it to be "the Handsomest Paper in the World" and "a representative and champion of American Art." While American artists were the focus, quality was the key factor in producing the work of such varied artists as Gustave Dore, Thomas Moran, Jules Tavernier, W.M. Cary, Granville Perkins, John S. Davis, F.O.C. Darley, Otto Gunther, J.W. Bolles, George H. Smillie and Paul Dixon. James Sutton entrusted the editorial management to Richard Henry Stoddard, who published the poetry and prose of writers such as George Sand, Coleridge, Longfellow, Emerson and Mark Twain.

 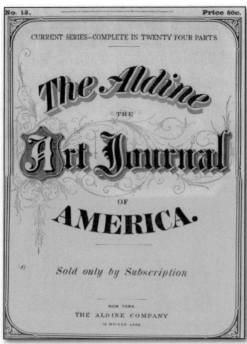

On June 22, 1872, due to an explosion at No. 18 Liberty Street, 20 firemen were injured, and Edward Burke, of Engine Company No. 4, was killed. James Sutton & Co. of **The Aldine,** No. 23 Liberty Street, got up a subscription for the sufferers. In a bizarre turn of events, as a result of labor troubles, the magazine was burned down years later and never resumed publication. The quality of **The Aldine** engravings were without peer in the American magazine field and even today are as vibrant and crisp as they were at their inception more than 100 years ago.

Single unremarkable issue	**$25**	October 1871 (Rockaway Beach)	**$30**
March 1872 (George Macdonald)	**$40**	August 1872 (Gustave Dore)	**$40**
April 1873 (Gustave Dore, Yellowstone, Thomas Moran)	**$50**	May 1873 (Edgar Allan Poe, Dore)	**$50**
July 1874 (Thomas Moran)	**$35**	January 1875 (Dore, Utah)	**$40**
January-December 1873 Volume VI bound volume	**$350**	January-December 1874 Volume VII bound volume	**$350**
January-December 1877 Volume VIII bound volume	**$400**		

All The Year Round (1859-1895)

In 1859, Charles Dickens closed down his successful publication **Household Words** after a dispute with the publishers. He became both editor and publisher for his new publication **All The Year Round**, which purported to be "The Story of our Lives from Year to Year." Similar in content to **Household Words,** each issue contained a serialized novel, some poetry and general articles on such topics as "The Poor Man and His Beer, " "Five New Points of Criminal Law," plus ghost stories of London. But it was the novel serializations that made **All The Year Round** an immediate and resounding popular success. The first novel serialized in **All The Year Round** was Dickens' own *A Tale of Two Cities* followed by *Great Expectations* (December 1860-August 1861). Other important novels serialized in **All The Year Round** were Wilkie Collins's *The Woman In White* and *The Moonstone*, Bulwer-Lytton's *A Strange Story* and Anthony Trollope's *Is He Popenjoy?*, *The Duke's Children*, and *Mr. Scarborough's Family*. At the time of Dickens's death, circulation of the publication was 300,000.

Single unremarkable bound volume	**$35**
April 1859-October 1859 (Dickens, "A Tale of Two Cities")	**$450**
October 1859-April 1860 (Dickens, "Great Expectations," Wilkie Collins, "Woman in White")	**$150**
April-October 1860 (Wilkie Collins, "Woman in White")	**$75**
December 1867-November 1868 (Wilkie Collins, "The Moonstone")	**$150**
October 1877-July 1878 (Anthony Trollope)	**$100**
October 1879-July 1880 (Anthony Trollope)	**$100**
May 1882-June 1883 (Anthony Trollope)	**$100**

American Boy (The Youth's Companion) (1827-1930s)

Founded by Nathaniel Willis, the **Youth's Companion** first appeared in 1827as a small periodical with overtly religious and instructional aims. Daniel Sharp Ford assumed ownership in 1867, and began an innovative premium marketing program that saw the magazine become one of the largest, in circulation, during the 1890s. **The Youth's Companion** magazine from 1892 to its demise in 1929, promoted the Pledge of Allegiance, first published in the Sept. 8 issue. The magazine claimed that its personnel had written the Pledge, and resented Francis Bellamy's claim that he alone had written the Pledge. William James, Willa Cather, O. Henry, Mark Twain, Bret Harte, William Dean Howells, Winston Churchill, Lincoln Steffens, William Cullen Bryant, Thomas Huxley, Theodore Roosevelt and, notably, Emily Dickinson all published in the magazine. It began a decline in 1907, and ceased publication in 1929 when it was absorbed into **American Boy. American Boy** was a fiction-based magazine similar to the pulps and continued nearly to World War II, featuring action and adventure stories for boys by such writers as Carl Carmer, Allan Swinton, Inglis Fletcher, Jaclund Marmur, Howard Brier, Carl H. Claudy and Neil Swanson.

Unremarkable single issue	$20	Unremarkable single issue w/American Boy	$10
Bound yearly volume publisher's consecutive numbers	$175	May 29, 1892 (Emily Dickinson)	$40
Sept. 29, 1892 (Emily Dickinson)	$40	Oct. 26, 1893 (Premium issue)	$50
April 23, 1896 (Kate Chopin's "Polydore")	$125	Dec. 15, 1898 (Queen Victoria)	$25
July 6, 1899 (Carolyn Wells)	$30	Nov. 30, 1899 (Jack London)	$80
Jan. 18, 1900 (Edith Wharton)	$125	April 12, 1900 (Sarah Orne Jewett)	$30
March 14, 1900 (Jack London)	$90	May 23, 1901 (Jack London)	$80
May 29, 1902 (Jack London)	$50	Dec. 18, 1902 (Winston S. Churchill)	$30
March 18, 1905 (John Burroughs)	$35		
Feb. 22, 1905-May 4, 1905 (Jack London's "Seven Tales of the Fish Patrol," first appearance) Single issue	$50	Complete run	$400
June 8, 1905 (Helen Keller)	$50	Dec. 15, 1910 (Kellogg's ad)	$25
March 16, 1914 (Post Toasties ad)	$50	July 16, 1919 (Jello ad)	$35
May 12, 1927 (Mt. Blanc)	$30		

American Magazine (1906-1940s)

In 1906, three muckraking journalists from **McClure's Magazine,** Ray Stannard Baker, Lincoln Steffens and Ida M. Tarbell, joined forces to produce a new magazine called **The American Magazine.** Their initial effort was published by the Phillips Publishing Company of Springield, Ohio, which later became The Crowell Publishing Company. The magazine focused on human interest stories, along with fiction. Early issues featured the Sherlock Holmes story "The Disappearance of Lady Francis Carfax" (1911), illustrated by Frederic Dorr Steele from "His Last Bow," "Boston Blackie Stories" by No. 6606, illustrated by N.C . Wyeth (1914), along with "Interesting People" such as Irving Berlin, Cecil Rhodes, Harold Bell Wright, Edgar Guest, Thomas Edison, John D. Rockefeller and Douglas Fairbanks. During the 1920s, writers as varied as Albert Payson Terhune, George Ade, Ellis Parker Butler, James M. Cain and Gene Stratton-Porter were contributors. Artists such as J. Knowles Hare, Norman Rockwell, Penrhyn Stanlaws, Nell Hott, Bradshaw Crandell, Diana Thorne, Lou Mayer, Clarence Underwood, Haskell Coffin, Andrew Loomis and Warren Davis illustrated the covers. In the 1930s, the magazine's fiction focused on the detective story genre. Some of the most important first appearances in print included: Dashiell Hammett's Sam Spade short story "A Man Called Spade,"(July 1932), Rex Stout's "Point of Death," (November 1934); the first Nero Wolfe story (later published in book form as *Fer-de-lance*), "Red Bull," and "Too Many Cooks" (recipes from the story were included as a giveaway with a three-cent stamp. The entire box is now worth a great deal); S.S. Van Dine's "The Bishop Murder Case" and "The Scarab Murder Case"; Agatha Christie's "13 For Dinner"; and Leslie Charteris' "The Pirate Saint" and "The Saint Thieves Picnic." Other important writers included Rafael Sabatini,

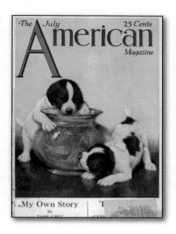

Max Brand, Zane Grey, P.G. Wodehouse, Don Marquis and H.G. Wells. While Rex Stout continued to publish his work well into the 1940s, the true heyday of **The American Magazine** and most valuable collectible issues were the earlier issues.

Single unremarkable issue **$10**	December 1911 (Arthur Conan Doyle) **$500**
August 1914 (Boston Blackie stories, N.C. Wyeth) **$175**	October 1914 (Boston Blackie stories, N.C. Wyeth) **$175**
April 1921 (Nikola Tesla interview) **$35**	June 1921 (George Ade, Norman Rockwell ads) **$25**
September 1922 (Doyle, F. Scott Fitzgerald) **$250**	July 1924 (Zane Grey, Gene-Stratton-Porter) **$30**
August 1924 (Robert Benchley, Coles Phillips ad) **$25**	September 1925 (Zane Grey, Penrhyn Stanlaws cover) **$30**
April 1926 (Albert Payson Terhune, Zane Grey) **$50**	December 1927 (Will James, Oliver Curwood) **$25**
June 1928 (Albert Payson Terhune, Houdini, Zane Grey) **$60**	October 1928 (S.S. Van Dine, Zane Grey, Edgar Guest) **$30**
January 1929 (Albert Payson Terhune, S.S. Van Dine, Charles Siringo, Ellis Parker Butler) **$60**	February 1929 (S.S. Van Dine, Ellis Parker Butler, Don Marquis) **$35**
September 1930 (Rafael Sabatini, Will Rogers, Babe Ruth) **$25**	December 1930 (Berton Braley) **$25**
February 1930 (S.S. Van Dine, Octavus Roy Cohen) **$30**	June 1931(P.G. Wodehouse, Octavus Roy Cohen) **$30**
July 1932 (Dashiell Hammett) **$100**	March-August 1933 (Agatha Christie's "Thirteen For Dinner") complete **$150**
September 1934 (Leslie Charteris "The Saint In New York") **$35**	November 1934 (Rex Stout's "Point of Death" first book, later known as *Fer de Lance*) **$200**
April 1935 (Norman Rockwell) **$30**	February 1935 (Ellery Queen) **$125**
December 1936-March 1937 (Rex Stout, "Red Box") complete **$150**	April 1936 (F. Scott Fitzgerald) **$45**
October 1936 (H.L. Mencken, Leslie Charteris, Rockwell) **$40**	May 1937 (Charteris, "Saint: Thieves Picnic") **$30**
November 1937-February 1938 (Max Brand, "Dust Across The Range") complete **$60**	March, April, May, June, July, August 1938 (Rex Stout, "Too Many Cooks") complete **$600**
March 1938 Complete Recipe Box "Too Many Cooks" **$900**	December 1938 (Rex Stout, *Red Bull* book published as "Some Buried Caesar") **$100**
September 1939 (Rex Stout) **$75**	December 1949 (Rex Stout) **$75**

American Mercury (1924-1980)

The **American Mercury** was the result of a proposal formulated by H. L. Mencken and George Jean Nathan while they were the editors of **The Smart Set** (qv.). Picked up by Alfred Knopf, the magazine had its debut in 1924 and became one of the most successful and influential magazines of the 1920s under the editorship of Mencken. Mencken and Nathan brought with them an impressive group of writers from their connections through **The Smart Set,** the New York Theater community and the *Baltimore Sun.* James Huneker, Eugene O'Neill, Samuel Chew, Theodore Dreiser, James M. Cain, Jim Tully, William Faulkner, F. Scott Fitzgerald, Sherwood Anderson, Sinclair Lewis and Edgar Lee Masters were all featured in various issues of the Mencken incarnation of the **Mercury,** which has been characterized as " a hip flask for the American mind."

In April of 1926, the **Mercury** published "Hatrack," from Herbert Asbury's forthcoming book *Up from Methodism.* The powerful Watch and Ward Society, known for book banning under the Rev. J. Frank Chase, found "Hatrack" immoral and placed the **Mercury** on its list of publications that were "banned in Boston." Mencken went to Boston to challenge the ruling and sold Chase a copy of the magazine, leading to his immediate arrest. Mencken's subsequent vindication in court was hailed as a victory against censorship and the **Mercury** was firmly established. As a result of the "Hatrack" affair, Walter Lippmann called Mencken "the most powerful influence on this whole generation of educated people."

Very much an intellectual reflection of the Jazz age, the **Mercury** declined rapidly with the Depression. Mencken resigned in 1933, and he was succeeded by Charles Angoff and Paul Palmer. Lawrence Spivak took over the editorship and the publishing of the magazine in 1936. The Spivak **Mercury** actually produced several collectible issues, having preserved a good deal of the Mencken/Nathan writing stable. Readership, however, continued to decline through World War II and the magazine went through two changes of ownership between 1950 and 1952. Clendenin J. Ryan published three issues under the title **The New American Mercury** and sold the magazine to William Bradford Huie in February 1951. In the issue of October 1951, Huie placed the legend "Founded by Henry L. Mencken" beneath the table of contents. The magazine reprinted several of Mencken's articles and ran a story by Herbert Asbury about the Hatrack affair. In August 1952, Huie sold the **Mercury** to J. Russell Maguire.

The Maguire **Mercury** became a standard bearer of what is now called the "religious right." J. Edgar Hoover wrote for the magazine, as did Billy Graham, whose portrait on the cover of the January 1957 issue has become collectible. The Maguire **Mercury** defended Sen. Joseph McCarthy along with states' rights, and attacked such things as the graduated income tax, the NAACP, the United Nations, NATO, the ACLU and Zionism. It was sold to Defenders of the Christian Faith, Inc. in 1962 and the Legion for the Survival of Freedom, Inc., the next year. Increasingly marginalized, the magazine struggled through several owners to publish its final issue, as a quarterly, in Winter 1980.

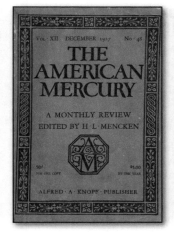 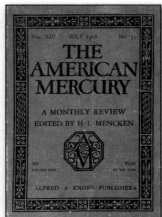 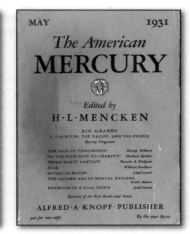

Mencken, Angoff, Palmer, Spivak Mercury unremarkable issue (1924-1950)	**$10**	Ryan/Huie Mercury unremarkable issue (1950-1952)	**$5**
Maguire Mercury unremarkable issue (1952-1962)	**$7.50**	Later Mercury various publishers unremarkable issue (1962-1980)	**$5**
January 1924 (Volume One #1)	**$45**	February 1924 (Eugene O'Neill First Publication)	**$55**
April 1924 (Article on Woodrow Wilson)	**$20**	May 1924 (James M. Cain)	**$15**
June 1924 (F. Scott Fitzgerald)	**$45**	July 1924 (Carl Sandburg)	**$15**
August 1924 (Theodore Dreiser)	**$20**	January 1925 (Edgar Lee Masters)	**$15**
September 1925 (James M. Cain)	**$15**	January 1926 (Upton Sinclair)	**$35**
April 1926 (Herbert Asbury's "Hatrack")	**$65**	December 1927 (Sherwood Anderson)	**$15**
January 1928 (Jim Tully's "California Holiday")	**$25**	July 1929 (Jim Tully)	**$15**
September 1929 (article on Walt Whitman)	**$15**	July 1930 (William Faulkner)	**$50**
January 1931 (Rockwell Kent)	**$15**	May 1931 (William Faulkner)	**$50**
October 1932 (F. Scott Fitzgerald)	**$65**	October 1933 (James T. Farrell)	**$15**
May 1938 (Havelock Ellis)	**$15**	November 1940 (Laurence Housman)	**$15**
Other issues containing William Faulkner	**$35**		

American Review, A Whig Journal
(January 1845-December 1852)

George Hooker Colton, an avowed Whig from New York City, established **The American Review: A Whig Journal of Politics, Literature, Art and Science** as "a five dollar monthly" in New York in January 1845, published by Wiley and Putnam. According to Colton, the purpose of the magazine was "To support freely and openly the principles and measures of the Whig Party" and "To establish a National Review" which would showcase "The writings of our own countrymen." The initial volume for 1845 had contributions by Horace Greeley, Donald Mitchell and Walt Whitman. However, it was the second number (February 1845) that established the magazine's fame and insured its collectible fortune with the publication in the issue of Edgar Allan Poe's poem "The Raven." Colton had bought "The Raven," probably for $15, which was fair compensation for space rates during that time. Poe, always hurting for funds, possibly sold it twice. The poem was published simultaneously in Nathaniel Parker Willis's *New York Evening Mirror* on Jan. 29, 1845, "in advance of publication," according to Willis. (However, Poe scholars consider **The American Review** publication to be the first appearance. The two periodicals, the former a monthly and the latter a daily, probably went on sale within a day or two of each other. Poe scholar Thomas Mabbott stated $15 is correct, and his guess is based on Colton family tradition and a note Colton wrote to James Russell Lowell, saying that the amount was less than $20). Poe chose to publish the poem under the pseudonym, Quarles, presumed to be a reference to Geoffrey Quarles, who wrote *Emblems*. Poe, also, may have intended the pun on quarrels. Other Poe material published in **The American Review** later included the first printing of "Some Words with a Mummy," "Eulalie," "The Facts of M. Valdemar's Case," as well as reprints of "The City in the Sea" and "Valley of Unrest."

Poe later wrote about **The American Review:** "A Whig magazine of higher (that is to say, of the five dollar) class. I must not be understood as meaning any disrespect to the work. It is, in my opinion, by far the best of its order in this country, and is supported in the way of contribution by many of the very noblest intellects. Mr. Colton, if in nothing else, has shown himself a man of genius in his successful establishment of the magazine within so brief a period. It is now commencing its second year, and I can say, from my own personal knowledge, that its circulation exceeds two thousand — it is probably about two thousand five hundred. So marked and immediate a success has never been attained by any of our five dollar magazines, with the exception of **The Southern Literary Messenger**." Nor, thanks to the publication of "The Raven," a more valuable periodical in magazine history.

1845.]   *The Raven.*   143

We dismiss this subject for the present, in the hope that it may receive that attention which is commensurate with its importance and proportionate to the value of the interests it involves. Whatever may be the result of these suggestions, we are sure that no patentee can be secure in the enjoyment of those rights for which he has expended his ingenuity or his capital, unless means of adjudicating disputes respecting these rights be provided, better and more efficient than those which are now available.

THE RAVEN.

BY —— QUARLES.

[The following lines from a correspondent—besides the deep quaint strain of the sentiment, and the curious introduction of some ludicrous touches amidst the serious and impressive, as was doubtless intended by the author—appear to us one of the most felicitous specimens of unique rhyming which has for some time met our eye. The resources of English rhythm for varieties of melody, measure, and sound, producing corresponding diversities of effect, have been thoroughly studied, much more perceived, by very few poets in the language. While the classic tongues, especially the Greek, possess, by power of accent, several advantages for versification over our own, chiefly through greater abundance of spondaic feet, we have other and very great advantages of sound by the modern usage of rhyme. Alliteration is nearly the only effect of that kind which the ancients had in common with us. It will be seen that much of the melody of "The Raven" arises from alliteration, and the studious use of similar sounds in unusual places. In regard to its measure, it may be noted that if all the verses were like the second, they might properly be placed merely in short lines, producing a not uncommon form; but the presence in all the others of one line—mostly the second in the verse—which flows continuously, with only an aspirate pause in the middle, like that before the short line in the Sapphic Adonic, while the fifth has at the middle pause no similarity of sound with any part beside, gives the versification an entirely different effect. We could wish the capacities of our noble language, in prosody, were better understood.—ED. AM. REV.]

Once upon a midnight dreary, while I pondered, weak and weary,
Over many a quaint and curious volume of forgotten lore,
While I nodded, nearly napping, suddenly there came a tapping,
As of some one gently rapping, rapping at my chamber door.
" 'Tis some visiter," I muttered, " tapping at my chamber door—
              Only this, and nothing more."

Ah, distinctly I remember it was in the bleak December,
And each separate dying ember wrought its ghost upon the floor.
Eagerly I wished the morrow ;—vainly I had tried to borrow
From my books surcease of sorrow—sorrow for the lost Lenore—
For the rare and radiant maiden whom the angels name Lenore—
              Nameless here for evermore.

And the silken sad uncertain rustling of each purple curtain
Thrilled me—filled me with fantastic terrors never felt before ;
So that now, to still the beating of my heart, I stood repeating
" 'Tis some visiter entreating entrance at my chamber door—
Some late visiter entreating entrance at my chamber door ;—
              This it is, and nothing more."

Single unremarkable issue	$20	Bound volume unremarkable	$35
Complete run 1845-52 bound 16 volumes	$3,800	January-June 1845 bound volume (Poe as "Quarles" for "The Raven" February 1845)	$2,500
January 1845 (Poe, review of Elizabeth Barrett's "Drama of Exile")	$300	April 1845 (Poe, "Some Words with a Mummy, "The City in the Sea" and "Valley of Unrest")	$350
August 1845 (Poe, "The American Drama")	$300	December 1845 (Poe, "Facts of M. Valdemar's Case")	$350
January-June 1846 bound (review of Melville's "Typee")	$100	December 1847 (Poe, "Ulalume")	$350
January-June 1848 bound volume (Emily Bronte review)	$150		

Analectic Magazine (1813-1820)

The Analectic Magazine "Containing Selections From Foreign Reviews And Magazines, Together With Original Miscellaneous Compositions" was a monthly publication based in Philadelphia. The first series of **The Analectic Magazine** was from 1813-1819. The first three years were edited by Washington Irving, who contributed a number of articles and reviews in the early issues. A New Series appeared in two volumes beginning in 1820 when James Maxwell took over as publisher.

The November issue of 1814 contains probably one of the most important and valuable first magazine appearances: the words to "The Star Spangled Banner," by Francis Scott Key published anonymously under the title of "Defence of Fort McHenry." The editor stated that "although these lines have previously been printed in several newspapers they may still, however, be new to many of our readers. Besides, we think their merit entitles them to preservation in some more permanent form than the columns of a daily paper. The annexed song was composed under the following circumstances. A gentleman had left Baltimore, in a flag of truce for the purpose of getting released from the British fleet a friend of his who had been captured at Marlborough. He went as far as the mouth of the Patuxent, and was not permitted to return lest the intended attack on Baltimore should be disclosed. He was, therefore, brought up the bay to the mouth of the Patapsco, where the flag vessel was kept under the guns of a frigate, and he was compelled to witness the bombardment of Fort M'Henry, which the Admiral had boasted he would carry out in a few hours, and that the city must fall. He watched the flag at the fort through the whole day with an anxiety that can be better felt than described, until the night prevented him from seeing it. In the night he watched the bomb-shells, and at early dawn his eye was again greeted by the proudly-waving flag of his country." All four verses were printed, with a note that they were sung to the "Tune–Anacreon in Heaven," the English drinking song composed by John Stafford Smith in the late 18th century.

Another important publishing landmark in **The Analectic Magazine** included the first lithograph published in America, a scene by Bass Otis dated 1820, though appearing in the July 1819 issue with an article on the "new" medium of lithography. Other valuable issues contain a description of the Lewis and Clark expedition, Washington Irving's review of the works of Robert Treat Paine; biographies of naval officers Oliver Perry, James Lawrence and Jacob Jones with portrait engravings; Traits of American Indian Character; Biography and engraving of Robert Fulton which included a controversy, and Negro Slavery Review of The Emigrant's Guide.

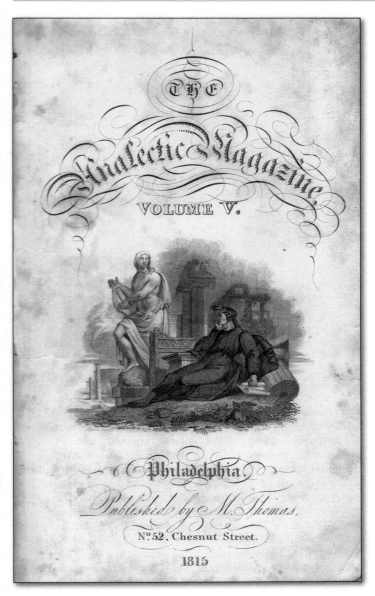

Rarely found as single issues in collectible condition 1813-1820, 16 volumes. Complete set	**$3,500**
January-June 1813 Washington Irving bound volume **$150**	July-December 1814 ("Defence of Fort M'Henry," Star-Spangled Banner in November issue) **$1,700**
January-June 1815 (Lewis and Clark Expedition in February issue) **$250**	July-December 1816 (Naval Chronicles War of 1812) bound volume **$150**
July-December 1817 (Slavery) **$100**	July-December 1819 (Bass Otis first U.S. lithograph) **$700**

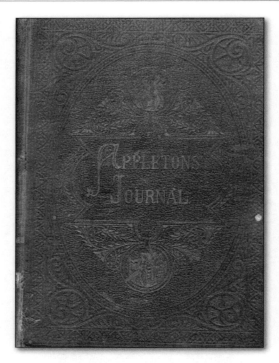

Appletons' Journal (April 3, 1869-December 1881)

Initially, it was a weekly periodical of literature, science and art, from April 3, 1869, until June 24, 1876. From July 1876 through December 1881, it became **Appletons' Journal: A Monthly Miscellany of Popular Literature.** According to publisher D. Appleton & Co.'s statement, the magazine was designed to encompass illustrations and fiction with literary and scientific papers. Its objective was to omit ordinary news and partisan politics. The illustrations were either steel engravings or woodcuts, and their combination with the literary content made **Appletons' Journal** a success. The literary content included both domestic and foreign luminaries including William Cullen Bryant, Victor Hugo, Bayard Taylor, Jules Verne, Alice Carey, Mrs. Oliphant, S. Baring-Gould and A.C. Swinburne. Issued as a Supplement to the Weekly, both Charles Dickens' "The Mystery of Edwin Drood" (1870) and Anthony Trollope's "Ralph The Heir" (1870) were serialized with illustrated engravings. Many of the early illustrations for **Appletons'** were done by American artists Thomas Moran and Winslow Homer. Along with Anthony Trollope, the issues containing Winslow Homer illustrations are among the most valuable and sought after by collectors.

Unremarkable single issues	**$30**	With Dickens/Trollope supplements **$50**	
With Winslow Homer illustrations intact	**$100**	Bound issues in publisher's consecutive numbers	**$65**

Appleton's Magazine (1906-1909)

Another incarnation of **Appleton's** as a monthly magazine was similar in tenor to **The Century** and **Harper's Monthly**, with both fiction and relevant non-fiction. Writing in **Appleton's** in 1908, Harold Bolce argued that most of the modern city's sanitary and economic problems were caused by the horse. Bolce charged that each year 20,000 New Yorkers died from "maladies that fly in the dust, created mainly by horse manure. John Philip Sousa wrote about "The Menace of Mechanical Music" (1906), and the April 1907 issue was devoted to Oklahoma and "The Fight For Statehood." One of the more sought after issues is February 1907 with Agnes & Egerton Castle's "The Debt of Honor," because of the illustrations of Joseph Clement Coll.

December 1906	$15	April 1907	$15
October 1907	$15	February 1907 (Coll)	$50

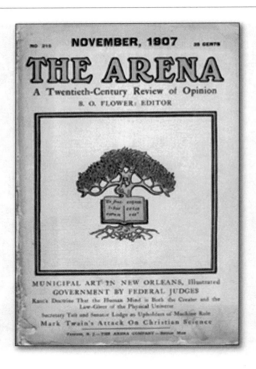

The Arena (1889-1909)

The Arena was an American monthly magazine founded in 1889 in Boston, by B.O. (Benjamin Orange) Flower, and has been identified with many progressive and populist causes, notably the New Thought movement. Under editors Flower and John Clark Ridpath, **The Arena** was an on-the-edge populist journal that took up reform and grass roots causes. Between 1904 and 1909, in his second tenure as editor, Flower turned to the techniques of an investigative journalist to obtain information and material to further his campaigns for social, economic and political reform. The editorial focus, which was similar in character to **McClure's Magazine** (qv.) of the same period, classified **The Arena** as one of the principal outlets for muckraking journalism. **The Arena** is collected under various headings, New Thought, muckraking and for original appearances of work by Flower, Ridpath, Ella Wheeler Wilcox and W.T. Stead.

Unremarkable single issues	**$15**	Volumes in publisher's consecutive numbers, editor B.O. Flower	**$50**
Volumes in publisher's consecutive numbers, editor John Clark Ridpath **$35**			

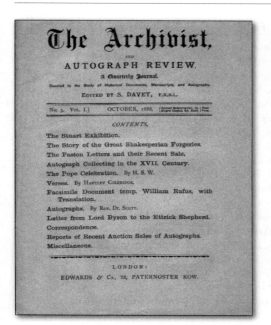

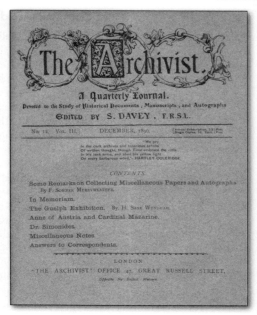

The Archivist and Autograph Review (1888-)

A little-known quarterly magazine, **The Archivist and Autograph Review** was published, starting in 1888, by Edwards & Co. in London. It is highly prized and collected by autograph and manuscript collectors for its original publications of historic letters and monographs, as well as its coverage of forgeries. In its initial year of publication it carried the first publication of a letter from Lord Byron to James Hogg, it was one of the first publications to extend a sympathetic look at William Henry and his Shakespeare forgery *Vertigen*, and it carried an unpublished work of DeQuincey, "Novels, 1830." Edwards & Co. was closely associated with Eliot Stock, who published **The Antiquary** and **The Book Worm,** which were the trade journals for used and antiquarian booksellers. The three magazines in concert formed the trade publications of the book trade through World War I, though neither of the two Stock publications has reached the importance and collectibility of **The Archivist and Autograph Review.**

Bought for research, primarily single issues   **$150**

The Ark/Odd Fellows (1815-present)

The Odd Fellows is a fraternal organization founded in England during the 18th century. The Patriotic Order in England was followed by the Union of United Orders and the Loyal Order. In 1813, various lodges organized the Manchester Unity of Odd Fellows. The first American Lodge was founded in Baltimore in 1819 by Thomas Wildey and recognized by the Manchester Unity in 1820. The Manchester Unity published both Quarterly and Monthly magazines from Manchester beginning as early as 1815. The first Odd Fellows magazine in the United States was published by J. Roach in 1825, in Baltimore. **The Ark, The Ark and Odd Fellows Monthly Magazine** and regional **Odd Fellows** magazines were basically locally produced magazines, some growing to cover larger areas of the country. The largest, perhaps, was **The Ark and Odd Fellows Western Magazine,** published from the Central Lodge in Columbus, Ohio, by Alex E. Glenn from 1844 and continuing today. Odd Fellows magazines, because they have been continually published since 1815, have become collectible in many areas. Many carried esoteric articles and are sought by occult collectors. In the western and southern United States, they are among the most comprehensive sources of marriages and obituaries, and are sought by collectors of genealogy and genealogists. One of the first societies to accept women on a nearly equal footing, the Rebekah Degree for women members, was established in 1851. Women, including early feminists, were regular features in Odd Fellows magazines on both sides of the Atlantic.

Ark and Odd Fellows Magazine, Columbus, Ohio			
Single issues	**$20**	Six-month bound publisher's numbers	**$75**
Companion and American Odd Fellow, New York			
Single issues	**$15**	Six-month bound publisher's numbers	**$65**
The Elblrm, an Odd Fellows Magazine, Boston			
Single issues	**$150**		
The Golden Rule, and Odd-Fellows' Family Companion, Westchester, N.Y.			
Single issues	**$55**		

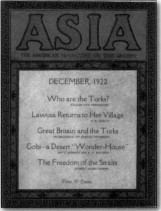

Asia (1898-1947)

Asia, The American Magazine On The Orient was originally established by J.P. Morgan's associates as the journal of the American Asiatic Society in 1898. The magazine had been closely associated with Willard Straight during his lifetime, and was owned outright by him from January 1917. Straight had married heiress Dorothy Payne Whitney, who financed the magazine and kept it going long after his untimely death in 1918. The magazine's heyday was the 1920s and early 1930s. In addition to the "Diaries" of Willard Straight, the magazine featured such prominent writers as Roy Chapman Andrews, Rose Wilder Lane, Frank Buck, T.E. Lawrence, John Dos Passos, Lowell Thomas, Arnold Toynbee and Pearl S. Buck. In the 1930s, it was operated for the Whitneys by Richard J. Walsh and his wife, who was known to the world as Pearl Buck. The Art Deco covers painted by artist Frank McIntosh through the 1920s and the '30s insured the collectible value of the magazine. In 1942, **Asia Magazine** changed its name to **Asia and the Americas.** In 1947, when Mike Straight (Willard's son) began a drive to "sell" the United Nations, the magazine was completely reorganized into **United Nations World.**

Single unremarkable issue	$10	August 1920 (T.E. Lawrence)	$35
September 1920 (Roy Chapman Andrews)	$20	November 1920 (Roy Chapman Andrews, Willard Straight)	$20
August 1922 (Rose Wilder Lane)	$50	October 1922 (Thornton Oakley, Frank Buck)	$15
March 1925 (Frank McIntosh cover, Rackham ad, Tibet)	$30	October 1925 (Frank McIntosh cover, Rackham ad)	$30
February 1925 (Frank McIntosh cover)	$25	February 1926 (Frank McIntosh cover, Roy Chapman Andrews, Tibet)	$30
October 1927 (Frank McIntosh cover)	$25	February 1931 (Frank McIntosh cover)	$25
January 1932 (Frank McIntosh cover, Pearl S. Buck)	$30		

Atlantic Monthly (1857-present)

The **Atlantic Monthly** was founded by James Russell Lowell, Ralph Waldo Emerson, Henry Wadsworth Longfellow, Oliver Wendell Holmes, Francis H. Underwood, John Lothrop Motley, James Elliot Cabot and Moses Dresser Phillips, publishing its first issue on Nov. 9, 1857, under the editorship of James Russell Lowell. Published in Boston, the magazine was a response to several factors, including the popular magazines published in New York and Philadelphia as well as the southern regional magazines **Southern Literary Messenger** (qv.) and **Russell's** (qv.). New England, especially Boston, had a stranglehold on American literature in the early- to mid-19th century. Attempts to break it came from the popular presses of New York and the southern establishment. John Neal's challenge from Baltimore had been exiled to Scotland, but regional writers continually assaulted the Boston establishment.

The **Atlantic** was a response. Uncredited, the major New England literary figures contributed to **The Atlantic** which, in the first volume, contained poems by Emerson, the serialization of Holmes' *Autocrat of the Breakfast Table* and Rose Terry Cooke's "Sally Parson's Duty." In 1869, Harriet Beecher Stowe published

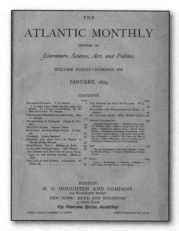

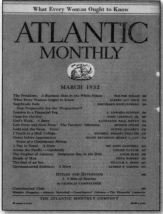

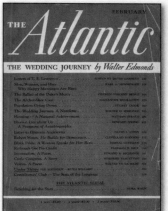

"The True Story of Lady Byron's Life," a feminist piece in which she crossed the decency barriers of the time, writing openly of Byron's incest with his half-sister. The piece almost destroyed **The Atlantic,** halving its circulation and leading to the replacement of James Thomas Fields with William Dean Howells as editor in 1871. The magazine recovered under Howells, who left in 1881. Thomas Bailey Aldrich managed to get a more popular appeal into **The Atlantic** when he succeeded Howells, and following editors, such as Bliss Perry, seem to have been able to secure enough of a popular following without losing the high brow image of **The Atlantic,** which continues to be published from Boston.

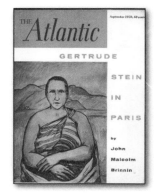

Normally collected in six-month bound volumes			
First four (Volumes One and Two)	**$100**	Others	**$68**
February 1862 (Julia Ward Howe, Battle Hymn of the Republic)	**$75**	June 1928 (Lord Dunsany)	**$25**
Unremarkable issue pre-1880	**$15**	Unremarkable issue 1880-WW II	**$10**
Unremarkable issue post-WW II	**$5**		

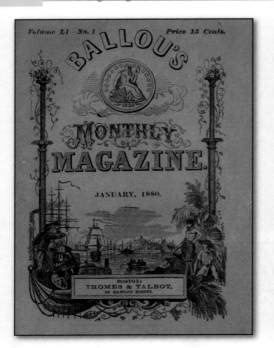

Ballou's Monthly (1866-1893)

Ballou's Monthly Magazine was an illustrated general interest magazine begun in 1855 as **Ballou's Dollar Monthly Magazine.** It was owned and edited by Maturin Ballou, and published by Elliott, Thomes & Talbot in Boston. The magazine featured fiction, poetry, travel, fashion and household hints, and a section for children. Joseph Edward Badger Jr., who established a reputation as a puzzler and puzzle solver, signed his contributions "Beau K." Charles Bertrand Lewis, the humorist, wrote under his pseudonym, "M. Quad." In addition to illustrated engravings by artists such as George Coomer, illustrated fiction and articles included "Luck and Pluck" by Horatio Alger Jr., "Ascent of Mount Shasta, "The Home of Victor Hugo," "Dresden on the Elbe," "Fingal's Cave" (which had served as the inspiration for Felix Mendelssohn's "Hebrides Overture"), "A Yankee in Mexico" (the adventures of a United States volunteer in Maximilian's Army), and "Pitcairn Island and the Mutineers."

Single unremarkable issue	$10	January-December 1856	$50
January-December 1864	$85	January-December 1867	$45
January-December 1869 (Horatio Alger)	$125	January-June 1873	$25

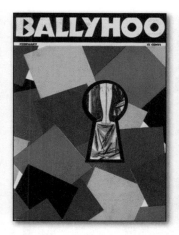

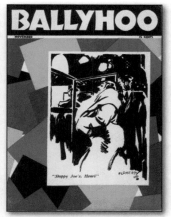

"Sloppy Joe's, Henri"

"Morning, Major"

Ballyhoo (1931-1939)

Ballyhoo was edited by Norman Anthony, former editor of the original humor **Life** magazine, and published in New York by Dell Publishing. **Ballyhoo** was the 1930s version of **Mad Magazine,** similar to **College Humor.** It contained cartoons, satire and satirical ads with illustrations and cartoons by artists such as Russell Patterson, Thomas Sanford Tousey, C.W. Anderson, Donald McKee, Frank Hanley, Jack Markow, Ralph Fuller, Ed Graham, Paul Reilly and Floherty, Jr. Typical **Ballyhoo** fare consisted of "Are You A Wet Or A Dry? Ballyhoo Referendum On Prohibition!" "Red Russia–A Trip with Pen and Insk from Minsk to Zinsk via Orkst," "211 Slain By Shovel In Penthouse Orgy," and a non-existent cartoon character called "Mr Zilch." Mr Zilch was never actually seen. He was always outside the frame of the cartoon, but scantily clad, wide-eyed girls would be seen reacting to something the unseen Mr Zilch had done or said, by crying out, "Oh, Mr Zilch!" Thus, the meaning of the word Zilch came to be seen as a nothing.

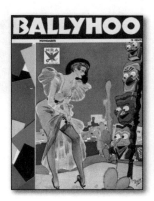

Unremarkable single issue	**$10**	December 1931	**$25**
November 1931	**$15**	January 1932	**$15**
April 1932	**$20**	July 1932	**$15**
November 1932	**$15**	July 1933	**$20**
January 1934	**$20**	July 1934	**$25**
August 1934	**$25**	October 1934 (Hollywood issue, W.C. Fields)	**$75**
February 1935	**$20**	April 1935	**$25**
May 1935	**$20**	June 1935	**$20**
July 1935	**$25**	August 1935	**$25**
October 1935	**$20**	December 1935	**$20**
March 1936	**$20**	April 1936	**$20**
May 1937	**$25**	July 1937	**$15**

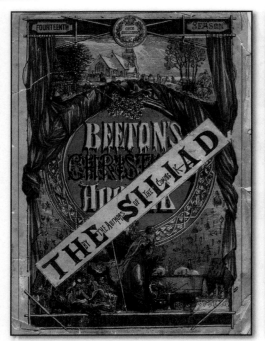 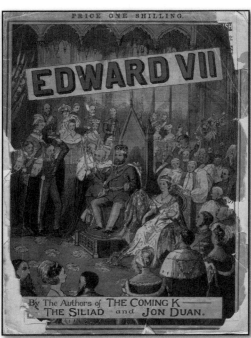

Beeton's Christmas Annual (1860-1898)

Published by Warde, Lock & Tyler, **Beeton's Christmas Annual** was a successful paperback magazine notorious for insulting satires on Queen Victoria, the Prince of Wales, the Court, the Ministers and the hangers-on of British Royalty. Published in November, each issue also carried a distinctive title reflecting the contents such as "The Siliad, or the Siege of the Seats" (Fourteenth Season 1873) and "Edward VII, A Play on the Past and Present Times with a View to the Future"(1876). Although published anonymously, the authors were alleged to be E.C. Grenville Murray, J. Ashby Sterry, F.C. Burnand, H. Sutherland Edwards, George Augustus Sala, Charles Townley and E. Dyne Fenton. In 1869, Samuel Orchart Beeton became the editor. Beeton had previously founded, edited and published **The Boys' Own Magazine** and **The Englishwoman's Domestic Magazine** and, in 1861, established **The Queen.** His wife was the enormously successful author of *Mrs. Beeton's Household Hints.*

The satire presented in **Beeton's Annual** was, however, creating problems. According to the press extracts, Beeton and the publishers had "a row in Beeton's (Ward, Lock's) office over the scurrility of the 'Authors of the Coming K.' Beeton personally split from the outraged Ward, Lock, & Tyler, perforce leaving them the title **Beeton's Annual,** but stating that he would start an annual of his own." The British courts found against Samuel Beeton. The most important issue of **Beeton's Christmas Annual** (Twenty-Eighth Season) was the 1887 edition entitled "A Study in Scarlet." It was written by a young, struggling doctor, Arthur Conan Doyle,

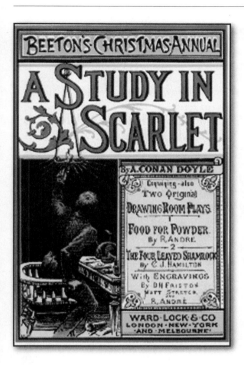

who was paid a mere 25 British pounds for his efforts. (The novel had been rejected elsewhere.) It introduced the detective, Sherlock Holmes, and Dr. Watson as the narrator of the stories. It was issued in November at a price of one shilling and sold out before Christmas.

1872 (The Coming of the K) 13th Season	**$50**	1873 (The Siliad or The Siege of the Seats) 14th Season	**$50**
1874 (English Knights Entertainment) 15th Season	**$50**	1874/1875 (Jon Duan)	**$75**
1876 (Edward VII)	**$50**	1887 (Study In Scarlet, Arthur Conan Doyle) 28th Season	**$200,000**

In 1990, a complete copy, while not in the best condition, sold for $57,200 at Sotheby's Auction in New York. A private sale for a copy in excellent condition had an asking price of $125,000 in 1990. The most current auction records are: 2001 for $15,000 (plus buyer's premium) at Christie's New York for a bound copy without the all-important cover or advertisements. A fair copy, complete, auctioned at Sothebys for $153,600 in December 2004.

1887 Study In Scarlet, Arthur Conan Doyle, Facsimile Baker Street Irregulars (1960) **$225**	1887 Study In Scarlet, Arthur Conan Doyle, Facsimile New York: Magico (1987) **$40**

Bentley's Miscellany (1837-1868)

Richard Bentley was a successful London printer who became a major force in London publishing. His first two famous editors were Charles Dickens (1837-1839) and William H. Ainsworth (1839-1841) with whom he had a "stormy" relationship. The magazine, with an emphasis on serialized fiction, was an enormous success from the beginning with the publication of the first installment of Dickens' "Oliver Twist"(February 1837-April 1839) illustrated by George Cruikshank. The illustrations of John Leech and George Cruikshank were a prominent feature of the magazine. Notable English and American writers included William Ainsworth, Samuel Lover, Sheridan Knowles, William Thackeray, William Maginn, Longfellow and James Fenimore Cooper (excerpt from "The Deerslayer" in September 1841). Edgar Allan Poe's "The Fall of the House of Usher" appeared anonymously (August 1840). During the 1850s, the magazine focus shifted to reviews and criticism, with high praise for the work of Herman Melville and lengthy discussions of Thomas De Quincey. In 1869, Bentley merged the **Miscellany** with Bentley's **Temple Bar.**

Prices are for bound volumes.	
February 1837-June 1839 (Dickens' "Oliver Twist," Cruikshank illustrations) **$1,200**	July-December 1839 (Ainsworth, "Jack Shepard") **$50**
January-December 1840 (Poe) **$200**	January-December 1841 (James Fenimore Cooper) **$150**
January-December 1842 (Cruikshank, John Leech) **$75**	January-December 1852 (Melville reviews) **$40**

Black Cat (October 1895-March 1922)

The Black Cat: The Monthly Magazine of Original Short Stories was published initially by Shortstory Publications of Boston. It was a general fiction magazine that featured a large amount of fantasy in its early years, and offered monetary prizes for the best short story. Jack London made his first commercial sale to **The Black Cat** with his macabre science-fiction story "A Thousand Deaths." It was published in the May 1899 issue and the $40 he was paid for it was, by his own account, the "first money I ever received for a story." The editor of **Black Cat** commented, however, that London's "A Thousand Deaths" was "more lengthy than strengthy." Other important writers that were published in **The Black Cat** included Ellis Parker Butler, Mary Austin, Clark Ashton Smith and Charles Fort. Interestingly, Henry Miller had his first story published in the May 1919 issue of **The Black Cat,** "The Unbidden Guest." Miller stories also appeared in June, August and October 1919.

Unremarkable single issue	**$30**	October 1895 first issue	**$100**
November 1895	**$50**	April 1897 (Geik Turner)	**$35**
February 1898 (Emma Wise)	**$35**	March 1899 (Mary Austin)	**$50**
May 1899 (Jack London)	**$175**	September 1905 (Charles Fort)	**$50**
August 1911 (Clark Ashton Smith)	**$75**	January 1912 (Ellis Parker Butler)	**$50**
May 1919 (Henry Miller)	**$100**		

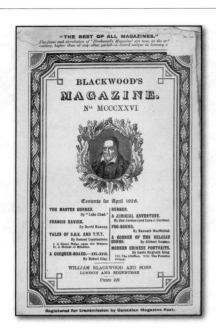

Blackwood's Magazine (1817-1980)

William Blackwood established himself as a bookseller and publisher in 1804. In 1817, after a fitful start of six issues under James Cleghorn and Thomas Pringle, he recast **Blackwood's Edinburgh Magazine,** in October, into the mold it would remain until its demise in 1980. **Blackwood's** had a major influence on British, and especially Scottish, writing. It even had a hand in directing the course of American literature, employing American literary rebel John Neal from 1824-1827 under the name Carter Holmes.

Distinguished writers from early issues include Walter Scott's son-in-law and biographer, John Gibson Lockhart, John Wilson (Christopher North), James Hogg, William Maginn, Samuel Ferguson and Thomas de Quincey. **Blackwood's** featured rather savage criticism, taking to task such notables as William Wordsworth, John Keats, William Hazlitt, the Cockney School of Poetry and Samuel Taylor Coleridge. The tradition continued: the **Blackwood's** review of *Jude the Obscure* in 1896, for example, drew this reaction from the author, Thomas Hardy: "Ever since the days of John Keats, to be bludgeoned by **Blackwood** has been the hallmark of an author of ideas." Nonetheless, **Blackwood's** regularly featured such authors as R.D. Blackmore, Elizabeth Barrett Browning, Anthony Trollope, Charles Lever and Edward Bulwer Lytton, in its first century, as well as introduced George Eliot (Mary Anne Evans) in 1857.

Internationally, in the late 19th and early 20th centuries, **Blackwood's** became the magazine of the British Empire, featuring such things as tiger hunts in India, as well the adventurous stories of John Buchan and Joseph Conrad, who serialized the first appearance of his *Heart of Darkness* in **Blackwood's** (1899). It was

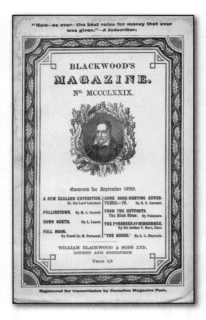

to be found in all corners of the Empire, from small African trading posts to the teeming cities of India. And, it seems, its fortunes were irrevocably tied to the rule of Britannia. As the empire declined, so did **Blackwood's.** An aging readership, changing taste, declining revenues and the downturn of the monthly literary magazine genre in the 1950s, 1960s and 1970s, proved an overwhelming combination for the magazine's directors. The magazine ended 163 years of regular publication in December 1980. Early **Blackwood's** and the period of its ascendancy as the magazine of the British empire are highly prized collectibles. Issues featuring original publications by both Buchan and Conrad are sought after.

Blackwood's is usually collected in bound volumes in six-month consecutive numbers:	
Volumes pre-1850 **$100**	Volumes containing Elizabeth Barrett Browning, Anthony Trollope or George Elliot **$125**
Volumes containing Joseph Conrad or John Buchan **$85**	Volumes 1850-1900 **$75**
Volumes 1900-WWII **$45**	Volumes post-WWII **$25**
Volume Two 1862 (Jefferson Davis) **$100**	Volume One 1868 (Impeachment of Andrew Johnson) **$150**
Volume One 1869 (Sir John Lawrence in India) **$150**	Volume One 1871 (The Fall of England?) **$175**
Volume One 1879 (The Himalayas) **$90**	Volume Two 1894 ("Poets and Geographers" and The Golfer) **$90**

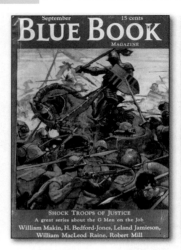

Achmed Abdullah, Edgar Rice Burroughs
William Makin, George Worts, H. Bedford-Jones
Beatrice Grimshaw, James Francis Dwyer

Achmed Abdullah, H. Bedford-Jones, George
Worts, William Chester, Beatrice Grimshaw.
"My Ten Years in the Foreign Legion"

Blue Book (1905-1952)

Blue Book Magazine began as **Monthly Story Magazine** with the May issue of 1905, as a publication of the Short Story Company, changed its name to **Blue Book** in September 1906, and was incorporated as Consolidated Publishers in May 1907. Originally it was a more adventure-oriented complement to the established romantic adventure magazine **The Red Book.** The first incarnation of **Blue Book** set the tone it would continue to follow as a fiction magazine of adventure, and fantastic stories and serials. William Hope Hodgson published what is considered his finest story "The Voice in the Night" in **Blue Book,** November 1907. Consolidated ran **Blue Book** until September of 1929, finding success publishing Edgar Rice Burroughs, Albert Payson Terhune, William MacLeod Raine, Gilbert Parker, Zane Grey and other adventure-oriented writers.

McCall's bought **Blue Book** in October 1929 to compete with **Argosy,** which featured many of the same writers. **McCall's** continued with the adventure and fantastic story formula with Burroughs and others, including Philip Wylie and Edward Balmer's *When Worlds Collide* (September 1932-February 1933). It added some mystery authors in the 1930s such as Michael Arlen, Achmed Abdullah and Octavus Roy Cohen to broaden the fiction base, always having a heavily male-oriented readership. **McCall's** changed gears with **Blue Book** in September 1941, cutting back on the fiction to add non-fiction of interest to men and changed to focus from adventure, fantastic fiction to a "man's magazine." Ultimately this approach failed and **Blue Book** published its final issue in January of 1952.

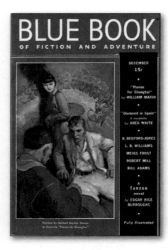

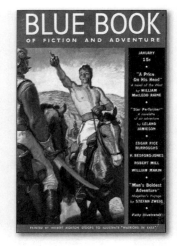

Unremarkable issue pre-1941	**$15**	Unremarkable issue post-1941	**$5**
Edgar Rice Burroughs serials:			
(Tarzan) Any single issue	**$25**	Complete run	**$175**
(Tanar of Pellucidar, March-August 1929) Single issue	**$100**	Complete run	**$800**
(A Fighting Man of Mars, April-September 1930) Single issue	**$50**	Complete run	**$450**
(Jungle Girl, May-September 1931) Single issue	**$45**	Complete run	**$350**
(The Swords of Mars, November 1934-April 1935) Single issue	**$40**	Complete run	**$350**
(When Worlds Collide, September 1932-Februry 1933) Single issue	**$30**	Complete run	**$250**
February 1917 (Edgar Rice Burroughs)	**$65**	March 1918 (Edgar Rice Burroughs)	**$75**
August 1918 (Edgar Rice Burroughs)	**$55**	October 1918 (Edgar Rice Burroughs)	**$55**
December 1918 (Edgar Rice Burroughs)	**$55**	January 1933 (Edgar Rice Burroughs)	**$40**
December 1935 (Edgar Rice Burroughs)	**$35**	October 1936 (Achmed Abdullah)	**$35**
August 1937 (Carl Sandberg)	**$35**	May 1940 (Nelson Bond)	**$40**
January 1942 (Edgar Rice Burroughs)	**$125**		

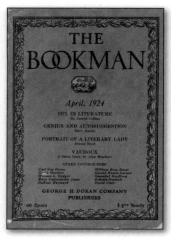

The Bookman (1891-1946)

The **Bookman** was the title of three separate magazines: one British and two American. The British magazine was published by Hodder and Stoughton, and conceived and edited by Sir William Robertson Nicholl from 1891 to 1923. It was a monthly literary journal that stood somewhere between the more academic journals such as **Literature, Academy** and **Atheneum,** and popular magazines without venturing as far in popular literature as **Cornhill's** and **The Strand. Bookman's** published J.M. Barrie, Thomas Hardy, A. T. Quiller-Couch and W.B. Yeats, providing a balance between the more literary journals and the magazines of popular fiction. During the early years of the 20th century, **The Bookman** published Arthur Conan Doyle, Walter de la Mare, G.K. Chesterton, Llewellyn Powys and one of the first works of Samuel Beckett, among others. Merged with **The London Mercury** in January of 1935, it effectively ceased to exist, though the organization continued through the **Mercury's** merger with **Life and Letters** in May 1939 and stayed in publication until February 1946.

An American version of **The Bookman** evolved from the house organ of George H. Doran into a literary magazine under the editorship of Arthur Burton Rascoe, and later John Farrar and Robert Cortes Holliday. Aside from Doran authors, the Doran version of **The Bookman** published Mary Austin, F. Scott Fitzgerald, Ellis Parker Butler, Amy Lowell, Babette Deutsch, Dubose Heyward, William Rose Benet and other major literary figures, becoming a major literary journal in the 1920s until allowed to languish after the Doubleday Doran merger in 1927. The Dodd Mead, American version of **The Bookman** began as **An Illustrated Magazine of Literature and Life** in 1894. Despite publishing such people as James Branch Cabell, the Dodd Mead **Bookman** gained neither the following nor the reputation of the Doran publication, possibly due to pushing Dodd authors who failed to stand the test of time such as Mrs. Roger A. Pryor and Robert Morss Lovett.

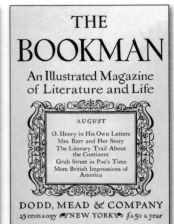

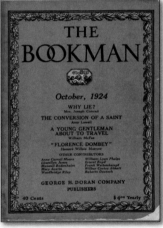

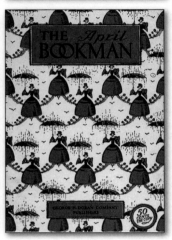

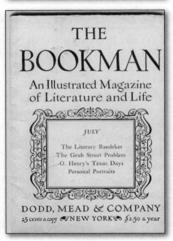

Hodder and Stoughton unremarkable issue	$10	Unremarkable Christmas issue	$10
Christmas Issue 1921	$100	Christmas Issue 1924	$125
Christmas Issue 1925	$50	Christmas Issue 1926	$125
Christmas Issue 1929	$50	Christmas Issue 1931	$100
Dodd Mead unremarkable bound volume	$10	Vol. 21 May-August 1905	$125
Vol. 22 September 1905-February 1906	$135	Vol. 24 September 1906-February 1907	$65
Vol. 25 March 1907-August 1907	$75	George H. Doran unremarkable issue	$15
July 1925	$30	August 1925	$45
September 1925	$30	September 1927	$20
February 1928	$25	May 1928	$25
November 1928	$35		

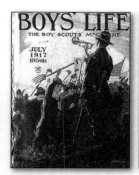

Boy's Life (1911-present)

Boys' and Boy Scouts' Magazine was founded by George S. Barton of Somerville, Mass., in 1911. At that time, there were three major competing scouting organizations in the United States: the American Boy Scouts, New England Boy Scouts and Boy Scouts of America. The first issue was published on Jan. 1, 1911, however very few of the 5,000 printed copies actually reached the public. Following its expansion from eight to 48 pages, a reduction in page size and the addition of a two-color cover, the March 1, 1911, issue is the generally accepted first issue. The Boy Scouts of America purchased the magazine in 1912. Dr. James E. West was the first editor under the BSA banner. **Boy's Life** has published original pieces by Alex Haley, Arthur C. Clarke, Ray Bradbury, Isaac Bashevis Singer, Van Wyck Brooks, Ernest Thompson Seton, Catherine Drinker Bowen, Robert Heinlein, Isaac Asimov, John Tolan and John Knowles, and featured cover art by Norman Rockwell and Salvador Dali.

Rockwell covers March 1934, February 1935, July 1935, February 1937, February 1948, February 1957, August 1959, February 1964			**$45**
August 1923	**$40**	September 1928	**$25**
March 1929	**$20**	August 1933	**$20**
June 1946	**$15**	July 1947	**$15**
August 1950-November 1950 (Robert Heinlein serial, "Farmer in the Sky") Single issue	**$35**	Full run	**$225**
May 1951	**$15**	December 1952	**$35**
February 1954	**$20**	May 1955	**$15**
August 1959	**$40**	March 1964	**$20**
April 1968	**$15**	June 1969	**$20**

THE "BOY'S OWN PAPER"]   Grover & Co., Nottingham.   [56, Paternoster Row, London.

THE PILOT'S YARN.
(EXHIBITED AT THE INSTITUTE OF PAINTERS IN OIL COLOURS, 1888)
Painted by GEORGE FOX.

Boy's Own Paper/Annual (1879-1967)

The Boy's Own Paper was a popular British boy's weekly magazine published by the Religious Tract Society of London. The weekly issues were bound in a collection and published as **The Boy's Own Annual.** In its later years, it became a monthly. Peak circulation reached about 250,000. The contents included serialized adventure stories, essays, sports (notably cricket), letters, puzzles and a variety of contests to stimulate the readership. Jules Verne was a frequent contributor to early issues, with serializations of his work published prior to book publication of "Barbicane & Co; Or, The Purchase of the Pole" and "Simon Hart–A Strange Story of Science and the Sea." Other important literary contributions were by G.A. Henty (1897), Algernon Blackwood (1906) and very early pre-Sherlock Holmes Arthur Conan Doyle stories such as "Crabbe's Practice" (anonymously 1884), "A Literary Mosaic (or Cyprian Overbeck Wells)" in 1886, "Uncle Jeremy's Household" (1886-87 with a character that was a precursor to Dr. Watson), "An Exciting Christmas Eve"(1887) and "Stone of Boxman's Drift" (1887). Accompanying the stories were hundreds of black and white engravings and numerous color chromolithos by illustrators such as the fantasy-oriented Sidney H. Sime, Louis Wain, Cecil Aldin, Warwick Goble and the humorist G.E. Studdy.

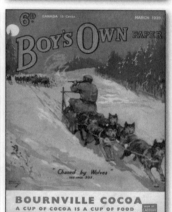

Boy's Own Paper for unremarkable single issues	**$5**
Boy's Own Annual for unremarkable bound volumes	**$7.50**
Boy's Own Paper Annual 1884-1885 (A.C. Doyle)	**$200**
Boy's Own Paper Annual 1886-1887 (A.C. Doyle)	**$250**
Boy's Own Paper Annual 1889-1890 (Jules Verne, Louis Wain)	**$150**
Boy's Own Paper Annual 1895-1896 (Henty, Wain)	**$150**
Boy's Own Paper Annual 1897-1898 (Henty, Sime, Goble, Wain)	**$150**
Boy's Own Paper Annual 1906-1907 (Algernon Blackwood, G.E. Studdy)	**$150**
Boy's Own Paper Annual 1914-1915 (Jules Verne)	**$75**
Boy's Own Paper Annual 1929-1930 (Jiu-Jitsu)	**$25**
Boy's Own Paper Annual 1932-1933 (Cricket)	**$50**
Boy's Own Paper Annual 1940-41 (Cricket)	**$35**
Boy's Own Paper Annual 1967	**$15**

Broom (1921-1924)

The **Broom, An International Magazine of the Arts,** was edited by Harold A. Loeb and Alfred Kreymborg, and published in Rome, Berlin and New York from November 1921 through January 1924. Matthew Josephson, Slater Brown, Lola Ridge and Malcolm Cowley all participated in producing the magazine at different times. Man Ray, Picasso, Modigliani, Stella, Weber, Derain, Strand, Arp, Kandinsky, Grosz, Matisse and Klee all contributed art to **Broom.** Writers included: William Carlos Williams, Gertrude Stein, Hart Crane, Jean Cocteau, Virginia Woolf, Robert Graves and John Dos Passos.

Full run 21 issues				$28,000
Volume One:	One	$350	Two	$575
	Three	$550	Four	$350
Volume Two:	One	$250	Two	$350
	Three	$450	Four	$350
Volume Three:	One	$350	Two	$250
	Three	$200	Four	$500
Volume Four:	One	$750	Two	$425
	Three	$475	Four	$350
Volume Five:	One	$350	Two	$375
	Three	$450	Four	$350
Volume Six: One		$550		

Burr McIntosh Monthly (1903-1910)

The Burr McIntosh Monthly was first published in April 1903, continuing monthly through 86 issues until May 1910. One of the first great pictorial magazines, it featured photography as its primary drawing card. Originally a collection of photographs bound by a ribbon strung so that individual pages could be removed and framed, it was originally 6¼" wide by 12" tall. With the August issue of 1907, the size was increased to 7¼" wide by 12¼" tall, but in January 1910, when the photography emphasis was dropped, the size was changed for the final five issues to 7" wide by 10" tall emphasizing text. The magazine featured the arts, with minor excursions into other areas such as sports and travel. Some issues featured a cover by Alphonse Mucha and several issues carried early Coca-Cola ads.

The nature of Burr McIntosh is such that few complete issues survive. Any complete issue in collectible condition sells for	**$150**
Those with Alponse Mucha covers sell for	**$250**

This is a magazine to be very careful of, as there are few ways to tell a complete issue without a collation.

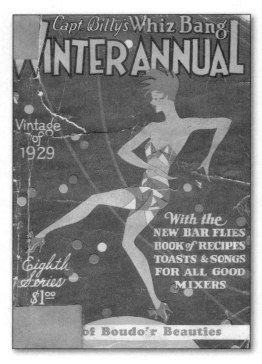

Captain Billy's Whiz Bang (1919-1930s)

Captain Wilford H. Fawcett began publishing **Whiz Bang** in October 1919 with an initial run of 5,000 copies. The title, **Whiz Bang,** was taken from the nickname for a World War I artillery shell. Fawcett initially distributed copies to hospitalized veterans, sending the remaining copies to a newsstand distributor. The public responded positively and immediately to the **Whiz Bang** and, within two years, the circulation approached 1 million. While **Whiz Bang** could certainly claim to be the most popular humor magazine of the 1920s, it always had the reputation of being slightly disreputable. A lot of that reputation, however, stems from later 1930s issues when circulation dwindled because of the Depression and competition from the more sophisticated **Esquire.** Raunchier jokes and some female nudity allowed the magazine to survive into the late 1930s, and gave it the raunchier reputation many people remember. Despite the fact that millions of copies of the **Whiz Bang** were printed, poor quality paper and a less than stellar reputation have combined to make it scarce in the collectible market. Surviving copies in good condition are few and far between, and bring a premium.

Unremarkable pre-1929 issue	$20	Unremarkable post-1929 issue	$10
Later 1930s issues containing nudity	$25	February 1928 (Louise Brooks)	$55

Cassell's (1867-1932)

Published by Cassell's, a newspaper publisher and later book publisher, **Cassell's Magazine** was originally **Cassell's Fiction Magazine** in April 1867. It became **Cassell's Family Magazine** in December 1874, **Cassell's Magazine** in December 1897, and **Cassell's Magazine of Fiction** from April of 1912 until its demise in December 1932 under Amalgamated Printers, its publisher from 1927. Early **Cassell's** featured Wilkie Collins, and later issues featured George Manville Fenn, Max Pemberton, E.W. Hornung, Rudyard Kipling and H. Rider Haggard. Under Max Pemberton's editorship (1896-1905), it tried to emulate **The Strand.** The final incarnation, **Cassell's Magazine of Fiction**, published Rafael Sabatini in a pulp format. Illustrations by both Arthur Rackham and Louis Wain bring large premiums in **Cassell's.**

Unremarkable issue	**$10**	Unremarkable six-month volume	**$50**
Volume or issue containing Louis Wain	**$150**	Volume or issue containing Arthur Rackham	**$175**
Serial "From a Surgeon's Diary" by Clifford Ashdown, December 1904-May 1905 Single issue	**$35**	Complete run	**$200**
Serial "Through the Magic Door" by Arthur Conan Doyle, November 1906-October 1907 Single issue	**$45**	Complete run	**$500**
June 1907 (P.G. Wodehouse)	**$100**	December 1908 (Jack London)	**$75**

Century (1881-1930)

"I was a child when we started to California, yet I remember the journey well and I have cause to remember it, as our little band of emigrants who drove out of Springfield, Ill., that spring morning of 1846 have since been known in history as the 'Ill-fated Donner party.' My father, James F. Reed, was the originator of the party, and the Donner brothers, George and Jacob, who lived just a little way out of Springfield, decided to join him." So began Virginia Reed Murphy's wrenching eyewitness account of "Across The Plains In the Donner Party" (1846), which appeared in **The Century Magazine** (July 1891) as part of an extensive series about "The Gold Hunters of California" (November 1890-October 1891).

The Century Illustrated Monthly Magazine was one of the most successful long-running "general interest" publications in American history. Single issues that sold for 35 cents could be exchanged, if in good condition, for corresponding bound volumes in gold cloth with gilt top for $1 per volume (six numbers); half Russia for $2.25; olive-green cloth, plain top, 75 cents. Originally published as **Scribner's Monthly,** it was renamed **The Century Magazine** by owner/editor Dr. Josiah Gilbert Holland after the death of book publisher Charles Scribner. Dr. Holland brought with him from **Scribner's** Richard Watson Gilder, who remained the editor of **The Century** from 1881-1909. Gilder was able to combine relevant topics of the time with fiction and poetry by American writers such as Mark Twain, Joel Chandler Harris, Jack London, Emma Lazarus, Paul Laurence Dunbar and Ella Wheeler

Wilcox, to name a few. The illustrators were the best, including
Timothy Cole, Winslow Homer, E.W. Kemble, Frederic Stuart
Church, Frederic Remington, Maxfield Parrish, J.C. Leyendecker
and N.C. Wyeth.

A unique feature of **The Century** was well-researched and
sometimes controversial historical series such as "The Life of
Napoleon" by William M. Sloane (November 1894-October
1896), "Abraham Lincoln: A History" by J.J. Nicolay and John
Hay (May 1887-April 1888) and the all-important "Battles and
Leaders of the Civil War." Leaders of both Union and Confederate
armies contributed to this extensive series, which appeared in
The Century from May 1884 through April 1888. James Edward
Taylor (1839-1901) was a battlefront artist who originally worked
for **Frank Leslie's Weekly. The Century** contracted him to provide
scenes of the recent Civil War from his memories. The series of
articles about the war were very popular, so the editors decided to
compile those articles and more, along with vivid illustrations by
various artists, for a set of four volumes in 1887, which became the
classic "Battles and Leaders of the Civil War."

The Century did not shy away from contemporary
controversy, either. America's first journalist-photographer,
Jacob Riis, was a turn of the century muckraker known as the
"Emancipator of the Slums." His shocking exposes of poverty
and life in the tenements on New York City's Lower East Side
appeared in **The Century** in "The Making of Thieves in New
York" (November 1894), "Merry Christmas In The Tenements"

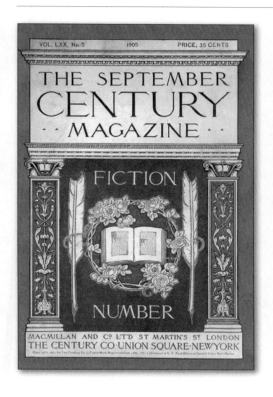

(December 1897) and "Feast-Day In Little Italy" (August 1899).

Science and technology were important to the readers of **The Century.** The Man of the Century was Thomas Edison. His "Invention of Kineto-Phonograph" was documented with photos in the May 1894-October 1894 volume. In the late 1800s, Nikola Tesla discovered a way to transmit power over long distances. The result was the alternating current system (AC) we use today. Tesla demonstrated the wireless transmission of power in 1899 and wrote the "Blueprint" for his concepts in "The Problem of Increasing Human Energy," which appeared in the June 1900 issue of **The Century.**

The crème de la crème of the American literati all had first appearances of their fiction published in **The Century.** The most pivotal was the pre-publication in parts of Mark Twain's *Huckleberry Finn.* Editor Richard Watson Gilder wanted to publish the entire novel serially. He talked Mark Twain into an excerpt for **The Century's** December 1884 issue. He then convinced Twain to let him print two further installments, in January and February, 1885. Although Twain participated in these publications, Gilder selected which parts to use, and also did most of the extensive editing by which aspects of the novel were "adapted to our audience." *Huck Finn* created an immediate sensation. It was banned by the Concord Library Committee, which thought the book was unsuitable for their shelves and viewed it as "trashy and vicious," "absolutely immoral in its tone," and "there is not a line in it which can be read by a pure-minded woman." The

New York Times reported that Huck "disfigured **The Century** magazine." The **Boston Literary World** stated it was happy to see that "**The Century** has received a check" for publishing "this sort of literature." The readers of **The Century** disagreed. Twain loved the ban because of all the free publicity. In retrospect, it was a successful literary alliance, as many other Twain creations were printed first in **The Century's** pages.

Perhaps the most valuable issues for collectors of **The Century** are the issues that featured illustrators. The July 1896 issue announced the winners of the Century Company's Poster Contest. The magazine offered three prizes of $125, $75 and $50 for the three best designs for a poster advertising its Midsummer Number. The offer was open to professional and amateur artists alike. Names or initials were not to appear upon the sketch, but a small "device" was to be drawn in the margin, and the full name and address of the artist placed in a sealed envelope bearing the same "device" and sent with the sketch, to be opened only after the award was made. Seven hundred designs were submitted in the competition. The winners were: first prize, J.C. Leyendecker, Chicago; second prize, Maxfield Parrish, Philadelphia; third prize, Baron Arild Rosenkrantz, New York. **The Century** sold the posters for 25 cents. An edition deluxe of 250 copies was printed on heavy paper and sold for $1 per copy. Parrish's poster was not published until 1897. It went on to become one of the most widely reproduced American posters of the era. Today if you can find one of the original lithos, your cost would be well over $1,000.

Arguably, the most sought after series published in **The Century** was the collaboration of Edith Wharton and Parrish in "Italian Villas and Their Gardens." It appeared in two volumes from November 1903-April 1904 (illustrated with 11 color plates and numerous black and white plates by Parrish), and April 1904-November 1904 (illustrated with five color plates and numerous black and white plates by Parrish). Both volumes also contain the first appearance of "The Sea-Wolf," serialized by Jack London. **The Century** was able to capture the essence of America during its long publishing history and create a legacy that was and still is an invaluable resource of the American experience. "Words cannot tell how beautiful the spring appeared to us coming out of the mountains from that long winter at Donner Lake in our little dark cabins under the snow…it was spring in California." –Virginia Reed Murphy, 1891.

Century Magazine unremarkable single issue	**$10**	Century Magazine unremarkable bound volume	**$20**
Century Magazine 1884-1885 (Mark Twain, "Huck Finn")	**$250**	Century Magazine 1886-1887 (Civil War series)	**$75**
Century Magazine 1887-1888 (Lincoln, Civil War Series)	**$75**	Century Magazine 1889-1890 (Mark Twain)	**$125**
Century Magazine 1894-1895 (Napoleon, Thomas Edison, Nikola Tesla)	**$75**	Century Magazine 1890-1891 (Donner Party, California gold hunters)	**$45**

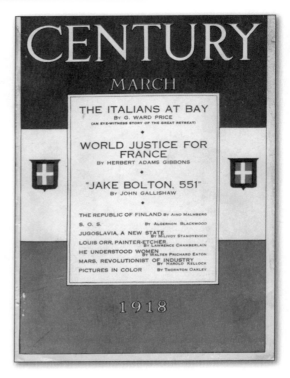

Century Magazine 1901-1902 (Maxfield Parrish, Milton's L'Allegro)	**$150**	Century Magazine 1902-1903 (Maxfield Parrish, Great Southwest)	**$550**
Century Magazine 1903-1904 (Maxfield Parrish, Edith Wharton, Italian villas)	**$750**	Century Magazine 1904-1905 (Alphonse Mucha, Parrish, Jack London)	**$125**
May 1883 (Emma Lazarus)	**$25**	June 1889 (Jack the Ripper)	**$35**
November 1894 (Jacob Riis)	**$25**	December 1897 (Jacob Riis)	**$25**
August 1896 (Leyendecker contest cover)	**$250**	August 1899 (Jacob Riis)	**$25**
June 1900 (Tesla)	**$75**	November 1904 (Parrish)	**$60**
December 1905 (Leyendecker color cover)	**$100**	December 1906 (Leyendecker color cover)	**$100**
August 1910 (Parrish color)	**$100**	April 1912 (Parrish frontispiece color)	**$100**
June, July, November 1912 (Booker T. Washington)	**$75**	December 1915 (Parrish frontispiece color)	**$100**
August 1917 (Parrish cover color)	**$100**	March 1918 (Algernon Blackwood)	**$25**

Century Guild/Hobby Horse (1884-1892)

A quarterly magazine, which emphasized printing as a craft in its own right, **The Century Guild/Hobby Horse** was edited by Herbert Horne, an architect, designer and poet. It was printed at the Chiswick Press by Kegan Paul, Trench and Co. The magazine was essentially the vehicle of The Century Guild, a group of artists, craftsmen and writers influenced by the Pre-Raphaelite School, known as the Arts and Crafts Movement. Members included magazine founders Arthur Mackmurdo, Selwyn Image and Herbert Horne, in addition to Smetham Allen and May Morris (daughter of William Morris). Other participants and/or affiliated artists were Dante Gabriel, Rossetti, Burne-Jones and Muir of the Blake Press. The magazine served as an inspiration to William Morris in setting up his Kelmscott Press, and to others in what became the private press movement. Issues printed on hand-laid paper contained articles and woodcuts by Herbert Horne, Selwyn Image, May Morris, Christina Rossetti, J. Henry Shorthouse and John Addington Symonds, with illustrations such as "Autumn Mists" mezzotinted by William Ward, after the picture by T. Hope McLachlan and one of the first appearances of three William Blake woodcuts "Pastorals of Virgil." Selwyn Image was responsible for the cover design for its first six volumes. Although it started as Mackmurdo's creation, from 1886 it was largely left to Horne to run. **The Century Guild** lasted only a few years, but as the first of the Arts and Crafts organizations, it had an importance far beyond its own productions as a precursor to art nouveau a decade or so later.

April 1884 Number 1	**$850**	1886 Volume I No.4 (William Blake)	**$750**
January, April, June, October 1888 complete year	**$800**		

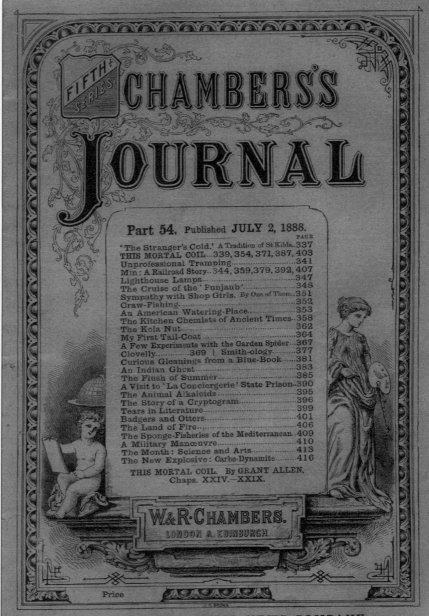

CHAMBERS'S JOURNAL

FIFTH SERIES

THIS MORTAL COIL. By GRANT ALLEN,
Chaps. XXIV.—XXIX.

W. & R. CHAMBERS.
LONDON & EDINBURGH.

Price

J. G. BROWN.

THE INTERNATIONAL NEWS COMPANY,
29 and 31 Beekman Street, NEW YORK.
FOR CANADA: Toronto News Co., Toronto and Clifton.—Montreal News Co., Montreal.

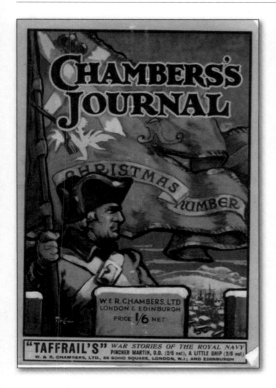

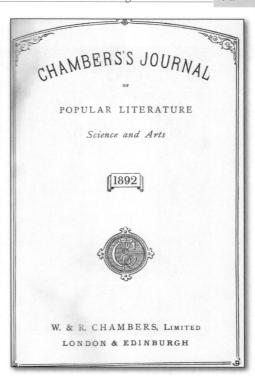

Chambers's Journal (1832-1956)

Originally a weekly tabloid, **Chambers's Edinburgh Journal** initiated in February 1832, became a magazine crafted after **Blackwood's** soon after. It changed its name in January 1854 to **Chambers's Journal of Popular Literature, Science and Arts,** finally becoming **Chambers's Journal** in December of 1897 through its demise in December 1956. William Strange, who published **Chambers's London Journal** from June 1841 through October 1843, was an attempted competitor and imitator using H.H. Chambers as the publisher, but was relatively unsuccessful. **Chambers's** aimed higher than most periodicals of its time and was noted as a major poetry publisher.

Unremarkable 19th century issue	**$15**	Unremarkable 20th century issue	**$7.50**
Unremarkable six-month volume	**$30**	June 22, 1839	**$50**
Feb. 29, 1840	**$25**	May 2, 1840	**$25**

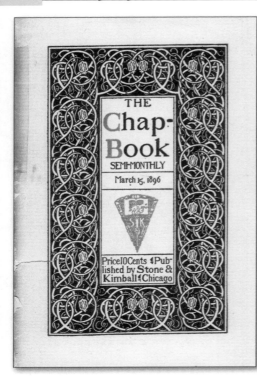

THE
Chap-Book
SEMI-MONTHLY

March 15, 1896

Price 10 Cents ¶ Published by Stone & Kimball ¶ Chicago

BY L. D. WILDMAN

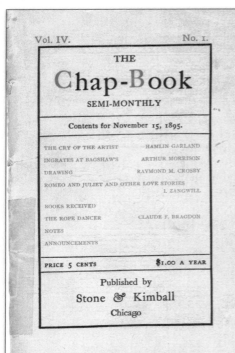

Vol. IV.   No. 1.

THE
Chap-Book
SEMI-MONTHLY

Contents for November 15, 1895.

THE CRY OF THE ARTIST   HAMLIN GARLAND

INGRATES AT BAGSHAW'S   ARTHUR MORRISON

DRAWING   RAYMOND M. CROSBY

ROMEO AND JULIET AND OTHER LOVE STORIES
    I. ZANGWILL

BOOKS RECEIVED

THE ROPE DANCER   CLAUDE F. BRAGDON

NOTES

ANNOUNCEMENTS

PRICE 5 CENTS $1.00 A YEAR

Published by
Stone & Kimball
Chicago

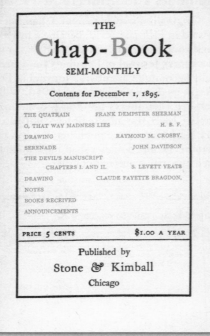

THE
Chap-Book
SEMI-MONTHLY

Contents for December 1, 1895.

THE QUATRAIN   FRANK DEMPSTER SHERMAN

O, THAT WAY MADNESS LIES   H. B. F.

DRAWING   RAYMOND M. CROSBY.

SERENADE   JOHN DAVIDSON

THE DEVIL'S MANUSCRIPT
    CHAPTERS I. AND II.   S. LEVETT YEATS

DRAWING   CLAUDE FAYETTE BRAGDON.

NOTES

BOOKS RECEIVED

ANNOUNCEMENTS

PRICE 5 CENTS $1.00 A YEAR

Published by
Stone & Kimball
Chicago

The Chap-Book (1894-1897)

The Chap-Book appeared on May 15, 1894, containing a commissioned drawing by Aubrey Beardsley. It was a finely printed, small format literary periodical with avant-garde illustrations, serving as a vehicle to advertise and promote Stone and Kimball authors. At its inception, Stone and Kimball began to do further advertising by commissioning posters for The Chap-Book as well as individual titles. Stone and Kimball commissioned Will Bradley to do their first poster, The Twins, for the first Chap-Book issue in the spring of 1894. They commissioned designers, notably Will Bradley, Claude Fayette Bragdon, Frank Hazenplug, E.B. Bird, J.C. Leyendecker, Felix Vallotton and Henri Toulouse-Lautrec, to do posters as well as illustrations, cover designs and decorations for their publications. The Chap-Book started a small magazine craze in the U.S., and gave a strong impetus to modern graphic design. The partnership dissolved in 1897 due to internal disagreements and the magazine ceased publication.

NOTE: Due to its artwork, **The Chap-Book** is frequently ripped and the prices given are for issues and volumes known to be complete. In buying it, it is imperative to check page by page for cuts.

Unremarkable issue	$20	Unremarkable six-month volume	$75
Volume III May 15-Nov. 1, 1895	$180	Volume IV Nov. 15, 1895-May 1, 1896	$150
Volume V May 15-Nov. 1, 1896	$145	Aug. 1, 1894	$35
Dec. 1, 1894	$50	Feb. 1, 1895	$35
Feb. 15, 1895	$35	July 1, 1895	$35
July 15, 1895	$35	Sept. 1, 1895	$75
Sept. 15, 1895	$30	Oct. 1, 1895	$35
Dec. 15, 1895	$75	Jan. 1, 1896	$35
April 15, 1896	$100	May 1, 1896	$50

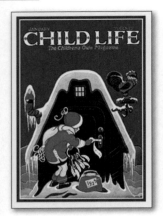 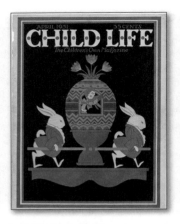 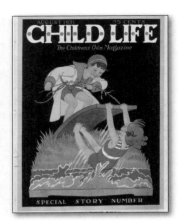

Child Life (1921-present)

Originally published by Rand-McNally in January 1921, **Child Life** was intended as a cheaper version of **St. Nicholas,** with a slightly younger audience. Rand McNally's connections with authors brought writers like Thornton Burgess, Carl Sandburg and Laura Ingalls Wilder to **Child Life,** and employed Harrison Cady, whose illustrations and covers bring a premium with collectors, as does the work of J. Allen St. John. A curious fact is that **Playboy** publisher Hugh Hefner began his magazine career with **Child Life.** Purchased by **The Saturday Evening Post** in 1977, **Child Life** began to languish, turning over increasingly larger portions of the magazine to filler such as games. **Child Life** continues to be published, with a significant portion of the content reprints of nostalgic children's stories from the Rand McNally era by the Children's Better Health Institute. Perhaps the most collectible issue is November 1932, which carries a small article by Alice Liddell Hargreaves, the girl Lewis Carroll patterned his Alice after, at age 81.

Unremarkable issue	$10	Unremarkable issue (with cover/ artwork by Harrison Cady)	$35
Unremarkable issue (with cover/ artwork by J. Allen St. John)	$50	June 1927	$55
April 1931	$25	July 1932	$20
September 1932	$20	November 1932 (Alice Hargreaves)	$125
March 1936	$25		

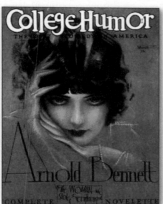

College Humor (1921-1943)

Debuting in December 1921, **College Humor** had a very impressive list of contributors until its demise during World War II in 1943. Both F. Scott and Zelda Fitzgerald were almost regular contributors; Scott would later attribute all of these stories with a shared byline to Zelda. Faith Baldwin, Michael Arlen, Ellis Parker Butler and Groucho Marx were all featured in **College Humor.** John Held Jr. contributed both covers and cartoons to **College Humor** in the style he made famous epitomizing the "Jazz Age." Most popular in the 1920s, the magazine declined with the Depression, following much the same trend as H. L. Mencken's incarnation of **The American Mercury.**

Unremarkable issue	**$15**	F. Scott/Zelda Fitzgerald stories (July 1929, October 1929, February 1930, April 1930, January 1931) **$250**	
Issues with cover/artwork by John Held Jr.	**$25**	Issues with cover/artwork by Rolf Armstrong	**$20**

Collier's Weekly (1888-1957)

Originally founded in 1888, as **Collier's Once a Week** by Peter Fenelon Collier, an Irish immigrant, it was a magazine of "fiction, fact, sensation, wit, humour, news." By 1892, it had a circulation of more than 250,000 and was one of the largest selling magazines in the United States. In 1895, its name was changed to **Collier's Weekly: An Illustrated Journal.** It later became known as **Collier's The National Weekly,** concentrating on news. The magazine became a leading exponent of the half-tone news picture. Collier recruited James H. Hare, one of the pioneers of photojournalism, to feature the new technology.

Norman Hapgood became editor of **Collier's Weekly** in 1903. Hapgood developed a reputation of employing the country's leading writers. For example, in May 1906, he had Jack London write extensively about the San Francisco earthquake. London also wrote about "The Trouble Makers of Mexico" (1914). Investigative journalists such as Ida M. Tarbell, Ray Stannard Baker, Samuel Hopkins Adams and Upton Sinclair wrote "muckraking" articles that brought on legal changes. Some of the most collectible Maxfield Parrish designs graced the **Collier's** covers from 1904 through 1936. Other important illustrators who appeared in **Collier's** were Frank X. Leyendecker, Phillip R. Goodwin and, of course, Joseph Clement Coll, who created the illustrations for the appearances of Sax Rohmer's "Fu Manchu" in the early issues. The magazine's circulation had reached 1 million by 1917. While early fiction had been published, such as Arthur Conan Doyle's "The Return of Sherlock Holmes" (1903-04), it wasn't until the late 1920s that **Collier's Weekly** began to concentrate on the serialization of novels. Produced in about 10 parts, the magazine ran two novels at a time featuring such authors as H.G. Wells, Sax Rohmer and P.G. Wodehouse. The 1930s issues carried the classic Damon Runyon stories and Zane Grey. Ernest Hemingway wrote first-hand accounts about the Spanish Civil War and later World War II. After the war, circulation diminished, and the magazine was closed down in 1957 after losing money for several years.

Serials: Arthur Conan Doyle, "The Return of Sherlock Holmes" Sept. 26, 1903; Oct. 31, 1903; Dec. 5, 1903; Dec. 26, 1903; Jan. 30, 1904; Feb. 27, 1904; March 16, 1904; April 30, 1904; Sept. 24, 1904; Dec. 31, 1904 and Jan. 28, 1905.			
Single issue	**$45**	Complete run	**$600**
Sax Rohmer, "Fu Manchu's Bride" (Coll Illustrations) May 13-July 1, 1933		Single issue	**$15**
Complete run	**$150**	Unremarkable issue	**$10**
July 17, 1900 (Kipling)	**$65**	Feb. 23, 1901 (Paul Laurence Dunbar) **$35**	
Nov. 3, 1903 (Parrish, Joel Chandler Harris)	**$60**	Dec. 30, 1905 (Jessie Wilcox Smith)	**$30**
Nov. 24, 1906 (Jessie Wilcox Smith)	**$45**	June 15, 1907 (Red Riding Hood) **$30**	

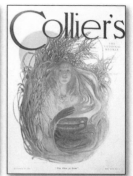

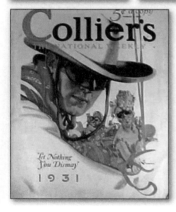

Nov. 23, 1907 (Remington, George Bernard Shaw)	$50	May 28, 1910 (P.G. Wodehouse)	$75
March 11, 1911 (Parrish)	$45	Oct. 13, 1916 (Parrish)	$40
June 6, 1925 (Willa Cather)	$40	Aug. 13, 1927 (Albert Payson Terhune)	$35
Jan. 30, 1932 (Runyon)	$45	June 4, 1932 (P.G. Wodehouse)	$65
Nov. 13, 1937 (Rohmer)	$45		

Cornhill Magazine (1860-1974)

The **Cornhill Magazine** was founded in 1860 by publisher George Smith (Smith Elder). Starting with pieces by William Makepeace Thackeray, the first editor, and Anthony Trollope the magazine combined criticism and serialized novels. The initial sales of the magazine marked it a success, the first number selling 110,000 copies. Especially under Leslie Stephen, who took charge in 1871, **Cornhill** maintained a remarkable level of literary distinction, publishing novels by Thackeray, Trollope, George Eliot, Mrs. Gaskell, Thomas Hardy, Henry James, Wilkie Collins, Charles Reade and James Payn, as well as articles by Robert Lewis Stevenson, Matthew Arnold and John Ruskin. Smith and Thackery pulled off a literary coup in 1862, luring George Eliot from **Blackwell's** to publish *Romola* as a **Cornhill** serial from July 1862

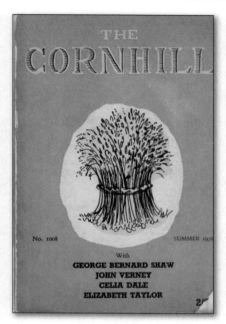

to August 1863. **Cornhill** also published the original appearances of James' *Daisy Miller* (June-July 1878) and Hardy's *Far from the Madding Crowd* (January-December 1874). Arthur Conan Doyle published an anonymous short story in **Cornhill,** "J. Habakuk Jephson's Statement" (January1884) at the beginning of his career and serialized the first appearance of *The White Company* (January-December 1891). Curiously, it was Doyle's first series of Sherlock Holmes stories in **The Strand** (qv.) that dethroned **Cornhill** as the major fiction outlet in England in 1891. Before a rather marked decline at the beginning of the 20th century under John Murray, spiraling down to a final issue in 1974, **Cornhill** published two of the last pieces by Stephen Crane in 1899, "A Self-Made Man" (March) and "God Rest Ye Merry Gentlemen" (May).

Unremarkable issue under Smith Elder	$15	Unremarkable yearly volume under Smith Elder	$45
Unremarkable issue under John Murray	$10	Unremarkable yearly volume under John Murray	$25
January 1884	$100	March 1899	$45
May 1899	$40	July 1932	$75
July 1945	$50	Summer 1947	$50
Winter 1949	$35	Summer 1956	$20
Serials by Trollope, Thackery and Wilkie Collins, complete run			$200
Serials by Thomas Hardy (*Far From the Madding Crowd* and *The Hand of Ethelberta*)			
Single issue	$40	Complete run	$375
Serial "The White Company" by A.C. Doyle January-December 1891			
Single issue	$25	Complete run	$200

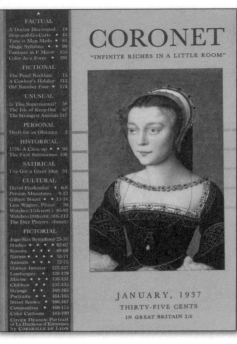

HEINRICH KLEY

THE ICE WALTZ

JANUARY, 1937

43

HEINRICH KLEY

FEBRUARY, 1937

43

Coronet (1936-1961)

The success of **Esquire** allowed David A. Smart to bring out a digest (pocket) sized magazine in imitation of **Reader's Digest** in November of 1936, entitled **Coronet**. Edited by Arnold Gingrich, the editor of **Esquire, Coronet** was an initial success, though it never approached the mass circulation of **Reader's Digest. Coronet** was not as adventurous in seeking out important literary pieces as **Esquire,** sticking with more popular writers of its time such as Rupert Hughes and Milt Gross. It did, however, introduce Heinrich Kley to America in three consecutive issues in 1937. Despite the magazine wrongly declaring Kley to have died in an insane asylum, Kley's satirical drawings, which used humans and anthropomorphic animals as metaphors, became influential in American illustration, especially at the Walt Disney studios. **Coronet** issues containing Kley have become highly desirable collectibles. **Coronet** declined in the early 1950s, publishing its final issue in October 1961.

Single unremarkable issue pre-1950s	**$8**	November 1936 first issue	**$50**
December 1936 (Saroyan)	**$15**	January, February, March 1937 Heinrich Kley issues, complete set	**$100**
October 1946 (Ku Klux Klan)	**$20**		

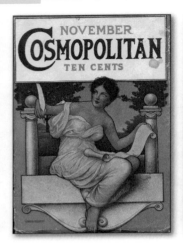

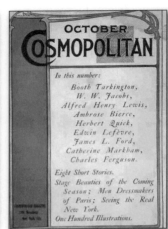

Cosmopolitan (1886-present)

Initially founded as the **Brooklyn Magazine** under the editorship of Edward Bok in 1883, then becoming **The Cosmopolitan An Illustrated Monthly** in 1886, it gained considerable circulation in 1889 under editor and publisher John Brisben Walker. Walker serialized the fiction of British authors such as Bram Stoker, "The Red Stockade" (1894); H.G. Wells with "The War of the Worlds" (1897) and "The First Men in the Moon" (1900-1901); Arthur Conan Doyle, "Tempted By The Devil"(1895) and "Uncle Bernac" (1897); Rudyard Kipling with "Mowgli Leaves the Jungle Forever" (1895); and Robert Louis Stevenson with "A Tragedy of the Great North Road." In 1905, William Randolph Hearst bought **The Cosmopolitan** for $400,000 and dropped the "The" from the name. "The Treason of the Senate" (1906) by David Graham Phillips, a landmark piece of journalistic "muckraking," was Hearst's first coup for the magazine. Hearst, who always bought and paid for the best, hired Ambrose Bierce to write two columns "The Passing Show" and "Small Contributions"(1905-1908). He also signed illustrator Harrison Fisher to an exclusive contract for the covers of **Cosmopolitan**, which lasted until Fisher's death in 1934. Although Jack London had published in **The Cosmopolitan** with "Diable-A Dog" (1902), once Hearst took over, a steady stream of London's work was published, including "Planchette"(1906), "Just Meat" and "Pinched" (1907), "Smoke Bellew" (1912), "Valley of the Moon"(1913) and "The Little Lady of the Big House"(1915). By the 1930s, the magazine had a circulation of 1.7 million and an advertising income of $5 million. Hearst, at this point, merged it with Hearst's International. Serializations by mystery writers such as S.S. Van Dine and Agatha Christie were featured along with short stories and articles by Somerset Maugham, Edith Wharton, Theodore Dreiser, Gertrude Stein, Edna St. Vincent Millay, P.G. Wodehouse and Damon Runyon. Bradshaw Crandell brought another dimension to the cover illustrations with his renderings of Hollywood stars such as Veronica Lake and Lana Turner into the 1940s. After the war, however, circulation dipped until 1965, when Helen Gurley Brown became the editor and changed the appeal of the magazine toward modern, independent and sexy women.

The Cosmopolitan unremarkable single issue **$10**	Cosmopolitan unremarkable single issue **$8**
Cosmopolitan unremarkable with Harrison Fisher cover, single issue **$50**	The Cosmopolitan October 1894 (Bram Stoker) **$75**
The Cosmopolitan September 1895 (Doyle) **$50**	The Cosmopolitan January 1896 (R.L. Stevenson, Eric Pape) **$50**
The Cosmopolitan January 1897 (Doyle) **$50**	The Cosmopolitan February 1897 (Doyle) **$50**
The Cosmopolitan March 1897 (Doyle) **$50**	The Cosmopolitan April 1897 (H.G. Wells) **$100**
The Cosmopolitan May 1897 (H.G. Wells) **$100**	The Cosmopolitan July 1897 (H.G. Wells) **$100**

The Cosmopolitan September 1897 (H.G. Wells) **$100**	The Cosmopolitan December 1898 (Doyle) **$65**
The Cosmopolitan October 1899 (Mark Twain) **$100**	The Cosmopolitan December 1899 (Doyle, Madame Blavatsky) **$95**
The Cosmopolitan April 1900 (Willa Cather) **$25**	The Cosmopolitan November 1900 (H.G. Wells, Jack London) **$150**
The Cosmopolitan December 1900 (H.G. Wells) **$100**	The Cosmopolitan January 1901 (H.G. Wells) **$100**
The Cosmopolitan June 1902 (Jack London) **$100**	The Cosmopolitan October 1905 (Ambrose Bierce) **$65**
The Cosmopolitan February 1904 (H.G. Wells, Oliver Herford) **$25**	Cosmopolitan May 1906 (David Graham Phillips, H.G. Wells, Ambrose Bierce) **$75**
Cosmopolitan August 1906 (Jack London, Ambrose Bierce) **$75**	Cosmopolitan December 1906 (Jack London, Ambrose Bierce) **$75**
Cosmopolitan March 1907 (Jack London, Ambrose Bierce, Blendon Campbell) **$100**	Cosmopolitan June 1907 (Jack London, Ambrose Bierce) **$75**
Cosmopolitan July 1907 (Jack London, Ambrose Bierce) **$75**	Cosmopolitan October 1907 (Jack London, Ambrose Bierce) **$75**
Cosmopolitan November 1907 (Jack London, Ambrose Bierce) **$75**	Cosmopolitan August 1908 (Ambrose Bierce, Fisher cover) **$65**
Cosmopolitan May 1913 (Jack London, Fisher cover) **$75**	Cosmopolitan June 1913 (Jack London, Fisher cover) **$75**
Cosmopolitan July 1913 (Jack London, Fisher cover) **$75**	Cosmopolitan August 1913 (Jack London, Fisher cover) **$75**
Cosmopolitan December 1913 (Jack London, George Ade, Fisher cover) **$75**	Cosmopolitan January 1914 (Robert W. Chambers, Fisher cover) **$50**
Cosmopolitan February 1914 (Robert W. Chambers, Fisher cover) **$50**	Cosmopolitan July 1915 (Jack London, George Ade, Fisher cover) **$75**
Cosmopolitan November 1915 (Jack London, Fisher cover) **$75**	Cosmopolitan July 1916 (Ella Wheeler Wilcox, Fisher cover) **$50**
Cosmopolitan December 1923 (Albert Payson Terhune, Fisher cover) **$75**	Cosmopolitan August 1927 (Don Marquis, Fisher cover) **$50**
Cosmopolitan August 1931 (Erte, John Held Jr., Fisher cover) **$50**	Cosmopolitan January 1931 (Harry Price, Doyle) **$50**
Cosmopolitan November 1932 (S.S. Van Dine, Fisher cover) **$50**	Cosmopolitan March 1933 (Harold Bell Wright, Fisher cover) **$50**
Cosmopolitan September 1933 (Evelyn Waugh, Fisher cover) **$50**	Cosmopolitan April 1934 (Ernest Hemingway, Fisher cover) **$75**
Cosmopolitan January 1935 (Damon Runyon, Mary Roberts Rinehart) **$30**	Cosmopolitan February 1935 (Gertrude Stein, P.G. Wodehouse) **$75**
Cosmopolitan November 1935 (Agatha Christie, Damon Runyon) **$150**	Cosmopolitan November 1937 (Somerset Maugham, Bette Davis) **$40**
Cosmopolitan November 1938 (Max Brand) **$25**	Cosmopolitan November 1941 (Veronica Lake, Damon Runyon, Bradshaw Crandell cover) **$40**
Cosmopolitan March 1942 (Lana Turner, Judy Garland, Bradshaw Crandell cover) **$40**	

What Am I Offered for Spuds? — By Hugh J. Hughes

THREE PER CENT MONEY

HENRY FORD ON FARMING

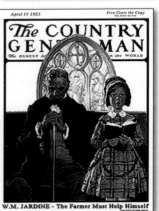

W.M. JARDINE - The Farmer Must Help Himself

O. E. Bradfute—Timberland Savings Banks

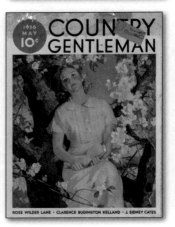

RADIO DEATH FIGHTERS — By PAUL DE KRUIF

ROSE WILDER LANE · CLARENCE BUDINGTON KELLAND · J. SIDNEY CATES

MARGARET WEYMOUTH JACKSON · BEN HIBBS · JAMES E. EDMONDS

Country Gentleman (1853-1955)

Country Gentleman was the successor to **The Genesee Farmer** and **The Cultivator**, founded by Luther Tucker. In 1853, he established **Country Gentleman,** a weekly, with which **The Cultivator** was finally combined in 1866 under the united title. Under Tucker and his sons, the magazine became America's rural general interest magazine and remained so after its purchase by Curtis in 1911. Under the Curtis banner, **Country Gentleman** published fiction by Zane Grey, Max Brand, Albert Payson Terhune, and other writers of Western and rural stories, as well as articles of rural and farming interest by such journalists and politicians as Bernard Baruch and Rose Wilder Lane. The last 21 issues from February-June 1955 were published as **Better Farming.**

Unremarkable issue	$10		
Serials: Erle Stanley Gardner serials featuring Doug Selby Single issue	$30	Complete run	$200
July 1, 1922	$20	Dec. 2, 1922	$50
Sept. 8, 1923	$45	Oct. 11, 1924	$25
Dec. 13, 1924	$25	May 16, 1925	$20
March 1929	$50	June 1931	$55
November 1931	$45	June 1932	$45
September 1933	$50	August 1935	$45
May 1936	$45		

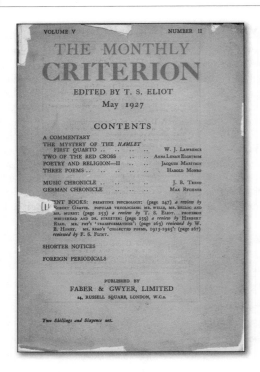

The Monthly Criterion (1922-1939)

A quarterly literary journal was published from 1922-1925 by Cobden Sanderson and from 1925 through 1939 by Faber, edited by T.S. Eliot. From 1922-1926, it was called **The Criterion,** it switched to **The New Criterion** in 1926 and 1927, and finally was **The Monthly Criterion.** Eliot's extended debate with John Middleton Murry on Classicism versus Romanticism and his attack on Bertrand Russell's anti-Christian philosophy as "merely a variety of Low Church sentiment" are two highly collectible topics, along with publications by Ezra Pound.

Unremarkable issue	$20	April 1925	$30
June 1926	$75	October 1926	$75
June 1927	$25	July 1930	$30
January 1931	$30	April 1935	$25

Das Plakat (1910-1921)

Das Plakat (The Poster) was edited by Hans Josef Sachs, a German dentist and poster collector. Although the art poster was born in Paris before the turn of the century, in 1905 Berlin was the capital of modern poster art. Dr. Sachs launched **Das Plakat** in 1910 as the official publication of the Verein der Plakat Freunde (The Society for Friends of the Poster). The society was one of a number of groups that advocated poster art and collecting. **Das Plakat,** as a magazine, explored aesthetic, cultural and legal issues about posters and graphic design. It featured original work in both commerce and politics. **Das Plakat** exhibited the finest poster examples from Germany and other European countries. Its high artistic standards and exquisite printing defined the decade of graphic design between 1910 and 1920, combining French art nouveau and German Jugenstil. While the first issue was only 200 copies, by 1914 the edition was up to 2,400 copies and its circulation reached 5,000 at its peak. The work of German graphic illustrators such as H.R. Erdt, Julius Klinger, Paul Leni and Heinrich Jager was featured with tipped-in cards on high quality papers on topics of advertising and war issues.

November 1914	$250	June 1920	$135
February 1921	$200	March 1921	$200
April 1921	$200	May 1921	$200
October 1921	$215		

The Delineator (1873-1937)

The Delineator (A Journal of Fashion, Culture, and Fine Arts) began in 1873 and was published until 1937, when it was merged into **Pictorial Review** by Hearst after its purchase from original publisher Butterick. Conceived primarily as a women's magazine with literary overtones, the magazine featured fashion illustrations along the order of those pioneered by **Godey's Lady's Book** earlier in the century. Under the editorships of Theodore Dreiser and Honore Willsie Morrow (1907-1920), both popular writers, the literary content of the magazine was raised considerably and it began publishing writers such as William Macleod Raine, Amelia Barr, Richard LeGallienne, Countess Van Arnim (Elizabeth), Joseph C. Lincoln, Zona Gale and Arnold Bennett. It switched gears in the early 1920s, turning to stronger romance authors such as Kathleen Norris, Maud Hart Lovelace, Albert Payson Terhune and Sophie Kerr. Margaret Sangster, Dorothy Canfield and Arthur Train also published in **The Delineator** before its merger with **Pictorial Review.** Illustrators of cover and interior decoration for the magazine included Rose O'Neill, John Held Jr., Howard Chandler Christy and Philip Boileau.

Serial: Kathleen Norris, "Margaret Yorke," February-July 1923			
Single issue	$25	Complete run	$175
Single unremarkable issue	$12		
July 1890 (Women's fashions)	$75	November 1890 (Women's fashions)	$65
May 1894 (Wedding dresses)	$40	December 1894 (Women's fashions)	$75
June 1901 (William MacLeod Raine)	$35	January 1904 (Jack London)	$100
December 1915 (Arthur Rackham)	$100	January 1916 (Arthur Rackham)	$100
July 1916 (Philip Boileau)	$85	December 1916 (Arthur Rackham)	$75
December 1921 (Zona Gale)	$30	February 1927 (Albert Payson Terhune, Arthur Train)	$55
June 1927 (Arthur Rackham)	$85	June 1928 (Rose O'Neill's Kewpies)	$45
October 1928 (Albert Payson Terhune, Rockwell Kent)	$65		

The Dial (1840-1929)

Originally a transcendentalist magazine founded in 1840, edited first by Margaret Fuller and later by Ralph Waldo Emerson, **The Dial** went through its first reorganization in 1880 as a liberal journal, becoming more radical under Martyn Johnston, then floundering both ideologically and financially from about 1916. Scofield Thayer bought the magazine in 1918, and by 1920 had transformed it into a journal of art and culture, with a liberal political agenda and clearly focused aesthetic agenda. Thayer's **Dial** was filled with illustrations of many new works of art as well as the best in poetry, prose and drama, publishing such people as: Sherwood Anderson, Djuna Barnes, Randolphe Bourne, Kenneth Burke, Hart Crane, e.e. cummings, Charles Demuth, Kahlil Gibran, Gaston Lachaise, Amy Lowell, Marianne Moore, Ezra Pound, Odilon Redon, Betrand Russell, Carl Sandburg, Van Wyck Brooks and W.B. Yeats. Thayer fell ill in 1927 and, although Marianne Moore kept **The Dial** going for two years, by 1929 the magazine was unable to continue. **The Dial** ceased publication in July of 1929.

May 1920 (e.e. cummings)	$65	July 1920 (Rimbaud, James Joyce)	$75
August 1920 (William Carlos Williams)	$55	September 1920 (Ezra Pound, D.H. Lawrence)	$55
June 1922 (Hart Crane, D.H. Lawrence, Picasso)	$100	October 1922 (W.B. Yeats, Chagall)	$75
February 1923 (D.H. Lawrence)	$50	November 1926 (W.B. Yeats)	$55
November 1927 (D.H. Lawrence)	$50	March 1928 (Ezra Pound, T.S. Eliot)	$55

 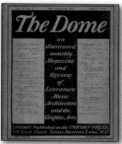  

The Dome Magazine (1897-1900)

The Dome was a London literary review on the order of
The Yellow Book and **The Savoy**, published and edited by the
owner of the Unicorn Press, Ernest J. Oldmeadow. Oldmeadow,
who fashioned the Unicorn Press based on the aesthetic ideals of
William Morris, contributed frequently to **The Dome** under the
pseudonym of J.E. Woodmeald. Initially published as a "Quarterly
containing Examples of all the Arts," **The Dome** became a monthly
after the first five issues. Important writers that contributed to
The Dome were Arthur Symons, Laurence Binyon, C.J. Holmes,
Gleeson White, Laurence Housman and William Butler Yeats.
Yeats was the most significant of the writers, with poems such as
"The Desire of Man and of Woman" and "Aodh Pleads With The
Elemental Powers," and essays like "A Symbolic Artist and the
Coming of Symbolic Art." Laurence Housman not only wrote
poems and stories but did illustrations for **The Dome** including the
endpapers for the quarterly issues. **The Dome** also showcased other
prominent illustrators such as Althea Gyles and Gordon Craig.

1897 Midsummer Day Quarterly issue (W.B. Yeats, Housman) **$75**	1897 Michaelmas Day Quarterly issue (Burne-Jones) **$60**
1898 New Year's Day Quarterly issue (Housman) **$60**	December 1898 (W.B. Yeats, Gordon Craig) **$75**
February 1899 (Gordon Craig) **$60**	March 1899 (Gordon Craig, Fiona Macleod) **$75**
June1899 (Burne-Jones) **$35**	July 1899 (Rossetti) **$40**
April 1899 (W.B. Yeats) **$50**	

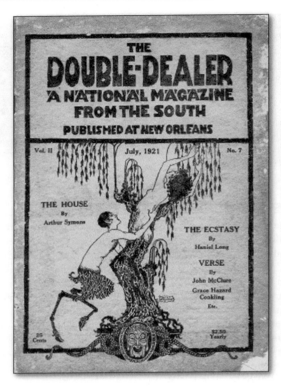

Double Dealer (1921-1926)

The Double Dealer was a little magazine published in New Orleans, 1921–1926, edited by John McClure. It was founded by Albert Goldstein, Julius Weiss Friend, John McClure and Basil Thompson, with the assistance of a dedicated group of Louisiana guarantors, who were tired of hearing the South described as a literary backwater by critics in other regions. Original publications of William Faulkner and early work by Ernest Hemingway has made The Double Dealer a sought after collectible.

Unremarkable issue	$20	June 1921 (Harte, Crane)	$125
July 1921 (Harte, Crane)	$100	January 1922	$65
May 1922 (Harte, Crane and Ernest Hemingway)	$350	June 1922 (Ernest Hemingway)	$200
July 1925	$55	Issues containing William Faulkner	$300

Electrical Experimenter/Radio News/Practical Electronics (1913-1971)

The **Electrical Experimenter** was first published in 1913, the name was changed to **Science and Invention** in 1920; the last issue was published in August 1931. **Practical Electrics** was begun in 1921 and the name changed to **The Experimenter** in 1924 and the last issue was in 1926, at which point it was merged into **Science and Invention**. **Radio News** was first published in 1919 as **Radio Amateur News,** dropping the word "Amateur" from the title in 1920. In 1948, the title changed to **Radio and Television News,** and finally becoming **Electronics World** from May 1959 to December 1971. These magazines were the basis of Hugo Gernsback's popular technical magazine line and complemented his science fiction pulps with hard science for the layman, with articles by and about such people as Nikola Tesla and Thomas Edison.

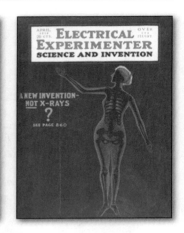

The Electrical Experimenter/Science and Invention

Unremarkable issue	$20	May 1918	$25
December 1918	$25	April 1919	$20
May 1919	$25	August 1919	$25
November 1919	$20	December 1919	$35
October 1927	$40	January 1928	$40
May 1928	$40	July 1928	$30
January 1929	$25	March 1929	$35
June 1931	$25	August 1931	$25

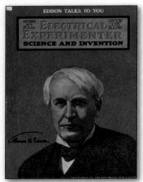

Practical Electrics/The Experimenter

Unremarkable issue	$10	November 1925	$20
December 1925	$15		

Radio Amateur News/Radio News/ Radio and Television News/Electronics World

Unremarkable issue	$10	September 1919	$40
May 1921	$20	July 1921	$25
March 1925	$35	April 1925	$30
May 1925	$45	October 1929	$20
November 1931	$20	July 1933	$40
September 1933	$20	March 1957	$20

Esquire (1933-present)

The magazine was founded in 1933 and became famous for contributions by literary writers such as Langston Hughes, Ernest Hemingway and F. Scott Fitzgerald. In the 1940s, it increased in popularity, partly because of the famous pin-up girls of George Petty and Alberto Vargas. In the 1960s, **Esquire** published writers such as Tom Wolfe, Norman Mailer and Gay Talese. **Esquire** took part in the so-called new journalism trend that takes on many of the devices of literary fiction such as: stream of consciousness, conversational speech (rather than quotations and statements), and the writer's opinions, thoughts and feelings (as opposed only to corroborated facts). Unlike **True, Esquire** weathered the storm of erotica/pornography, begun by **Playboy** and augmented by **Penthouse** and **Hustler,** to remain a viable magazine property as an over-the-counter men's magazine without being forced to adopt overtly erotic or pornographic features.

Unremarkable issue pre-WW II	$20	Unremarkable issue post-WW II	$10
Unremarkable issue post-1960	$7.50	Issues containing original Hemingway	$65
Issues containing original Hemingway plus other features:			
January 1935	$100	October 1935	$75
September 1939	$75		
Issues containing original F. Scott Fitzgerald before 1939	$85	Issues containing original F. Scott Fitzgerald "Pat Hobby," 1940-1941	$55
Issues containing F. Scott Fitzgerald after 1941	$35	Volume One #1, Autumn 1933	$150
With either Varga or Petty calendar intact	$50	September 1941	$45
September 1951	$55	November 1958	$55
December 1961	$50	October 1973	$35

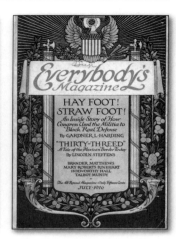
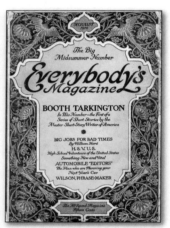
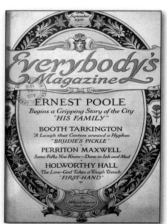

Everybody's (1899-1930)

Everybody's Magazine was founded in 1899. The editor, John O'Hara Cosgrave, was fully committed to investigative journalism and social justice, sometimes described as muckraking journalism. Frank Norris, Charles Edward Russell, Upton Sinclair, Ambrose Bierce, Lincoln Steffens and C.P. Connolly all contributed exposes to **Everybody's.** A massive advertising campaign for Thomas Lawson's "Frenzied Finance" series in 1908 saw **Everybody's** circulation climb to more than 750,000. **Everybody's** argued for America's support of Britain in World War I, printing pro-war articles by Theodore Roosevelt and Samuel Hopkins Adams, as well as a series on American neutrality in 1916 by British authors including H.G. Wells, G.K. Chesterton and George Bernard Shaw. The magazine declined rapidly after the war and combined with **Romance Magazine** in a fiction format from March 1929 to January 1930 before ceasing publication.

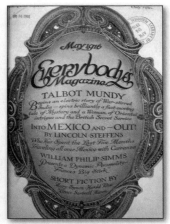

Unremarkable issue	$10		
Serials: Jack London, "Before Adam," October 1906-June 1907			
Single issue	$25	Complete run	$200
Talbot Mundy, "King of the Khyber Rifles," May 1916-January 1917			
Single issue	$50	Complete run	$500
Victor Rousseau, "The Messiah of the Cylinder," June 1917-September 1917			
Single issue	$45	Complete run	$200
December 1901	$35	May 1903	$35
September 1903	$15	March 1908	$45
July 1908	$30	March 1910	$20
January 1914	$35	October 1914	$15
October 1916	$55		

The Galaxy (1866-1878)

The Galaxy was founded by William C. and Francis P. Church in 1866, and sold to Sheldon & Co in 1868. It was chiefly remarkable for two columnists, Mark Twain for "Memoranda" from 1868 through 1871, and George Edward Pond who wrote the "Driftwood" essays, which were published in **The Galaxy** under the signature of "Philip Quilibet." And for George Armstrong Custer, "My Life on the Plains" was published in installments from 1872-1874. Bought by Tichnor and Fields, **The Galaxy** was merged into **The Atlantic Monthly** in 1878.

Unremarkable issue without Mark Twain	**$25**	Unremarkable issue with Mark Twain	**$50**
Serial: " My Life on the Plains" by George Armstrong Custer, January 1872-December 1874			
Single issue	**$30**	Complete run	**$650**
NOTE: The following two issues must be examined carefully, as their collectible feature is often ripped and framed:			
December 1869 (Winslow Homer)	**$250**	July 1870 (Mark Twain's fold-out map of Paris)	**$65**

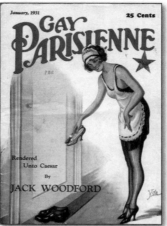

Gay Parisienne/Snappy/Paris Nights (1925-1938)

GlamArt magazines included **Gay Parisienne** by Deane Publishing Company 1930-1938; **Snappy** and its various incarnations as **Snappy Love Stories, Snappy Stories**, etc., by Lowell Publications Inc. from 1929 to 1932, then by Merwill until 1934 and finally by D. M. Publishing until 1938; and **Paris Nights** published by Paris Nights starting in 1925, then by Shade Publishing from 1928 until 1938. They featured pin-up illustrations, occasional nude art photos and stories that were suggestively on the edge. Many of the writers are collectible under their pseudonyms. Some, such as Achmed Abdullah (Michael Romanoff), Octavus Roy Cohen and Jack Woodford used their own names or popularly known pseudonyms. Many collectors have claimed to have found some well-known writers in GlamArt magazines of the Depression era, and quite a few remain to be discovered.

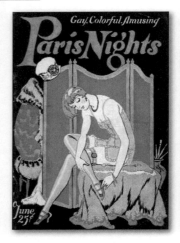

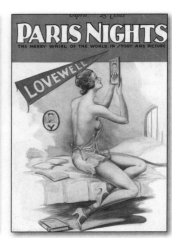

Gay Parisienne in collectible condition with photographs intact			**$75**
Snappy unremarkable single issue			**$85**
Snappy Stories, Fun and Fiction, etc., unremarkable single issue			**$30**
Snappy May 1931	**$125**	April 1933	**$100**
May 1933	**$125**	June 1934	**$150**
Paris Nights in collectible condition with photographs intact			**$125**

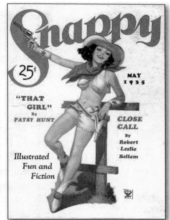

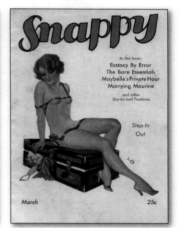

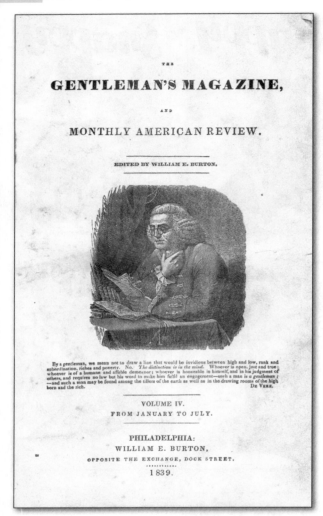

THE

GENTLEMAN'S MAGAZINE,

AND

MONTHLY AMERICAN REVIEW.

EDITED BY WILLIAM E. BURTON.

By a gentleman, we mean not to draw a line that would be invidious between high and low, rank and subordination, riches and poverty. No. The distinction is in the mind. Whoever is open, just and true; whoever is of a humane and affable demeanor; whoever is honorable in himself, and in his judgment of others, and requires no law but his word to make him fulfil an engagement—such a man is a gentleman; —and such a man may be found among the tillers of the earth as well as in the drawing rooms of the high born and the rich. DE VERE.

VOLUME IV.
FROM JANUARY TO JULY.

PHILADELPHIA:
WILLIAM E. BURTON,
OPPOSITE THE EXCHANGE, DOCK STREET.

1839.

Gentleman's Magazine/ Burton's (1837-1840)

In 1834, actor William E. Burton fled his home in England for America amid a public domestic scandal. While working as an actor in Philadelphia, Burton founded and edited **The Gentleman's Magazine** in 1837. **The Gentleman's Magazine and Monthly American Review** was later simply called **Burton's Gentleman's Magazine.** The astute Burton hired Edgar Allan Poe as co-editor in June of 1839, although Poe left the magazine's employ in May 1840. While there is some controversy among Poe scholars as to which of the early material in the magazine is attributed to Poe, many of Poe's first short stories and poems first saw publication there. In addition to Poe's book reviews and articles, stories such as "The Fall of the House of Usher" (1839) and "The Journal of Julius Rodman" (1840) were published in **Burton's.** Poe's friend, John Sartain, contributed engravings to the magazine. Other contributors, according to Burton, were Davy Crockett with "Adventures on the Scottish Moors," and "A Ramble In The Philippines In 1837" by William W. Wood, as well as articles on the theater and theatrical careers. In October 1841, George R. Graham, the publisher of **The Casket** and the principal owner of **The Saturday Evening Post,** bought **Burton's** magazine for $3,500. Burton used the money to build a new theater, which he managed, and continued his successful theatrical career. George Graham in 1841 replaced **Burton's Gentleman's Magazine** and **The Casket** with **Graham's Magazine.** The contents of the final issue of **Burton's Gentleman's Magazine** are identical to the final issue of **The Casket.** Interestingly, Graham hired Poe as book review editor for his new magazine.

January-June 1839 (Poe, possibly Davy Crockett)	**$250**	July-December 1839 (Poe, "The Fall of the House of Usher")	**$550**
January-June 1840 (Poe, "Julius Rodman")	**$350**	July-December 1840 (Poe, "Man In The Crowd")	**$350**

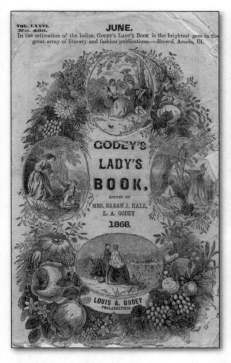

Godey's Lady's Book (1830-1898)

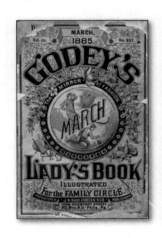

Godey's Lady's Book was founded in Philadelphia by Louis A. Godey in 1830. It was not until 1836, however, when Godey convinced Sarah Hale to become the editor, that **Godey's** found widespread success as a monthly magazine. Under the direction of Mrs. Hale and her championing of women's independence, the magazine thrived among the women of America, with an eventual Civil War circulation of 150,000. The popularity of **Godey's** was so great that women joined together to form clubs in order to afford the magazine subscription rate. While many European and American magazines included hand-colored fashion plates, Sarah Hale made sure the fashion designs for the ladies of **Godey's** were Americanized. The fashion plates also provided work for 150 female hand tinters, and at least one plate was included in every issue, along with steel and copper engravings illustrating the text. Mrs. Hale demanded quality fiction for **Godey's**. The first story publication by Edgar Allan Poe to appear in a national magazine was "The Visionary" in the January 1834 issue of **Godey's.** Throughout his brief career, Poe's work such as "The Oblong Box" (1844), "The Cask of Amontillado" (1846) and "The Literati of New York City" (1846) was consistently published in **Godey's.**

However, it was the recipes, household hints and pattern instructions for fashionable clothes for women and children, handbags, beadwork, lace, quilts and even architectural plans that were the crux of the magazine. Although, **Godey's** editorial policy was to stay out of the political arena, the magazine was frequently smuggled to the ladies in the South who just had to "have their

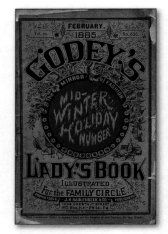

GODEY'S FASHIONS

GODEY'S FASHION

GODEY'S FASHIONS

SUB ROSA : A VALENTINE.

GODEY'S FASHIONS.

Godey's." Mrs. Hale also did make an elaborate statement on the death of Abraham Lincoln. Godey eventually sold the magazine and Mrs. Hale retired as editor in 1877. Its publication ended in 1898. Interestingly, **Godey's** today is sought by collectors not only for the literature of Poe, but for its recipes and fashions that are coveted by re-enactment enthusiasts.

Single unremarkable issue with hand-colored plate intact	**$25**	January-June 1834 (Poe's "The Visionary")	**$1,400**
January-December 1844 (Poe)	**$400**	January-December 1846 (Poe)	**$400**
January-December 1849 (Poe)	**$450**	January-June 1851	**$75**
January-December 1858 (National Cushion)	**$150**	January-December 1862 (Bridal fashions)	**$250**
January-December 1865 (Civil War)	**$250**	January-December 1867 (Civil War)	**$250**
January-December 1868 (Civil War)	**$250**	January-December 1869	**$200**
January-June 1874	**$75**		

Good Housekeeping (1885-present)

First published in May 1885 by George W. Bryan, and owned since 1911 by Hearst, **Good Housekeeping** evolved from a women's magazine into a consumer testing and product testing medium inside a women's magazine. In terms of longevity at a successful level, it is one of the most successful American magazines. Highlights have included covers and illustrations by such artists as Jessie Willcox Smith and Coles Phillips; fiction and articles by such writers as Kathleen Norris, James Oliver Curwood, Frances Hodgson Burnett, Margaret Sangster, Basil King, Gene Stratton-Porter, Octavus Roy Cohen, Albert Payson Terhune, Rose Wilder Lane, Gertrude Atherton, Pearl S. Buck, Katherine Mansfield, Max Brand, Stephen Vincent Benet, Sinclair Lewis, Vera Caspery, Agatha Christie, as well as Rose O'Neill's collectible Kewpies. Many issues of **Good Housekeeping** are worth keeping.

Unremarkable issue	$10	November 1910 $100	
January 1932	$65	February 1932	$75
September 1932	$75	October 1932	$125
November 1932	$100	January 1935	$45
May 1935	$60	June 1937	$45
September 1937	$40	October 1944	$50
February 1948	$175	December 1954	$55
December 1955	$35	November 1959	$150

Graham's Magazine (1841-1858)

In 1841, **Burton's Gentleman's Magazine** and **The Casket** were merged into **Graham's Magazine** by publisher and owner George R. Graham of Philadelphia. The new magazine, **Graham's American Monthly Magazine of Literature and Art,** embellished with mezzotint and steel engravings, music, etc., appealed to a more literary audience than its Philadelphia rival, **Godey's Lady's Book.**

Edgar Allan Poe, who had been an associate editor at **Burton's,** was hired as the book review editor for **Graham's Magazine** at an annual salary of $800. The second edition of **Graham's Magazine** for January 1841 published eight engravings by Poe's friend, John Sartain. During his lifetime, Poe's work that was

published in **Graham's Magazine** not only contributed to the magazine's popularity, but included some of his most important literary output. The April 1841 issue of **Graham's Magazine,** for example, featured Poe's "Murders in the Rue Morgue," the first modern detective story. During Poe's tenure, the circulation of **Graham's Magazine** increased from about 5,000 to nearly 37,000 subscribers. Although Poe only held his editorial position with **Graham's Magazine** for about a year, much of his important writing, "The Mask of the Red Death" (1842), "The Conqueror Worm" (1843), "The System of Dr. Tarr and Prof. Fether" (1845) to name a few, was published in the magazine until his death.

Interestingly, one of his editorial successors was the Rev. Rufus W. Griswold, who became one of Poe's more virulent detractors and rivals. George R. Graham, in fact, in his Poe obituary took Griswold to task for his anti-Poe remarks and treatment of Poe. Other important contributors to **Graham's** included James Fenimore Cooper, Nathaniel Hawthorne, Longfellow, Lowell and Francis Osgood (Poe's alleged lover). The magazine supposedly declined when Graham published a harshly unfavorable review of Harriet Beecher Stowe's *Uncle Tom's Cabin.*

January-June 1841 (Poe, "Murders in the Rue Morgue")	**$750**	January-June 1842 (Poe, "The Mask of the Red Death")	**$550**
January-June 1843 (Poe, "The Conqueror Worm")	**$450**	January reprints	**$250**
July-December 1845 (Poe, "The Imp of the Perverse," "The System of Dr. Tarr and Prof. Fether")	**$450**	January-June 1846 (Poe, "Marginala")	**$200**
July-December 1846 (Poe, "Marginala")	**$200**	January-June 1848 (Poe, "Marginala")	**$200**
January-June 1849 (Poe, "Fifty Suggestions")	**$200**	January-June 1850 (Poe, "Critics and Criticism")	**$200**
July-December 1850	**$110**	June 1844 (Poe, "Dreamland," reviews)	**$400**
January-June 1845 (Poe poem)			

Harper's Bazar/Bazaar (1867-present)

"A Repository of Fashion, Pleasure and Instruction" was published in New York by Harper & Brothers. **Harper's Bazar** was a weekly fashion-oriented magazine for well-heeled Victorian women. It contained fashion reports from New York and Paris, columns giving personal advice and gossip about "Society" in "Sayings and Doings," fiction, recipes, beadwork, knitting and needlework. The highlights of the early issues were the fold-out fashion patterns. Unfortunately, most of them were well used and they have not survived. In 1901, the magazine became a monthly. William Randolph Hearst bought it in 1913. Russian art deco fashion designer and illustrator Erte got his first break in America with his cover designs and illustrations for the magazine. Starting with his first cover on Jan. 1, 1915, his fashion illustrations were published in **Harper's** for more than 22 years. About 1930, the spelling of the name was changed to **Bazaar** and, in 1934, Carmel Snow became the editor and a fashion publishing legend. She hired Diana Vreeland as the fashion editor in 1936 and also got Cassandre (Adolphe Mouron), another Russian illustrator, to sign a contract to do cover art for **Harper's Bazaar.** Cassandre's covers displayed his Dali-like influence (1937). Snow also featured the surrealistic photography of Man Ray from 1934-1942. Today the magazine still publishes under the publishing empire that Hearst built.

Harper's Bazar unremarkable single issue without the fashion pattern	**$10**	Harper's Bazar unremarkable single issue with the fashion pattern	**$30**
Harper's Bazar Sept. 25, 1875 (Hand-colored cover)	**$35**	Harper's Bazar July 29, 1882 (Thomas Nast)	**$65**
Harper's Bazar July 5, 1884 (Hand-colored cover)	**$55**	Harper's Bazar August 1911 (Clark Hobart cover)	**$30**
Harper's Bazar Aug. 29, 1891	**$35**	Harper's Bazar January 1915 (Erte cover, first)	**$150**
Harper's Bazar February 1920 (Erte cover)	**$75**	Harper's Bazar June 1922 (Erte cover)	**$75**
Harper's Bazar November 1923 (Erte cover)	**$75**	Harper's Bazar May 1925 (Erte cover)	**$75**
Harper's Bazaar unremarkable single issue pre-1940	**$30**	Harper's Bazaar July 1930 (Benigni cover)	**$35**
Harper's Bazaar March 1931 (Benigni cover)	**$35**	Harper's Bazaar September 1932 (Dorothy Parker, Robert Benchley)	**$50**
Harper's Bazaar May 1934 (Erte cover)	**$75**	Harper's Bazaar March 1935 (Erte cover)	**$75**
Harper's Bazaar May 1936 (Erte cover)	**$75**	Harper's Bazaar August 1937 (Cassandre cover)	**$110**
Harper's Bazaar January 1938 (Man Ray, Cassandre cover)	**$145**		

Harper's Monthly (1850-present)

Originally published by the New York book-publishing firm Harper & Brothers as **Harper's New Monthly Magazine,** the name was changed to **Harper's Monthly Magazine** for the Christmas 1900 issue and finally **Harper's Magazine** for the March 1913 issue. The magazine presented fiction, essays, fashions (in the early issues), book reviews, and cultural and political commentary. Even though the earliest issues mainly reprinted material that had already been published in England, the first printing of 7,500 copies sold out. The magazine began to print the works of American artists and writers, and circulation rose within six months to 50,000.

One of the most important American writers that **Harper's** published was Herman Melville. The first appearance of Melville's "The Town-Ho's Story" from " The Whale" (*Moby Dick*) was published in the magazine in 1851. Other Melville stories published in **Harper's** included "Cock-A-Doodle-Doo! Or the Crowning of the Noble Cock Beneventano" (1853-1854), "Poor Man's Pudding and Rich Man's Crumbs," "The Happy Failure–A Story of The River Hudson" and "The Fiddler" (1854). Other American writers that appeared in the early issues were Horace Greeley, Horatio Alger, Stephen A. Douglas, Mark Twain's "Petition to the Queen of England" (1887), Frederic Remington as both a writer and illustrator, Theodore Dreiser, John Muir, Booth Tarkington, Henry James' "New York Revisited" (1906), William Dean Howells, Jack London's "The Sun-Dog Trail" (1905), "The Chinago"(1909), and Albert Payson Terhune's "The Better I Like Dogs" (1926). The tradition of literary greatness continued with William Faulkner (1931) and Thomas Wolfe (1939).

It was not until Edward Penfield, the influential New York illustrator and designer, became the art editor of **Harper's Monthly** that the magazine came into its own as an artistic medium. Penfield gave the magazine an art direction with his brilliant cover illustrations. Other artists attracted by Penfield included Howard Pyle, Elizabeth Shippen Green and Maxfield Parrish (December 1900). **Harper's** remains one of the oldest American magazines that is still published today, with the first issue in June of 1850.

Unremarkable volume	**$15**	Volume 1	**$200**
Volume 3 (First appearance of a version of *Moby Dick*)	**$650**	Volume 9	**$250**
Volume 10	**$150**	Volume 11	**$150**
Volume 12	**$325**	Volume 13	**$175**
Volume 16	**$250**	Volume 21	**$200**
Volume 99	**$125**	Unremarkable issue	**$5**
September 1854 (Melville)	**$70**	February 1866 (Melville)	**$70**
February 1867 (Wild Bill Hickok)	**$135**	February 1874 (Whitman)	**$125**
April 1893 (Bison)	**$65**	June 1895 (Twain)	**$70**
October 1895 (Twain)	**$75**	August 1896 (W.D. Howells)	**$70**
September 1897 (Remington)	**$75**	August 1898 (Stephen Crane)	**$75**
September 1902 (Parrish)	**$125**		

Harper's Weekly (1857-1912)

In 1842, the **Illustrated London News,** in a technological breakthrough, found a way to quickly illustrate the latest news stories with quality wood block engravings. Frank Leslie (Henry Carter), an entrepreneurial engraver, brought the technique to America and published the first issue of **Frank Leslie's Illustrated Newspaper** (qv.) on Dec. 15, 1855, in New York. Seeing the instant success of **Leslie's,** the astute Harper Brothers under the guidance of Fletcher Harper published the first issue of **Harper's Weekly** on Jan. 3, 1857. Different than the flamboyant **Leslie's, Harper's Weekly** appealed to middle- and upper-class Americans with a serious cultural bent and satire.

The importance of the early **Harper's Weekly** issues was their coverage of the Civil War. Editor George William Curtis (1863-1892) helped shaped public opinion with his editorials and content during the Civil War (although critics called it "Harper's Weakly" because of its middle-of-the-road stance on certain topics). However, also featured were illustrations and cartoons by artists like Winslow Homer and Thomas Nast that boosted the magazine's circulation from 100,000 to 300,000, with readership figures that exceeded half a million. Nast's cartoons satirized the political arena from President "King Andy" Johnson during the impeachment proceedings to blasting New York's "Boss" Tweed. Winslow Homer's exquisite illustrations graced the pages of **Harper's** beginning in 1857, and then chronicled the Civil War. Homer's last contribution to the magazine appeared in 1875.

In the area of the "new" photography, **Harper's Weekly** emerged as a leading contender with the publication of the work

of William Henry Jackson. Forty Jackson articles were published in **Harper's** during 1895 and 1896. Jackson's photographs were among the very first halftones ever to appear in **Harper's** or any other popular American periodical. Jackson did a famous series on India for **Harper's,** even though he was considered the leading photographer of the American West in the 19th century. In fact, his photographs helped turn Yellowstone into the first national park. While photography became a staple of the magazine in the later years, several color covers by Maxfield Parrish (1895-1900) carried on the **Harper's** tradition of presenting fine illustrations to the American public.

Note: Be careful of *Harper's Weekly* and check each issue carefully, as the illustrations of Winslow Homer, Thomas Nast and Maxfield Parrish were featured and these are frequently ripped for framing. Also, be aware that it was originally bound in yearly volumes of 52 issues.

Unremarkable volumes	$50	Volume 2 (1858)	$1,200
Volume 3 (1859)	$1,800	Volume 4 (1860)	$2,000
Volume 9 (1865)	$1,500	Volume 10 (1866)	$2,000
Volume 11 (1867)	$1,500	Volume 12 (1868)	$2,000
Volume 15 (1871)	$1,100	Volume 16 (1872)	$1,600
Volume 30 (1886)	$1,000	Unremarkable issues	$15
Nov. 10, 1860 (Lincoln elected)	$375	Oct. 4, 1862 (Emancipation Proclamation)	$575
Nov. 15, 1862 (Army of the Potomac)	$275	April 15, 1865 (Last article on Lincoln alive)	$375
April 29, 1865 (Lincoln death issue)	$625	Dec. 19, 1868 (First article on the KKK)	$150
Sept. 14, 1872 (Winslow Homer's "Catskills")	$450	Nov. 24, 1888 (H.R. Haggard, Remington)	$275
Oct. 14 and 21, 1893 (A.C. Doyle's "Naval Treaty," two issues)	$200	Dec. 23, 1905 (Mark Twain's birthday)	$250
With original Thomas Nast covers	$100		

Harmsworth's/London Magazine (1898-1933)

This magazine was founded by Alfred (Lord Northcliffe) and Harold (Viscount Rothermere) Harmsworth as a competing magazine to **The Strand** in July 1898 as **The Harmsworth Monthly Pictorial Magazine.** It became **The Harmsworth London Magazine** from July 1901 to August 1903, **The London Magazine** from August 1903 to October 1930 and, finally, **The New London Magazine** before its final issue in May of 1933. Part of the Harmsworth's publishing empire, Amalgamated Press, the magazine attempted to copy the success of Newnes' **Strand,** often publishing the same writers including H.G. Wells, Robert Eustace collaborations and Arthur Morrison, as well as employing illustrator Sidney Paget. It never reached the height of **The Strand,** but the backing of the Amalgamated empire, once the largest periodical/newspaper firm in the world, kept it from going under.

Unremarkable issue	$10	Unremarkable six-month volume	$25
Volume I (Winston Churchill, Arthur Rackham)	$65	Volume II (Meade/Eustance, Arthur Rackham)	$75
Volume VII	$50	Volume VIII	$50
January 1899	$75	February 1899	$75

Household Words (1850-1859)

A "Weekly Journal" published by Bradbury & Evans, **Household Words** was the mouthpiece of Charles Dickens, geared toward a middle-class audience. Dickens wrote much of this original material pertaining to social issues of the day, such as the plight of the poor and working class, informational articles such as the gold rush in Australia and, of course, fiction. For the most part, contributors were anonymous. In fact, there is an entire book based on the **Household Words,** *Office Book,* which deciphers the list of the contributors and their contributions. Dickens' work consisted of such articles as "A Child's Dream of A Star," "Pet Prisoners," "The Heart of Mid-London," "A Detective Police Party," "Three 'Detective' Anecdotes," "A Walk In A Workhouse" and the serialization of "A Child's History of England." Later issues featured the writing of Wilkie Collins with "Gabriel's Marriage," "The Fourth Poor Traveller," "The Yellow Mask" and "Sister Rose." Other contributors included the hilarious "Illustrations of Cheapness" by Charles Knight and "A Paper-Mill" by Mark Lemon, who later became the editor of **Punch, Or the London Chiavari. Household Words** was extremely popular with a weekly circulation of 40,000 copies. Dickens ended its publication because of a dispute with the publishers, and went on to establish **All The Year Round** (qv.).

March-September 1850, first issues	$35	March-September 1851 (Dickens, "A Child's History of England")	$50

| March-September 1853 (Dickens, Wilkie Collins) **$50** | August-January 1855 (Dickens, Wilkie Collins) **$50** |
| June-November 1858 plus Christmas Number (Dickens, Wilkie Collins) **$75** | |

The Idler (1892-1911)

The Idler Magazine, An Illustrated Monthly, was published in London by Chatto and Windus. Basically a literary magazine edited by Jerome K. Jerome and Robert Barr, it was geared to the Victorian middle class, similar in some respects to **The Strand Magazine** (qv.). The magazine featured satire by Barr like "The Adventures of Sherlaw Kombs," plus short pieces and serializations. Arthur Conan Doyle contributed "The Doctors of Hoyland," "Sweethearts" (which was later published as *Round the Red Lamp*), "The Case of Lady Sannox" and "The Stark Munro Letters." Fergus Hume stories included "The Ivory Leg and the Twenty-four Diamonds" and "The Jesuit and the Mexican Coin." Marie Corelli became a regular contributor after her essay "Why Did I Write Barabbas?" created a sensation.

The series "My First Book" had successful authors such as Doyle, Bret Harte and Corelli describe their difficulties in getting published. Another popular feature was The Idler's Club, which was a Victorian-style round table with commentary by Oscar Wilde, Bernard Shaw, W. Pett Ridge, Barry Pain, Jerome J. Jerome, Eden Phillpotts and Corelli on topics ranging from "Duels" to "Policemen." Illustrations were also an important part of **The Idler**, featuring the work of Sidney H. Sime (who actually controlled the periodical for a short period), Walter Sickert (Patricia Cornwell's candidate for Jack the Ripper) and Frank Brangwyn.

Bound volumes in original green and gilt publisher's binding:	
February-July 1892 Volume I (Mark Twain, Doyle) **$100**	August 1892-January 1893 (Doyle, Twain, Annie Bessant) **$100**
February-July 1893 (H. Rider Haggard, Kipling) **$75**	August 1893-January 1894 (Doyle, Hornung, Hume, Corelli) **$75**
February 1894-July 1894 (Doyle, Cruikshank, Hume) **$50**	August 1894-January 1895 (Robert Louis Stevenson) **$50**
February 1895-July 1895 (Doyle, Wilde, Dore) **$65**	February 1897-July 1897 (Aubrey Beardsley) **$110**

Judge (1881-1939)

Established by James Wales and Livingston Hopkins in 1881 as a rival to **Puck,** after internal disagreements with **Puck** founder Joseph Keppler, the first issue appeared on Oct. 29, 1881. While the magazine sold well, it came off as an imitation of **Puck** and had trouble financially until Wales sold it to William J. Arkell. Arkell's personal fortune and politics changed **Judge** by persuading talented people like cartoonists Eugene Zimmerman and Bernard Gilliam to draw for **Judge,** and to champion the Republican Party, in contrast to the Democratic **Puck.** Art Young, Richard Outcault, Norman Rockwell and James Montgomery Flagg all joined **Judge** in the early 1900s. **Judge** remained a popular humor magazine through the 1920s, with both cartoon art and articles by humorists and commentators Ellis Parker Butler and Heywood Broun. In 1932, it became a monthly for reasons of economy during the Depression. It ceased publication in 1939.

Unremarkable issue	$10	Aug. 8, 1893	$45
Nov. 10, 1894	$45	Feb. 15, 1919	$25
Dec. 9, 1926	$20	Jan. 11, 1930	$30
March 1, 1930	$30	April 12, 1930	$25
October 1937	$30	May 1938	$45

Jugend (1896-1940)

Jugend was an illustrated weekly published by George Hirth in Munich, Germany. Although each issue was only about 20 pages, it was a success because of its novel and fashionable colored lithographic covers and witty cartoons. The artistic style portrayed in the magazine was a German version of the popular European art nouveau. The name of the art movement "Jugendstil," which means "style of youth" in German, came from the magazine's name. German artists who illustrated **Jugend** included Walther Caspari, Fritz Erler, Bernhard Pankok, Hans Eichrodt, Ludwig Raders, Hans Rossmann, Fritz Rehm, Maximilian Dasio, Franz Christophe, Jan Toorop, Jean Jacques des Valeurs, Franz Stuck, Reinhold Begas, Anton Werner, Angelo Jank, Sar Peladan, Anton Werner and even the Englishman Burne-Jones.

July 18,1896	**$95**	Aug. 29, 1896	**$95**
Oct. 3, 1896	**$95**	Sept. 11,1897	**$95**
Feb. 19, 1898	**$95**	June 4, 1898	**$95**
December 1924	**$20**	April 1924	**$15**
November 1929	**$20**	December 1929	**$15**

Juvenile Miscellany (1826-1836)

Founded by Lydia Maria Child in 1826, **The Juvenile Miscellany** was one of the earliest children's magazines in the United States and a powerful influence on subsequent children's literature. In 1829, through her husband's newspaper, the *Massachusetts Journal,* she met William Lloyd Garrison and became committed to the abolitionist cause, writing more and more of her children's stories on the subject of slavery. Nearly every issue of the **Miscellany** from September 1830 on carried some reference to slavery. She published an anti-slavery book that called for immediate emancipation and the integration of blacks as equal citizens, *Appeal in Favor of That Class of Americans Called Africans,* in 1833. Parents canceled subscriptions to the **Miscellany.** The magazine was taken over by Sarah Josepha Hale, who had published "Mary Had A Little Lamb" as "Mary's Lamb" in the issue of September 1830. Sarah Hale was unable to keep the magazine afloat beyond 1836, but did manage to introduce the original publications of Frances Hodgson Burnett during that period.

Issues edited by Lydia Maria Child, 1826-1833	**$45**
Issues edited by Sarah Josepha Hale, 1833-1836	**$55**
September 1830 containing "Mary had a Little Lamb"	**$3,750**

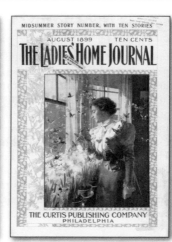

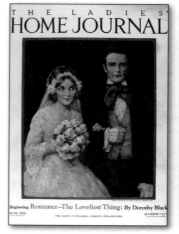

Ladies' Home Journal (1884-present)

Originally a supplement to the **Tribune and Farmer** (1879–1885), published by Cyrus Curtis and edited by his wife Louisa Knapp, **The Ladies' Home Journal** became an independent publication in 1884. Under the editorship of Edward Bok from 1889 to 1919, its circulation surpassed that of any other women's magazine. It had a running battle to maintain that position with **Woman's Home Companion**, edited by Gertrude Battles Lane, after 1911.

Bok's innovations in the women's magazine field included offering high-quality fiction and non-fiction, and establishing service departments that answered letters from readers, conveying a sense of intimacy. Bok's activism shocked some sensibilities, publishing reformers such as Jane Addams. Fiction was contributed by W.D. Howells, Frank Stockton, Frances Hodgson Burnett, John Kendrick Bangs, Marietta Holley (Josiah Allen's wife), Sarah Orne Jewett, James Whitcomb Riley, Paul Laurence Dunbar, Frank Norris, Gellet Burgess, Sarah Bernhart, Kate Douglas Wiggin, Mark Twain, Bret Harte and Rudyard Kipling. Articles by reformers, politicians and several American presidents initially set **The Ladies' Home Journal** apart from women's magazines until imitated by Lane with **Woman's Home Companion.** Covers and illustrations by known artists such as Palmer Cox, C.D. Gibson, Howard Pyle, Philip Boileau, Kate Greenaway, Maud Tousey Fangel and Harrison Fisher also add to the collectibility of **Ladies' Home Journal.** Purchased by the Meredith Corporation in 1984, **The Ladies' Home Journal** continues to be published.

Unremarkable single issue prior to 1984	**$8**	June 1901 (Parrish)	**$40**
July 1901 (Frank Lloyd Wright)	**$350**	May 1904 (Jessie Wilcox Smith)	**$100**
April 1905 (Jessie Wilcox Smith)	**$55**	June 1909 (Harrison Fisher)	**$45**
May 1911 (Harrison Fisher)	**$45**	December 1914 (Jessie Wilcox Smith)	**$100**
September 1917 (H.G. Wells)	**$45**	March 1918 (Betty Bonnet)	**$90**
August 1918 (Charlie Chaplin)	**$65**	July 1924 (N.C. Wyeth)	**$250**
December 1925 (Arthur Rackham)	**$100**	April 1927 (Albert Payson Terhune)	**$60**
April 1933 (Rose Wilder Lane)	**$100**	June 1935 (Agatha Christie)	**$60**
September 1940 (Vivian Leigh)	**$45**		

Lady's World/Woman's World (1887-1946)

Two unconnected publications share the name **The Lady's World,** one British, one American. The British version, under the editorship of Oscar Wilde from 1887 through October 1889, was changed to **The Woman's World** in 1889 on the suggestion of Dinah Mulock Craik and survived Wilde's resignation by only a year, ending publication in October of 1890. Revived by Amalgamated in 1906, **The Woman's World** remained in publication until 1946. It is collected chiefly for Wilde's contributions, such as "The Happy Prince" in 1888.

The American **Lady's World** was published between December 1898 and September 1926 by the S.H. Moore Company. A minor entry in the woman's magazine market, it attempted to emulate the success of **The Ladies' Home Journal** and **Woman's Home Companion,** but lacked the resources for quality writers and artists. This is one to be careful of as some dealers are unaware of it and sell it as edited by Wilde.

Lady's World, U. K., 1886-December 1887		**$65**
Woman's World, December 1887-October 1889 (Oscar Wilde, editor)		
Single issue **$400** Complete run		**$12,500**
Woman's World, October 1889-October 1890 (John Williams, editor)		
Single issue **$80** Complete run		**$1,000**
Woman's World, 1906-1946, unremarkable issue		**$8**
Lady's World, U.S., December 1898-September 1926, unremarkable issue		**$8**

Lady's Realm (1896-1914)

An important British women's magazine, **The Lady's Realm An Illustrated Monthly Magazine** was published by Hutchinson from 1896 to 1909, then by Stanley Paul from 1909-1910. It was bought by the Amalgamated chain and continued until 1914. Aimed at upper middle- and upper-class women readers, a great deal of space was given to stories by and about titled ladies. Publications by Marie Corelli were frequent in both fiction and non-fiction. The more romantic efforts of many major writers including E.F. Benson, George Gissing and H. Rider Haggard were featured in both story and serial form, such as Haggard's serialization and first appearance of *Margaret* in the magazine from November 1906 through October 1907. A good deal of **The Lady's Realm** concerned hostessing and fashion information in articles by noted women of the period. A shorter run magazine than most periodicals of the era, the magazine is scarce and, for that reason, tends to be worth a bit more than general interest and fiction magazines of the same era.

Unremarkable issue	**$15**	Unremarkable six-month volume bound by publisher pre-WWI	**$85**
Unremarkable six-month volume bound by publisher post-WWI	**$55**	Volume One	**$200**
Volume Two	**$150**	Volume Three	**$175**
Volume Five	**$100**	Volume Twenty-One	**$125**
Volume Twenty-Two	**$85**	Volume Twenty-Three	**$65**
Volume Twenty-Four	**$60**	Volume Twenty-Five	**$75**
Volume Twenty-Six	**$100**	Volume Twenty-Seven	**$75**

Land of Sunshine/Out West (1893-1917)

The Land of Sunshine was the first illustrated monthly centered in and on Southern California culture. Charles Lummis became the editor in 1893 and expanded the scope of **The Land of Sunshine** into natural history and the ethnology of the indigenous peoples of California, the Southwest, northern Mexico and the Great Basin. In 1898, the magazine began to include literature and adopted the subtitle "The Magazine of California and the West." In 1902, the title was changed to **Out West, A Magazine of the Old Pacific and the New.** It ceased publication with the issue of May 1917, merging with **Overland Monthly.** The combined magazine continued until 1935.

Land of Sunshine			
Unremarkable issue	**$30**	March 1897	**$65**
April 1897	**$65**	November 1897	**$75**
January 1899	**$65**	September 1899	**$50**
April 1901	**$40**	June 1901	**$45**
July 1901	**$40**		

Out West

Unremarkable issue	$20	June 1903	$50
November 1903	$45	May 1904	$75
June 1904	$50	August 1904	$50

Laughing Horse (1922-1938)

Censorship in the U.S. has not been limited to banning books. Magazines have also had their fair share of the censor's wrath, including and not limited to burning and court appearances. Interestingly, in the home of the "Free Speech Movement" of the 1960s, the University of California at Berkeley, a small student publication called **The Laughing Horse** had been banned in 1922. Edited by Willard "Spud" Johnson and owned and copyrighted by James T. Van Rensselaer, Roy Chanslor and Willard Johnson, **The Laughing Horse** appeared on the Berkeley campus in April 1922.

The goal of the magazine was to be satirical and critical of, among other things, education in America and in California in particular. To that end, the first three issues were done under the pseudonyms of Jane Cavendish, Noel Jason, Bill Murphy and L13, in order to maintain their freedom to criticize without fear of reprisal. The three, however, revealed their identities in Issue No. 4, which was subsequently banned at Berkeley. The banned issue included excerpts of Upton Sinclair's new book, *The Goose Step: A Study of American Education* (Pasadena, 1923), which was an attack on American higher education and the "militarization" of the University of California. The university, however, alleged that the publication was banned because of an obscene contribution by D.H. Lawrence, a letter that was a condemning review of Ben Hecht's *Fantazius Mallare.* (Hecht, a journalist and writer, published his work in 1922, which prompted the federal government to charge Hecht with obscenity.)

In the D.H. Lawrence review, the editors substituted long dashes for "offending" words. Chanslor, the only remaining student participant, was found guilty of the charge and expelled from the university. Consequently, issue No. 5 reprinted a lengthy letter from Upton Sinclair chastising the university for its treatment of Chanslor and reiterating Sinclair's objections to the university administration and policies. The "offensive" banned issue was, according to Chanslor, dismissed by the "Police" courts in less than a minute. Two more issues were published at Berkeley without claiming any affiliation.

With the publication of Issue No. 8, the tenor of the magazine changed. Subsequent issues were published in Santa Fe and Taos, N.M., and the magazine now stated it was **The Laughing Horse–A Magazine of the Southwest.** "Spud" Johnson, the editor, had moved to Santa Fe, and the magazine attracted contributions from the literary and artistic communities of Santa Fe and Taos. Writers and poets such as D.H. Lawrence, Mary Austin, Witter Bynner, William Rose Benet, Mabel Dodge Luhan, Haniel Long and Margaret Larkin contributed first appearances to **The Laughing**

Horse. Throughout its history, **The Laughing Horse** always maintained an outspoken voice on censorship issues. On Oct. 10, 1929, Sen. Bronson Cutting of New Mexico gave a speech before the U.S. Senate condemning the power given to customs clerks to censor reading and artistic material. The U.S. Tariff Law of 1890 gave clerks at the Bureau of Customs the power to confiscate "obscene" material and Congress was attempting to amend the law to include "treasonable and insurrectionary matter." (Fear of foreign writers like Engels and Karl Marx was rampant.) Senator Cutting, one of the first Anglo politicians in New Mexico who supported Hispanics, was trying to have the amendment stricken. (Cutting was eventually killed in a mysterious plane crash in 1935.) In support of the issues that Senator Cutting publicized, the February 1930 issue published from Taos was titled "Censorship!" This infamous issue was presented as "A Symposium of Criticism, Comment and Opinion on the Subject of Censorship." Prominent members of the American intelligentsia such as Carl Sandburg, Maxwell E. Perkins, John Dewey, Sherwood Anderson, Alfred A. Knopf, Upton Sinclair, Lincoln Steffens, Harriet Monroe and Mary Austin lent their support and voiced their outrage of United States censorship policy in **The Laughing Horse.** Will Irwin succinctly stated: "A twenty-five-dollar-a-week clerk sits as court of final judgment on Voltaire!" W.W. Norton: "Boston was the second best book town in America. Where it is today I do not know, but it certainly is not the book town it was. And anyone can guess the reason why." Upton Sinclair: "I almost always find myself opposing censors; and sometimes the censors have been opposed to me."

The Laughing Horse's irreverent approach and unique contributors made it one of the most influential and important of the "little" literary magazines of the 1920s through its last issue in December 1938, 21 issues. It is truly one of the most scarce and valuable American publications in both content and availability.

Issue 1	$200	Issue 2	$225
Issue 3	$225	Issue 4	$275
Issue 5	$175	Issue 6	$150
Issue 7	$150	Issue 8	$150
Issue 9	$135	Issue 10	$125
Issue 11	$125	Issue 12	$150
Issue 13	$160	Issue 14	$150
Issue 15	$125	Issue 16	$150
Issue 17	$140	Issue 18	$150
Issue 19	$125	Issue 20	$175
Issue 21	$175		

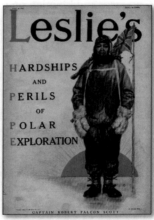

Leslie's Illustrated (1855-1922)

Frank Leslie was two people at various times in the publishing history of the various incarnations of **Leslie's Illustrated Weekly.** The original "Frank Leslie" was Henry Carter who, while working for the **London Illustrated News** in 1842, learned the latest techniques for printing illustrations. In December 1855, he produced the first issue of **Frank Leslie's Illustrated Newspaper.** The success of Leslie's original paper led to several satellite publications by Leslie's company: **Frank Leslie's Boys' and Girls' Weekly, Frank Leslie's Boys of America, Frank Leslie's Ladies' Journal, Frank Leslie's Lady's Magazine, Frank Leslie's Monthly, Frank Leslie's New Family Magazine** and **Frank Leslie's Popular Monthly.** On Carter's death in 1880, his wife, Miriam Squier, assumed control of the publishing empire and legally became "Frank Leslie." She sold the magazines to the Judge publishing company in 1889, which became Judge-Leslie in 1898. Judge-Leslie continued to publish **Leslie's Illustrated Newspaper** until June 1922.

Leslie's has been, for more than a century, one of the most frequently ripped publications. The value of **Leslie's** hangs on the prints that can be ripped from any issue, ranging in price from **$15-$150** for issues with hand-colored illustrations.

Liberty (1924-1950)

Liberty magazine was founded as a general interest weekly by the McCormick/Patterson newspaper chain in 1924. Originally edited by J.M. Patterson in New York and published in Chicago, it became one of the largest circulation magazines of the late 1920s. The McCormick/Patterson Liberty featured popular writers such as Kathleen Norris, Rex Beach, Achmed Abdullah and Adela Rogers St. John. Leslie Thrasher's covers and illustrations by James Montgomery Flagg, especially of P.G. Wodehouse serials, are also collectible. Liberty was sold to the McFadden chain in 1931, and became the largest circulation magazine in the United States until World War II.

McFadden inherited Fulton Oursler as editor of Liberty and, as was usual with McFadden, gave his editor a great deal of editorial freedom. Oursler was able to combine the popular appeal of Liberty's writers, adding such popular authors as Faith Baldwin, with on-the-edge editorial content by Pierre Van Paasen, Margaret Sangster, Anthony Eden and his publisher, Bernarr McFadden, among others. Morris Markey's article on Alcoholics Anonymous (Sept. 30, 1939) was the first national coverage of the organization and is very collectible. McFadden sold Liberty in 1942, and it never recovered its former prominence. Oursler moved on to Reader's Digest and the magazine died a slow death, publishing its final issue in July of 1950 as a monthly, having been a monthly since 1947.

Unremarkable McCormick/McFadden issues (pre-1942) **$7.50**	Unremarkable issues post-1942	**$4**
Serials:		
Erle Stanley Gardner, "Perry Mason" serials Single issue **$15** Complete run		**$125**
Dashiell Hammett, "Lady in the Dark," April 8-April 22, 1933 Single issue **$55** Complete run		**$200**
Edgar Rice Burroughs, "Tarzan and the Lion Man," Nov. 11, 1933-Jan. 6, 1934 Single issue **$25** Complete run		**$175**

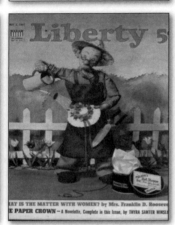

Oct. 13, 1923	$35	July 5, 1924	$65
Oct. 3, 1925	$25	April 17, 1926	$25
Dec. 24, 1927	$65	June 9, 1928	$55
March 2, 1929	$30	Aug. 16, 1930	$35
Aug. 27, 1932	$35	Aug. 12, 1933	$25
May 25, 1935	$20	May 16, 1936	$25
Aug. 10, 1936	$35	June 8, 1938	$55
Feb. 9, 1939	$75	Aug. 10, 1940	$20
Dec. 6, 1941	$25	June 1951	$50
March 1953	$50		

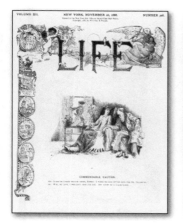

Life (1883-1936)

In January 1883, the first issue of **Life** magazine was published by John Ames Mitchell. The masthead slogan was "While There's Life There's Hope." The "Winged Life" cherub logo appeared on the early covers. It was not the folio-sized, photo-oriented **Life** familiar to the "modern" world, but a small 9" by 12" periodical devoted to satirizing the times in both words and cartoons. **Life** took its cue from the British publication **Punch, Or the London Chiavari,** but its attacks focused primarily on American society.

Mitchell, a talented artist, had gone to the Harvard Scientific School for two years, and then went off to France to study art at Ecole Des Beaux Arts. Upon his return to the United States, he felt there was a need for more public artistic expression in the area of black-and-white drawing. Consequently, he took his entire life savings of $10,000 and started publishing **Life** magazine. A "joke" magazine in 1883 was normally relegated to barber shops and the lower class, not "respectable" families. **Life,** however, managed to thrive against all odds. Mitchell had strong opinions about a variety of issues and minced neither words nor cartoons in voicing them in **Life's** pages. **Life's** writers and artists during the

Mitchell era railed against Prohibition, politics, Teddy Roosevelt, the Czar, the Kaiser, Anthony Comstock and even "Herr" Hearst. By today's standards, it was also politically incorrect, with cartoons and cover art that promoted stereotypes of both Jews and blacks. Authors such as H. Rider Haggard, Hall Caine and Mark Twain were continually slammed. Twain's *Huck Finn* was critiqued for its "coarseness" in the Feb. 26, 1885, issue. In the April 9, 1885, issue, **Life** even joined the news media that praised the Concord Library for banning the novel from its shelves. Ironically, Twain hired a **Life** artist, Edward Kemble, to illustrate *Huck Finn*.

As a result of the controversial viewpoints he portrayed in **Life,** Mitchell and the magazine were frequently at the center of lawsuits. He emerged victorious from the majority of his legal battles. This in turn increased the popularity of Mitchell and **Life** as a champion of public issues. In fact, his interest in French orphans during World War I created the Fresh Air Fund (still a vital charitable organization) with the *New York Tribune's* Horace Greeley. In addition to controversy, Mitchell spotlighted the poetry of Ella Wheeler Wilcox, featured the satire of John Kendrick Bangs and brought countless artists to the forefront for the American public. **Life's** artists through its publication history included such greats as: W.A. Rogers, Walter Granville-Smith, William H. Walker, Thomas King Hanna, Edward Kemble, Albert D. Blaishfield, C. Clyde Squires, Orson Byron Lowell, Otho Cushing, Henry Hutt, Will Crawford, Victor C. Anderson, A.B. Frost, H.W. Phillips and T.S. Sullivant. Sullivant and H.W. Phillips collaborated on the series called "Fables For The Times," which had excerpts later published in book form. It was Sullivant's only book published in his lifetime. Others were F.T. Richards, W.T. Benda, Penrhyn Stanlaws, Harrison Cady, Oliver Herford, James Montgomery Flagg, F.X. Leyendecker, J.C. Leyendecker, Angus Macdonnell, Anton Otto Fisher, C. Coles Phillips, F.G. Cooper, B. Cory Kilvert, Rea Irvin, Norman Rockwell, McClelland Barclay, John La Gatta, John Held Jr. and, of course, Charles Dana Gibson.

Probably Mitchell's most influential artistic "find" was the young Roxbury, Mass., artist, Charles Dana Gibson. In the fall of 1886, Gibson sold to **Life,** for $4, a small drawing of a dog chained to his doghouse, baying at the moon. Thus began a life-long career as artist, editor and eventually publisher of **Life** magazine spanning 30 years. In 1893, Gibson built the home and offices of **Life** magazine at 19 West 31st St. in New York City. (Today it is a New York City landmark known as the Herald Square Hotel, which houses a collection of **Life** magazines and the "Winged Life" sculpture by Philip Martiny). **Life** magazine continued publication from this site through the mid 1920s. Gibson took over as editor of **Life** after the death of Mitchell. The creator of America's Sweetheart, "The Gibson Girl," Gibson brought a whole new vitality and anti-establishment agenda to the pages of **Life.** John Held Jr. (1889-1958) had sold his first drawing to **Life** at the age of 15. His flapper drawings and cover art took the place of the Gibson Girl in the public's mind during the Roaring Twenties. Held, Russell Patterson, Rea Irvin, Maxfield Parrish and Coles Phillips were among the artists who dominated the covers of **Life** during the Gibson era.

On the editorial side, Gibson brought in playwright Robert E. Sherwood. Sherwood wrote "The Silent Drama" column, where he reviewed movies. A typical Sherwood commentary was, "All America is divided into two parts: (1) the great evil city of New York, where vice runs rampant, where hopes are shattered and ideals crushed, where wolves are clad in hired dress suits, where innocence is submerged in the mighty whirlpool of sin; (2) the great open spaces, where men are men (nine times out of ten)." Sherwood, in turn, enticed two of the all-time great Algonquin wits: Robert Benchley, who became **Life's** drama critic, and Dorothy Parker, who was, well, Dorothy Parker.

Benchley's drama column barely made the weekly deadline. He was usually at the Algonquin Round Table or the theater. His reviews were priceless: "Animal Crackers": "Several Marxes at play, much to the general amusement." "Diamond Lil": "One of the less revolting of Mae West's operas, containing the whimsical authoress

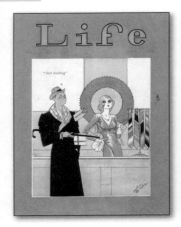

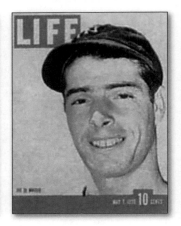

herself as a member of the cast–unless the police have other plans for her." "Abie's Irish Rose" was one of the most successful long-running plays on Broadway. It had a record run from May of 1922 to November of 1927. Robert Benchley hated it with a passion: "Opened in May 1922, and was immediately condemned by this department. There has been almost a year of this now, and yet we claim to have the best sense of humor of any nation in the world." On the first anniversary of the play, the producers sent a cake to Benchley at the **Life** office. At every opportunity he panned the play. His comment on the 1926-27 Broadway season: "264 openings with 250 of them terrible," and of course he included "Abie's Irish Rose" as one of the 250.

In 1928, **Life** proposed its own candidate for president: Will Rogers. The magazine presented his platform which, of course, included the repeal of Prohibition. Rogers challenged Hoover "To Joint Debate–in Any Joint You Name."

The Twenties could well be considered **Life's** Golden Age. The Thirties and the Depression changed the magazine into a monthly. Benchley, Sherwood and Parker left for stints at **The New Yorker** and other publications, and eventually wound up in Hollywood. Gibson retired and sold the magazine to Claire Maxwell, who had been the vice president. **Life** had its share of talent in the 1930s. Writers and illustrators included Dr. Seuss, Rube Goldberg, Ogden Nash and George Jean Nathan, to name a few. But it never regained the sizzle and riotousness of the Twenties, or the playful satire of the Sullivant turn-of-the-century **Life.** The Maxwell family sold the magazine to Henry Luce in 1936. The first issue of the new **Life** appeared Nov. 23, 1936, thus signaling both the end and beginning of a publishing era. Dorothy Parker once collided with Clare Booth Luce in a doorway. "Age before beauty," cracked Mrs. Luce. "Pearls before swine," said Parker, gliding through the door.

Single unremarkable issue pre-1936	**$15**	Will Rannels "Dog" covers	**$25**
Oct. 22, 1885 (Oliver Herford, J.K. Bangs)	**$25**	Nov. 22, 1888 (Jack The Ripper)	**$25**
April 23, 1891 (T.S. Sullivant cover)	**$35**	July 1894-December 1894 bound volume (T.S. Sullivant covers, cartoons, Doyle satire)	**$360**
January 1896-June 1896 bound volume (T.S. Sullivant, "Fables For the Times" series)	**$360**	Dec. 2, 1899 (Maxfield Parrish, first color cover)	**$100**
May 21, 1903 (Teddy Roosevelt)	**$25**	Nov. 27, 1903 (Charles Dana Gibson, Thanksgiving cover)	**$25**
July 2, 1908 (James Montgomery Flagg cover)	**$25**	July 29, 1909 (J.K. Bangs, Coles Phillips)	**$35**
Oct. 26, 1911 (Coles Phillips cover)	**$45**	Feb. 22, 1917 (Black Americana, Paul Stahr)	**$30**
Dec. 27, 1917 (Gertrude Stein, Harrison Cady)	**$50**	Oct. 3, 1918 (Anton Otto Fischer, Oliver Herford)	**$30**
March 17, 1921 (Parrish, "Humpty Dumpty" cover)	**$150**	June 14, 1923 (Movie Number, Dorothy Parker, Penrhyn Stanlaws cover)	**$35**
Nov. 1, 1923 (P.L. Crosby, T.S. Sullivant, Benchley)	**$35**	Nov. 8, 1923 (T.S. Sullivant cartoons)	**$35**
Nov. 22, 1923 (Norman Rockwell Thanksgiving cover)	**$75**	March 20, 1924 (Dorothy Parker, Robert Benchley)	**$35**
Nov. 13, 1924 (Dorothy Parker, John Held Jr. cover)	**$45**	April 28, 1927 (John Held Jr. cover)	**$45**
May 24, 1928 (Berton Braley, Benchley)	**$25**	Nov. 2, 1928 (Will Rogers for President)	**$30**
Feb. 14, 1930 (Dr. Seuss)	**$30**	Oct. 18, 1929 (Russell Patterson)	**$25**
November 1932 (Berton Braley, Lester Gaba cover)	**$25**	April 1933 (Jefferson Machamer, Ellis Parker Butler, Lester Gaba cover)	**$25**
June 1935 (Ogden Nash)	**$25**		

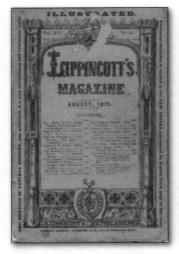

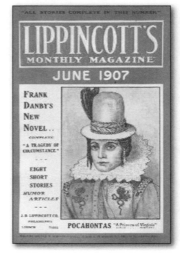

Lippincott's Magazine (1868-1914)

Published by Lippincott, a Philadelphia publishing house, from 1868 through 1914, **Lippincott's Monthly Magazine** was a major literary outlet for American and British writers. James Branch Cabell, Sarah Orne Jewett and James Russell Lowell all published in **Lippincott's. Lippincott's** was also the American outlet for Arthur Conan Doyle and Oscar Wilde, publishing Doyle's "Sign of the Four" and Wilde's "Picture of Dorian Gray" in 1890. **Lippincott's** also introduced Mary Roberts Rinehart. The magazine was sold to McBride-Nast in 1914 and renamed **McBride's Magazine** in 1915. It was sold again in 1916 to Scribner's and merged with **Scribner's Magazine.**

Unremarkable issue	$15	February 1890 ("Sign of the Four") December 2004 Sotheby's auction price	$63,000
July 1890 ("Dorian Gray")	$1,000	November 1877	$35
June 1880	$35	August 1887	$65
April 1888	$40	May 1890	$40
January 1891	$75	August 1892	$75
December 1892	$45	February 1894	$20
January 1907	$25	August 1910	$75

Macmillan's Magazine (1859-1907)

Macmillan's was the second major book publisher to found a magazine, following **Blackwell's** (qv.) lead in 1859, preceding Smith Elder's **Cornhill** (qv.) by two months. Like the other book publishers' magazines, Macmillan could draw on its strong stable of established authors to put out its magazine. Alfred Tennyson, Charles Kingsley, Thomas Hughes, Margaret Oliphant, Charlotte Yonge and R.D. Blackmore, however, did not fare well in comparison with the initial **Cornhill's** publications of Thackery and Trollope. This created a sort of competition between the two magazines, as **Macmillan's Magazine's** non-fiction featuring Matthew Arnold, F.D. Maurice and G.O. Trevelyan tended to be more popular than **Cornhill's** articles.

Macmillan's fiction did not begin to compete effectively with **Cornhill's** until the 1880s, with the publication of Henry James' *Portrait of a Lady* (1880-81) and Thomas Hardy's *The Woodlanders* (1886-87). In non-fiction, however, **Macmillan's** was unmatched. Starting in the January issue of 1864, an extended correspondence between Charles Kingsley and John Henry Newman was eagerly watched in **Macmillan's.** Newman's side eventually became *Apologia Pro Vita Sum.* **Macmillan's** also seemed to have the edge in poetry, publishing Alfred Lord Tennyson, Christina Rossetti and Matthew Arnold among others.

Of the book publishers' magazines, **Longman's** seemed to cut most deeply into **Macmillan's** popularity and circulation. **Macmillan's** just appeared to hit its stride in fiction when **Longman's** appeared. **Longman's** lower price, with fiction of like quality, cut into **Macmillan's** audience more deeply than it did **Cornhill's** or **Blackwoods.** The advent of **The**

Strand in the 1890s further cut into Macmillan's audience. In 1905, with the demise of Longman's, Macmillan's cut its price to six pence in an attempt to pick up Longman's market. The tactic failed and Macmillan's ceased publication in 1907.

Unremarkable six-month volume	$25	Volume I	$100
Volume II	$50	Volume III	$75
Volume XIII	$200	Volume XVII	$75
Volume XXIV	$120	Volume XXVIII	$75
Volume XLI	$75	Volume XLIII	$75
Volume XLIV	$225	Volume LX	$250

McCall's (1876-2001)

James and Belle McCall, after emigrating from Scotland in 1874, started a tailor shop and a pattern company. In 1876, they issued the first pattern pamphlet The Queen–Illustrated Magazine of Fashion. In 1884, after the death of James McCall, the magazine was renamed McCall's Magazine, the Queen of Fashion. In 1897, it was renamed McCall's Magazine. Though always based in part on fashion and patterns, the magazine evolved into a more general interest magazine along the lines of The Delineator and the Pictorial Review. It published such writers as Zona Gale, Ellis Parker Butler, Joseph Louis Vance, Gene Stratton-Porter, Rafael Sabatini, Laura Z. Hobson, Booth Tarkington, Faith Baldwin, Robert W. Chambers, Rupert Hughes, Harold Bell Wright, Zane Grey and Rudyard Kipling. Neysa McMien and Norman Rockwell did McCall's covers. In 1987, McCall's was sold to publisher Dale Lang, in 1989 to the *New York Times* and then to Gruner & Jahr in the mid-1990s. From there it became part of a sad episode as a joint venture with television star Rosie O'Donnell, where it became Rosie in April 2001 and went out of publication soon after, amid much ado. McCall's is collected for patterns and recipes, as well as other features.

Unremarkable single issue	$7.50	July 1905	$25
May 1908	$35	April 1910	$40
March 1913	$25	December 1919	$25
March 1923	$25	June 1923	$25
September 1923	$25	July 1924	$75
December 1932	$20	June 1935	$65
April 1936	$65	June 1937	$30
December 1965	$50	April 1967	$20

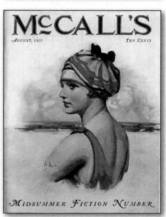

McClure's Magazine (1893-1929)

Founded by Samuel McClure in June 1893, **McClure's Magazine** was both a literary and a political journal. Run by Hearst from 1926 to 1928, then by James Quick from 1928 to 1929, **McClure's** published and, in some cases, introduced: Rudyard Kipling, Jack London, Arthur Conan Doyle, G.K. Chesterton, W.B. Yeats, O. Henry, John Kendrick Bangs, James Whitcomb Riley, Bret Harte, Robert Louis Stevenson, Eugene Field, W.D. Howells, Paul Verlaine, Walt Whitman and Stephen Crane on the literary side. In 1902, with journalists Licoln Steffens, Ida Tarbell and Ray Stannard Baker, **McClure's** became the original investigative magazine, with the journalists called muckrakers. The magazine declined in the early 1920s and neither Hearst nor Quick could bring it back to prominence. The final issue appeared in March 1929.

Unremarkable single issue	**$15**	May 1894	**$50**
June 1894	**$35**	June 1895	**$45**
November 1896	**$125**	March 1897	**$60**
April 1897	**$40**	May 1897	**$85**
June 1897	**$75**	October 1897	**$45**
May 1898	**$150**	November 1898	**$35**
October 1900	**$100**	September 1901	**$40**
November 1904	**$150**	December 1904	**$100**
January 1905	**$100**	March 1905	**$125**
May 1905	**$100**	March 1906	**$50**
June 1907	**$50**	January 1909	**$75**
December 1910	**$85**	November 1912	**$60**

Munsey (1889-1929)

Founded by Frank A. Munsey in 1889, **The Munsey Weekly** was a 36-page quarto magazine intended as "a magazine of the people and for the people, with pictures and art and good cheer and human interest throughout." John Kendrick Bangs was the first editor. In 1891, it was re-named **Munsey's Magazine** as a monthly and the following year began including "a complete novel in each number." In October 1893, the price of the magazine was reduced to 10 cents. When it began printing pictures of works of art, it was attacked for its "half-dressed women and undressed statuary." However, the change made the magazine more popular. It declined starting in 1906 and in July 1921, **Munsey's Magazine** was made an all-fiction monthly without illustrations. In October 1929, the magazine was merged with **Argosy All-Story** to form **All-Story Combined.**

Munsey was a fragile pulp magazine and few single copies of it exist in collectible condition. It is generally collected in bound volumes of publisher's consecutive numbers in six-month volumes: April-September and October-March	**$65**
Two volumes or single issues June-November 1922 (E.R. Burroughs, "Girl from Hollywood")	**$800**

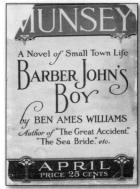

National Geographic (1888-present)

A publication of the National Geographic Society, **The National Geographic** magazine debuted in September 1888. It continues to be published by the society with this mission statement: "The 'National Geographic Society' has been organized 'to increase and diffuse geographic knowledge,' and the publication of a Magazine has been determined upon as one means of accomplishing these purposes. As it is not intended to be simply the organ of the Society, its pages will be open to all persons interested in geography, in the hope that it may become a channel of intercommunication, stimulate geographic investigation and prove an acceptable medium for the publication of results."

Unremarkable issues before 1908	**$10**	Unremarkable issues 1908-WWII	**$5**
Unremarkable issues after WWII	**$3**	Unremarkable volumes before 1908	**$100**
Unremarkable volumes 1908-WWII	**$35**	Unremarkable volumes after WWII	**$8**
First 20 volumes	**$3,500**		
Machu Picchu, The Peruvian Expeditions: April 1913, February 1915, May 1916.			
Single issue	**$300**	As a set	**$1,000**

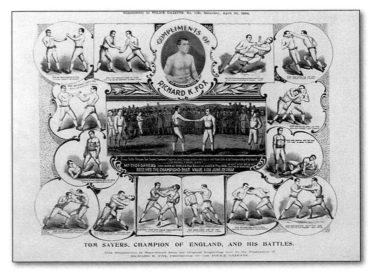

National Police Gazette (1845-)

Of the several publications with the name **Police Gazette,** including official organs of British and Commonwealth police forces, the best known is the American publication, officially **The National Police Gazette,** although commonly referred to as simply **The Police Gazette.** It was founded in 1845. The editor for the last quarter of the 19th century was Richard Kyle Fox, an influential boxing promoter, who defined weight classifications, offered championship belts and virtually created modern boxing. It was a sensational tabloid, supposedly devoted to matters of interest to the police, with lurid coverage of murders, prostitution, Wild West outlaws and sports, notably boxing, for which it was the major media outlet before the advent of **Ring** (qv.). At one point it was estimated that more than half of the circulation went to barber shops. It was well known for its "pin-ups": engravings and photographs of scantily clad young ladies posing as strippers and prostitutes. **The National Police Gazette** enjoyed considerable popularity in the late 19th century and through the Second World War, when some **Police Gazette** pin-up girls rivaled Hollywood stars with GIs. In 1937, the magazine was the subject of a popular song, "The Girl On The Police Gazette," written by Irving Berlin.

Boxing accounts, Jack the Ripper coverage in 1888 and some pin-up girls are extremely sought after by collectors, and the fragile tabloid nature of the magazine, along with the many readings it sustained in barber shops nationwide, combine to make earlier issues very scarce.

Unremarkable issue pre-1922	**$30**	Unremarkable issue 1922-1940	**$15**
Unremarkable 1940s pin-up issues	**$20**	Unremarkable post-WWII issues	**$5**
1888-89 Jack the Ripper issues	**$145**	Pre-1922 championship heavyweight bouts	**$65**
Pre-1922 other weight class championship bouts	**$50**	1920 "Black Sox" scandal coverage	**$75**

Oct. 25, 1847 (Madame Restell) **$155**	Nov. 18, 1848 (Patent Office robbery) **$145**
July 21, 1883 (Tombstone) **$125**	Jan. 12, 1884 (A novel execution) **$125**
April 18, 1885 (White slavery) **$75**	May 22, 1886 (Belle Starr) **$75**
April 9, 1887 (White slavery) **$100**	July 10, 1887 (Sullivan/Kilrain) **$250**
Dec. 21, 1889 (Lumber camps) **$45**	May 28, 1892 (Industrial accidents) **$55**
June 6, 1892 (Homestead riots) **$50**	Sept. 30, 1893 (George Dixon) **$75**
Sept. 22, 1894 (Forest fire) **$45**	June 11, 1895 (Bob Fitzsimmons) **$75**
Dec. 24, 1904 (Bob Fitzsimmons) **$85**	Sept. 12, 1925 (Gene Tunney) **$55**
March 1929 (Max Schmeling) **$25**	February 1931 (Young Stribling) **$25**
August 1931 (Primo Carnera) **$25**	October 1931 (Jack Sharkey) **$25**
November 1931 (Harness racing) **$25**	June 1940 (Burlesque) **$20**
January 1941 (Burlesque: Ann Corio pin-up) **$35**	October 1946 (Jeanne Lewis) **$20**
April 1947 (Lana Turner) **$15**	November 1947 (Hedy Lamarr) **$15**
January 1951 (Ernest Hemingway on Ezzard Charles) **$25**	February 1951 (Willy Pep/Sandy Sadler) **$15**
December 1957 (Jayne Mansfield) **$20**	

New Masses (1926-1948)

When the American Communist Party, under the leadership of Robert Minor, took over the left wing magazine, **The Liberator,** many of the artistic and literary contributors to it took offense and refused to continue their support. Michael Gold, John Sloan and Max Eastman got together and bought a defunct magazine, **Masses,** which had been published from 1911-1918. In 1926, they re-christened it **New Masses** as an outlet for art, literature and opinion previously available in **The Liberator.** Eastman became the publisher. From 1926 until 1948, **New Masses** published the work of Gold, Sloan and Eastman, as well as that of well-known leftist leaning writers and artists such as: Upton Sinclair, Sherwood Anderson, Erskine Caldwell, Richard Wright, Ernest Hemingway, Alvah Bessie, James Agee, Ralph Ellison, Langston Hughes, John Dos Passos, Josephine Herbst, Theodore Dreiser, Floyd Dell, Art Young, William Gropper, Albert Hirshfeld, Carl Sandburg, Waldo Frank and Eugene O'Neill.

Unremarkable issues	$15	Oct. 12, 1931 (Langston Hughes)	$75
Dec. 9, 1932 (Sherwood Anderson)	$45	Jan. 30, 1934 (Edward Dahlberg)	$35
Feb. 6, 1934 (Jose Clemente Orozco)	$35	May 15, 1934 (Langston Hughes)	$50
March 5, 1935 (Jacob Burck)	$25	April 9, 1935 (William Randolph Hearst)	$20
May 12, 1936 (Richard Wright)	$40	Aug. 1, 1936 (Richard Wright, Langston Hughes)	$65
Oct. 13, 1936 (Granville Hicks)	$20	Dec. 15, 1936 (Richard Wright)	$35
June 8, 1937 (James Agee)	$75	Sept. 14, 1937 (James Agee, Rockwell Kent)	$125
March 7, 1939 (Father Lobo)	$25	July 18, 1939 (Alvah Bessie)	$20
Oct. 3, 1939 (Alvah Bessie)	$20	Dec. 5, 1939 (Ralph Ellison)	$35
March 5, 1940 (Marion Greenspan)	$20	June 18, 1940 (Ralph Ellison)	$30
Aug. 6, 1940 (William Carlos Williams)	$25	April 1, 1941 (Theodore Dreiser)	$25
June 8, 1943 (William Gropper)	$20		

The New Yorker (1925-present)

The first issue of the magazine that was "not edited for the old lady in Dubuque" hit the newsstands on Feb. 21, 1925. Harold Ross founded and edited the magazine. Marc Connelly, Dorothy Parker, Alexander Woollcott and Heywood Broun all joined **The New Yorker** at its inception. Ross kept an impressive group of writers at the magazine during his tenure as editor, including E.B. White, James Thurber, Robert Benchley, Ogden Nash and S.J. Perelman. **The New Yorker** was conceptualized as a weekly humor magazine for local consumption, and was one of many city-based magazines that were springing up around the country in the 1930s. It rapidly developed a mass market of educated and sophisticated readers nationwide. **The New Yorker** also featured distinguished fiction typified by the story, "Only the Dead Know Brooklyn," by Thomas Wolfe in the issue of June 15, 1935. **The New Yorker** continues to be published.

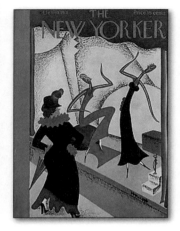

Unremarkable Ross/Shawn issues (pre-1981)	$20	Unremarkable issues (post-1981)	$5
July 27, 1929	$150	Oct. 17, 1931	$75
Nov. 7, 1931	$75	April 23, 1932	$100
May 5, 1933	$55	Aug. 26, 1933	$55
March 23, 1935	$75	June 15, 1935	$300
Oct. 14, 1939	$55	Sept. 15, 1943	$55
Aug. 31, 1946	$75	May 17, 1947	$65
June 21, 1947	$75	Jan. 31, 1948	$175
June 5, 1948	$150	March 19, 1949	$125
Sept. 2, 1950	$50	Jan. 29, 1955	$100
May 29, 1955	$100	June 5, 1959	$125
May 9 and 16, 1964 (two issues, Nabokov's "Luzhin Defense")	$125	Dec. 10, 1966	$50

North American Review (1815-present)

Founded in Boston in 1815, **The North American Review** was a principal reprinter of British literature in the United States. Part of the Boston/New England literary establishment that dominated American literature before the Civil War, the magazine was a principal source of British literature and criticism during that period. While making a specialty of British reprints, the magazine published some work by American writers, notably Walt Whitman. In 1870, the magazine moved to New York and attempted to compete with more successful popular magazines. During this period the magazine published Henry James, carried commentary by Andrew Carnegie and tried to capitalize on more popular British authors such as Joseph Conrad. The magazine was never a popular success, but maintained a niche among the intelligentsia until 1940. Revived in 1964 at Cornell (Iowa) College, and moved to the University of Northern Iowa in 1968, the magazine continues to be published. However, despite inclusions in a few award anthologies, the Iowa incarnation has not become popular with collectors.

Pre-Civil War unremarkable issues	**$35**	Post-Civil War to 1900 unremarkable issues	**$20**
Twentieth century to 1940 unremarkable issues	**$15**	Modern (post-1968) unremarkable issues	**$10**
June 1815 (first issue)	**$400**	July 1815	**$300**
October 1833 (John Jay biography)	**$65**	July 1838 (Oliver Wendell Holmes)	**$75**
October 1851 (Slavery)	**$100**	October 1854	**$30**
April 1880 (The Irish question)	**$100**	June 1882 (Walt Whitman)	**$75**
December 1888 (Henry M. Stanley, James G. Blaine)	**$175**	April 1903 (Mark Twain, Christian Science)	**$25**
April 1905 (Henry James)	**$45**	May 1905 (Havelock Ellis)	**$45**
May 1907 (Henry James)	**$40**	April 1912 (Henry James)	**$45**
July 1912 (Henry Cabot Lodge)	**$45**	July 1915 (Centenary)	**$25**
December 1916 (W.D. Howells)	**$25**	November 1933 (John Steinbeck, "The Red Pony")	**$200**
December 1933 (John Steinbeck, "The Great Mountains")	**$150**	April 1934 (John Steinbeck, "The Murder")	**$150**
October 1934 (John Steinbeck, "The Raid")	**$150**	January 1935 (William Saroyan)	**$25**
March 1935 (John Steinbeck, "The White Quail")	**$150**	Bound volume by the publisher's numbers (Usually six months)	**$55**
Complete run 1815-2001	**$11,000**		

Overland Monthly (1868-1935)

The Overland Monthly was a San Francisco-based publication edited by Bret Harte from 1868 to 1875. Harte made the magazine an instant success with the publication of his stories: "The Luck of Roaring Camp" (1868), "The Outcasts of Poker Flat"(1869) and "The Idyl of Red Gulch"(1869). He attracted important Western writers such as his friends Mark Twain, with the series "A Californian Abroad" (1868), and Ambrose Bierce. Within the first six months, **The Overland Monthly** had a circulation of 3,000 and by 1870, had reached 10,000. An early printed account of the Donner party tragedy (1870), which preceded McGlashan's work on the subject by nine years, was another factor in the magazine's success. Although it suspended publication in 1875, it was published for a time as **The Californian.** It became **The Overland Monthly** again in January 1883 with Millicent Shinn as the editor, although she chose not to put her name on the masthead. Jack London also published stories and articles in **The Overland Monthly** including "To the Man on the Trail" (A Klondike

Christmas), "The White Silence," "The Son of the Wolf" and "The Men of Forty-Mile" (1899). Memorial editions were produced for Bret Harte, the first editor, and of course the coverage of the San Francisco Earthquake was massive. In 1917, **The Overland Monthly** published an entire memorial issue on Jack London after his untimely death. By 1923, the magazine merged with **Out West**. The magazine finally ceased publication with the July 1935 issue.

First series 1868-1875

Unremarkable issue	$25	Complete run	$725
Volumes	$125	October 1869	$175
December 1869	$165	July 1870	$250
September 1870	$225	July 1871	$300

Second Series 1883-1923

Unremarkable issue	$15	December 1885 (Yosemite)	$40
December 1886 (Beet sugar)	$35	February 1886 (Chinese immigration)	$35
November 1886 (Tombstone, Ariz.) $45		February 1888 (San Diego)	$35
July 1899 (Jack London)	$200	September 1902 (Bret Harte)	$100
July 1903 (John Neihardt)	$75	March 1906 (Luther Burbank)	$35
October 1910 (Clark Ashton Smith)	$125	November 1910 (Clark Ashton Smith)	$100
December 1912 (Charles Taze Russell)	$100		

Pagany (1933)

Pagany was one of the most important small literary magazines of the Depression era. Founded by Robert Johns with the help of William Carlos Williams, Sherry Mangan and Charles Henri Ford, **Pagany** published, and in some cases introduced, William Carlos Williams, Ezra Pound, Gertrude Stein, Mary Butts, Kenneth Rexroth, Dudley Fitts, Hilda Doolittle, Kenneth Rexroth, Erskine Caldwell, John Dos Passos, Charles Henri Ford, Conrad Aiken, e.e. cummings and Louis Zukofsky. **Pagany** contributed to the growth, development and recognition of many major writers. However, Johns did not hesitate to reject the work of noted writers when he believed the quality of the writing was inferior, including submissions by D.H. Lawrence, William Saroyan and William Faulkner. Johns made **Pagany** a publication of lasting value through stubborn devotion to good literature and a refusal to be bound by commercial pressure. The attitude, however, coupled with the Depression, tolled the death knell for **Pagany.** Only 12 issues of **Pagany** were published before the lack of funds forced Johns to cease publication in February 1933.

Pagany issues	$40 each	Set of 12 **Pagany** issues	$750

Pall Mall (1893-1914)

The **Pall Mall Magazine** was a **Strand**-like magazine founded by a wealthy American, William Waldorf Astor. The contents were geared towards the upper class of late Victorian England by its first editors, Lord Frederick Hamilton and Sir Douglas Straight. Contributors with important first appearances included writers such as Arthur Conan Doyle with "The Green Flag and Other Stories of War and Sport," "St. Ives" by Robert Louis Stevenson, "Joan Haste" by H. Rider Haggard, "Huguenin's Wife" by M.P. Shiel, "Bolinas Plain" by Bret Harte, "Quod Erat Demonstrandum" by Guy Boothby and "Fox Hunting" by George Roller. Later writers included "Chris Farrington: Able Seaman" by Jack London, as well as work by G.K. Chesterton, P.G. Wodehouse, Rudyard Kipling, and Joseph Conrad's "Typhoon." Important illustrators whose work appeared in **Pall Mall** were Aubrey Beardsley, Arthur Rackham, Edmund Dulac, Sidney Paget and regular contributor Sydney H. Sime. After a decline in readership and revenue, **Pall Mall** was absorbed by **Nash's** in 1914.

Unremarkable bound volume original publisher's pictorial binding **$25**	May-December 1893 (Doyle, "Green Flag") **$75**
January-April 1895 (Haggard, "Joan Haste," M.P. Shiel) **$75**	May-December 1895 (Haggard, "Joan Haste," M.R. James) **$75**
January-April 1897 (Jubilee) **$50**	May-December 1897 (R.L. Stevenson) **$30**
September-December 1899 (Sydney Sime) **$50**	January-August 1900 (Sydney Sime) **$50**
January-March 1902 (Joseph Conrad, "Typhoon") **$60**	May-December 1905 (Arthur Rackham) **$75**
July-October 1906 (Joseph Conrad, "Gasper Ruiz") **$50**	January-April 1908 (Jack London) **$40**

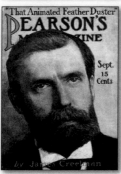

Pearson's (1886-1939)

Perhaps the only imitator of Newnes' **Strand** to make the expected impact, C. Arthur Pearson's self-named magazine at times rivaled **The Strand** for circulation and carried an impressive stable of writers including George Griffith, W.W. Jacobs, C.J. Cutcliffe Hyne ("Captain Kettle" stories), Sax Rohmer, Max Pemberton, Rudyard Kipling, H.G. Wells ("The War of the Worlds," 1897), Allen Upward, Baroness Orczy and Rafael Sabatini.

In terms of international impact, **Pearson's** editorially separate American edition, especially under the editorship of Frank Harris from 1916-1923, outstripped any other international publication. Harris' transformation of the magazine into a leftist leaning mixture of politics and fiction featured such writers as Floyd Dell alongside British leftists such as George Bernard Shaw. It also had investigative journalism ("muckraking") by such writers as Upton Sinclair. The combination made **Pearson's Magazine,** during Harris' editorship, one of the top circulation magazines in the United States. A series on the deficiencies of New York City's courts and judicial corruption led to certain reforms and, **Pearson's Magazine,** under Harris rivaled **McClure's Magazine** as an investigative journal. The American edition, however, only survived two years after Harris' tenure as editor, folding with the April issue of 1925. The British magazine continued until the beginning of World War II, ceasing publication with the June issue of 1939.

Unremarkable U.K. issue	**$20**	Unremarkable U.S. issue	**$15**
Serials: Rudyard Kipling, "Captains Courageous," July 1886 to June 1888			
Single issue	**$35**	Complete run	**$1,800**
H.G. Wells, "War of the Worlds," April to December 1897			
Single issue	**$75**	Complete run	**$850**
H.G. Wells, "The Sea Lady," July to December 1901			
Single issue	**$45**	Complete run	**$300**
Unremarkable U.K. volume	**$55**	Volume I	**$200**
Volume II	**$135**	Volume III	**$150**
Volume IV	**$200**	Volume V	**$150**
Volume IX	**$250**	Volume X	**$250**
American issues			
January 1902	**$30**	May 1911	**$50**
April 1917	**$35**	January 1920	**$35**
August 1922	**$45**	September 1936	**$50**

Peterson's Magazine (1842-1898)

Peterson's Magazine, published in Philadelphia by Charles Peterson, was variously known as the **Ladies National Magazine, Lady's World** and simply **Peterson's.** It was a fashion magazine similar to **Godey's Lady's Book,** but without the editorial vision of Sarah Hale. **Peterson's** contained similar departments for women such as recipes, household hints, parlor games, embroidery, lace patterns, Berlin work, crochet instructions, point lace stitches, children's fashions, purses, morning caps and beadwork. But it never pioneered for women's independence or published serious literary contributions by innovators like Edgar Allan Poe. The hand-colored fashions and foldouts were called Les Modes Parisiennes in an attempt to bring the latest Paris fashions to American women. In contrast, Sarah Hale consciously Americanized the fashions in **Godey's.** Nevertheless, **Peterson's** was successful and valued for its hand-colored fashions and by Civil War reenactment enthusiasts.

Single unremarkable issue with hand-colored fashion plate	**$20**	January-July 1855	**$135**
January-June 1857	**$135**	January-December 1863	**$150**
July-December 1867 (Civil War)	**$125**	January-December 1869	**$150**
January-June 1871	**$65**	January-December 1874	**$120**
January-December 1876	**$135**	January-June 1881	**$125**

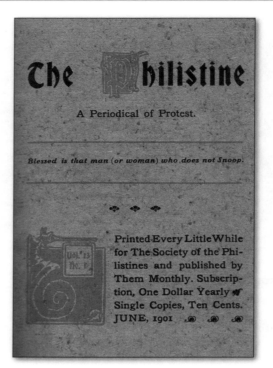

Philistine/Fra (1895-1915)

Published by Elbert Hubbard from his Roycrofters commune beginning in 1895, **The Philistine,** along with his inspirational essay "Message to Garcia," formed the financial backbone of the Roycrofters commune from 1895, eventually reaching a paid circulation of 200,000. An inspirational magazine, **The Philistine** was written, almost in its entirety, by Hubbard, as was its larger counterpart, **The Fra.** The publications of Roycrofters, a commune founded by Hubbard to emulate the fine editions produced by William Morris at Kelmscott Press, have become collectible in their own right, though reprints of several titles and the large circulation of **The Philistine** have dented the value somewhat. Of the two magazines, **The Fra** is more desirable in the collector's community. The most desirable issues of the Philistine carry early illustrations and decorations by W.W. Denslow, who began his career at Roycrofters and designed the "Seahorse" logo. The death of Hubbard on the Lusitania in 1915 ended the publication of both magazines, as they were essentially Hubbard's personal projects.

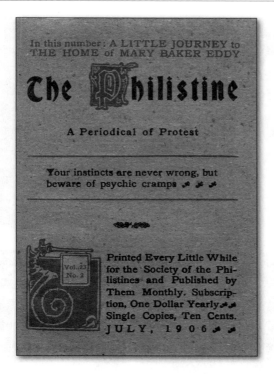

The Philistine:

Unremarkable single issue	$5		
Volumes:			
I (June-November 1895)	$200	III (June-November 1896)	$125
IV (December 1896-May 1897)	$50	VI (December 1897-May 1898)	$50
VII (June-November 1898)	$50	IX (June-November 1899)	$50
X (December 1899-May 1900)	$45	XIII (June-November 1901)	$30
XV (June-November 1902)	$75	XVI (December 1902-May 1903)	$65
XVIII (June-November 1903)	$40		

The Fra

Unremarkable single issue	$10	Complete run	$1,200
June 1908	$30	November 1908	$35
May 1911	$25	August 1911	$20
November 1911	$40	December 1911	$20
February 1912	$20		

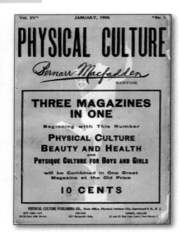
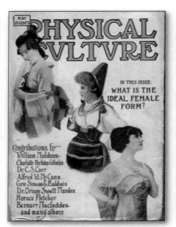
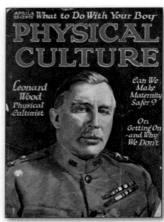
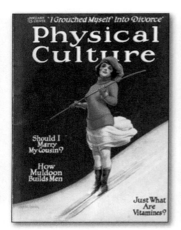
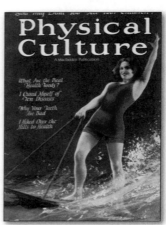
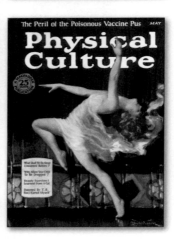

Physical Culture (1899-1933)

Physical Culture first appeared March 1899, sold for five cents and focused on bodybuilding. The magazine was a success and, by 1903, monthly sales were more than 100,000 copies. Articles about natural foods and the natural treatment of disease were featured along with bodybuilding. There were also drawings and photographs showing people (frequently publisher Bernarr Macfadden himself) wearing minimal or no clothing. In 1905, Anthony Comstock brought legal action against Macfadden to have him arrested, beginning a long feud between Macfadden and public "moralists." The feud continues even today, with Internet auction companies censoring issues of **Physical Culture** due to "nudity."

In 1907, Macfadden was arrested and convicted for a story in **Physical Culture Magazine** judged to be "obscene material" about a young man who had venereal disease. Combating the spread of venereal disease was a major cause for Macfadden. His object was to raise the public's awareness of the problem. Macfadden accurately assessed the problem: to control venereal disease, the medical profession had to stop avoiding it simply because it was an embarrassing or "obscene" subject. He campaigned nationally to have his conviction overturned and finally, in 1909, received a presidential pardon from President Taft. Through **Physical Culture,** Macfadden was one of the first publishers to challenge laws that restricted freedom of speech and the press. He viewed prudery as the source of many social ills, and taught that feelings of guilt and shame were destructive to a person's overall physical health. Macfadden was an important influence in changing attitudes toward sex and his legal battles opened the door for much of today's publishing freedom.

Unremarkable issue	$20	January 1906 (Comstock, "King of the Prudes")	$35
May 1914 (Jack London, Orison, Swett Marden)	$50	April 1920 (Johnny Gruelle)	$35
January 1922 (Tod Robbins)	$50	November 1928 (Haskell Coffin cover)	$25
January 1931 (Edgar Wallace)	$25	April 1931 (Zane Grey, Harold Bell Wright)	$30
May 1933 (Nudists "Banned")	$30		

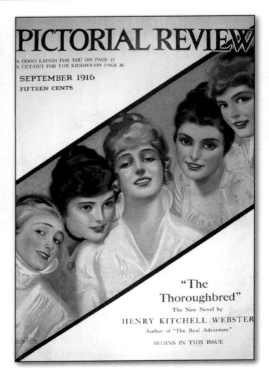

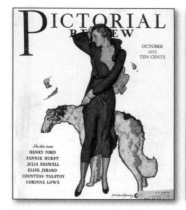  

Pictorial Review (1899-1939)

First published in 1899 by William Paul Ahnelt as a women's/ family magazine, early issues of the **Pictorial Review** featured a British import along with an American romance, and articles and features of interest to women such as: "What Every Woman Needs" (Laura S. Rabb, February 1912). Early British imports included Richard Marsh and P.G. Wodehouse. Dorothy Canfield and Ellis Parker Butler also contributed to early issues of the magazine. During the 1920s, Donn Byrne, Gertrude Atherton, Sophie Kerr, Carl Sandburg and Edith Wharton all published in **Pictorial Review.** Artists included Frederick Remington, Howard Chandler Christy, Rose O'Neill and Rolf Armstrong. Paper dolls are a big feature of the collectibility of **Pictorial Review.** Dolly Dingle, perhaps the most popular paper doll and precursor of the "Campbell Kids" in advertising, by Grayce Drayton appeared in **Pictorial Review** in March 1913, and from 1916 to 1933. Other popular paper dolls were: Peggy Pryde and friends in 1926, flappers Bonnie and Betty Bobbs in 1925 and 1926, and the Polly and Peter Perkins series by Gertrude Kay in 1934. Merged by Hearst with **The Delineator** in 1937, the combined magazine only lasted two years, ceasing publication in 1939.

Unremarkable single issue	$10	September 1910	$65
March 1912	$75	September 1916	$55
January 1918	$50	September 1918	$50
August 1925	$25	April 1926	$25
July 1926	$20	June 1930	$35
March 1931	$15	August 1932	$25
October 1932	$35	July 1933	$20
March 1934	$60	February 1935	$30

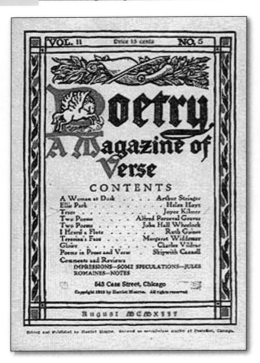

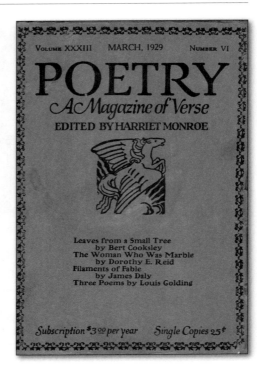

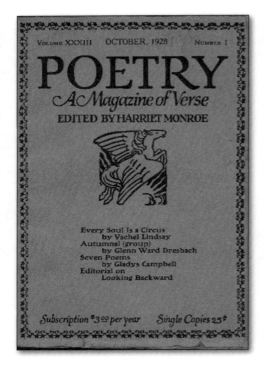

 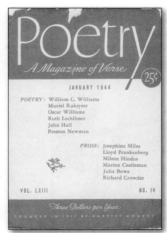 

Poetry (1912-present)

Claiming to be the oldest monthly devoted to verse in the English-speaking world, **Poetry A Magazine of Verse** was founded in Chicago by Harriet Monroe in 1912. Harriet Monroe's "Open Door" policy, set forth in 1911, remains the most succinct statement of **Poetry's** mission: "to print the best poetry written today, in whatever style, genre, or approach." **Poetry** published the first important poems of T.S. Eliot, Ezra Pound, Marianne Moore, Wallace Stevens, H.D., William Carlos Williams, Carl Sandburg and other now-classic authors. The magazine, which continues to be published, has published works by virtually every significant poet of the 20th century. It was edited by Monroe until her death in 1936.

Unremarkable issue pre-1936	$10	Unremarkable issue post-1936	$5
August 1913 ("Trees" by Joyce Kilmer)	$75	August 1914	$20
December 1915	$100	January 1918	$35
July 1918	$75	January 1919	$25
December 1919	$20	July 1920	$25
June 1923	$35	February 1924	$15
December 1925	$20	April 1926	$20
June 1926	$20	November 1926	$30
January 1927	$20	February 1927	$20

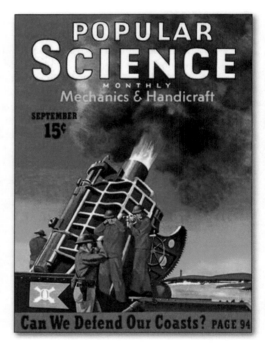

Popular Science (1872-present)

Founded in 1872 as **Popular Science Monthly** by Edward L. Youmans, the magazine was originally a serial outlet for Herbert Spencer's social Darwinist tract, *The Study of Sociology*. Maintaining an emphasis on evolution as a popular cause celebré, the magazine prospered through the 19th century. **Popular Science** was scoped toward the educated reader, but not necessarily the trained scientist, as was **Scientific American** (qv.). Earlier issues tended to rely on British popular science writers, such as Grant Allen, rather than scientists and inventors. Throughout the 20th century, the magazine benefited from popularizing gadgetry and an emphasis on technology rather than hard science. The "what's new" section featured all manner of new and innovative consumer products. Collectible modern issues feature gadgets that have become well known, as **Popular Science** was most likely the breakthrough into national media for them.

Unremarkable issue pre-World War II	$15	Unremarkable issue post-WWII	$5
Unremarkable volume pre-WWII	$45	Unremarkable issue post-WWII	$15
Volumes:			
63 (January-June 1903)	$125	64 (June-December 1903)	$100
65 (June-December 1904)	$65	66 (January-June 1905)	$75
68 (January-June 1906)	$65	69 (June-December 1907)	$275
72 (January-June 1908)	$50	73 (June-December 1908)	$75
74 (January-June 1909)	$90	75 (June-December 1909)	$65
76 (January-June 1910)	$50	77 (June-December 1910)	$50

Portrait Monthly (1863-1864)

Published by Legget & Co. of New York in 1863-1864, **The Portrait Monthly** featured woodcut engraved portraits of the prominent figures of the Civil War period. In all, 18 issues were distributed and they are highly prized collectibles in Americana as well as magazines. The magazine carried portraits and short blurbs for many of the major figures of the era, Abraham Lincoln and Jefferson Davis, Grant, Lee, Stanton, Custer, Clay, along with many forgotten characters such as Madame Guerrabella, an actress and singer also known as Genevieve Ward. Subtitled: "Sketches of Departed Heroes, and Prominent Personages of the Present Time, Interesting Stories, Etc.," it is often found in contemporarily bound volumes.

Single issue	$125

A FATAL GIFT

"THE PUBLIC BE DAMNED"

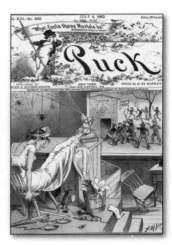

Puck (1876-1918)

Puck began as a German language weekly published by Joseph Keppler, a cartoonist who apprenticed with Frank Leslie's organization, in 1876. An English language version was begun in March 1877 and was, in actuality, supported by the German version until the early 1880s. Much of **Puck's** humor was political in character, poking fun at such subjects as women's suffrage and showing support for the growing labor movement of the era. **Puck** often attacked for the sake of attack, making fun of President Grant's drinking and Rutherford B. Hayes' tee-totaling. Keppler's death in 1896 brought the magazine under control of his son, who employed humorist Harry Leon Wilson and John Kendrick Bangs as editors before the magazine's decline in circulation and purchase by Hearst in 1917. Hearst ran the magazine for a year as a separate entity before making it the Sunday cartoon section of the Hearst newspaper chain. The center double truck from **Puck** is frequently ripped for framing, so check all issues carefully.

A SKELETON OF HIS OWN

BRIC-A-BRAC

Unremarkable single issue	$15	Unremarkable volume	$45
Volume XI	$125	July 4, 1877	$35
July 18, 1877	$25	Aug. 4, 1880	$40
May 30, 1881	$40	July 6, 1890	$20
May 22, 1895	$35	Dec. 8, 1897	$75
April 10, 1907	$35	June 22, 1910	$25
July 6, 1910	$35	May 31, 1911	$35
Oct. 10, 1914	$35		

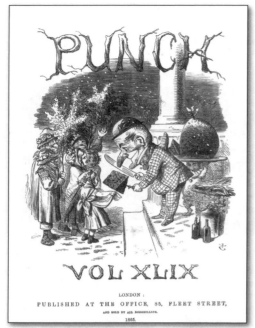

THE REAL IRISH COURT; OR, THE HEAD CENTRE AND THE DIS—SENTERS.

Punch, Or the London Charivari (1841-2002)

Although engraver Ebenezer Landells and writer Henry Mayhew got the idea for the weekly magazine from a satirical French paper, *Charivari,* **Punch** was the ultimate purveyor of British satirical humor. Its first editor, Mark Lemon, shaped its irreverent attitude with cartoons by John Leech, Charles Keene, George du Maurier and John Tenniel (of *Alice in Wonderland* fame). The artists satirized subjects such as "Oxford In The Future," "Erin's Little Difficulty," "The Re-United States," "Fenians In A Fix" and "The Jamaica Question." In addition to Lemon and Mayhew, early great comic writers included William Thackeray and Shirley Brooks (the magazine's second editor). Staff members and contributors held weekly editorial dinners around a wooden table that held their carved initials. In fact, most of the work that appeared in **Punch** was done either anonymously or with initials. Readers often had to wait for the end of year issues to decipher the contributors.

In 1888, **Punch** took up the cause of the poverty-stricken residents of London's East End with a classic series of devastating cartoons about the White Chapel Murders of Jack The Ripper. Under the editorship of Owen Seaman and later E.V. Knox, **Punch** presented early cartoons by Arthur Rackham. It also had the first appearance of editor A.A. Milne's *Winnie-The-Pooh* (1923) and "When We Were Very Young" (1924), illustrated by E.H. Shepard. **Punch** was thought of as more than a mere magazine. It was considered a national institution during its long publication history.

Single unremarkable issue pre-1940	**$10**	July-December 1865 (John Tenniel)	**$100**
January-June 1866 (John Tenniel)	**$100**	Sept. 15, 22, 29, 1888, Oct. 13, 20, 1888, July 27, 1889 (Jack The Ripper issues)	**$350**
July 5, 1905 (Arthur Rackham)	**$25**	Aug. 30, 1905 (Arthur Rackham)	**$25**
Sept. 6, 1905 (Arthur Rackham)	**$25**	Sept. 27, 1905 (Arthur Rackham)	**$25**
Oct. 11, 1905 (Arthur Rackham)	**$25**	Oct. 25, 1905 (Arthur Rackham)	**$25**
Nov. 15, 1905 (Arthur Rackham)	**$25**	Nov. 29, 1905 (Arthur Rackham)	**$25**
Jan. 3, 1906 (Arthur Rackham)	**$25**	Feb. 14, 1906 (Arthur Rackham)	**$25**
January-June 1924 (Milne, "When We Were Very Young")	**$250**		

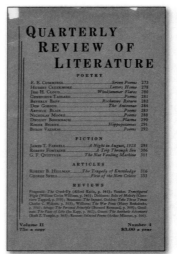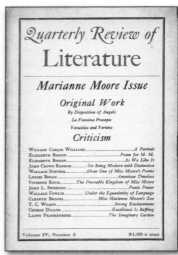

Quarterly Review of Literature (1943-present)

Founded in 1943 by Warren Carrier, the **Quarterly Review of Literature** has become the standard among American small literary magazines. Carrier turned the magazine over to a young poet and teacher, Theodore Weiss, in 1948. He was joined almost immediately by his wife, Renée, who is credited with making the magazine pay for itself entirely from sales and subscriptions. Though it has never received university funding, the magazine maintains loose affiliations with the universities where Theodore Weiss taught, currently Princeton University, which does give it office space. Early in its existence, the magazine made the decision to concentrate on original writing at the expense of criticism. It has published original work by Henry Miller, Wallace Stevens, e.e. cummings, Marianne Moore, Ezra Pound, William Carlos Williams, Denise Levertov and Robert Duncan. Among the writers introduced in **Quarterly Review of Literature** are John Ashbery, Robert Coover, James Dickey, John Gardner, W.S. Merwin, Linda Pastan and James Wright.

Unremarkable single issue	$10	Volume 7 #2 (1953)	$20
Volume 7 #4 (1954)	$20	Volume 10 #4 (1960)	$20
Volume 12 #3 (1963)	$25	Volume 14 #2 (1969)	$20

Red Book, Redbook (1903-present)

Established as a publication of the Short Story Company, which was incorporated as Consolidated Publishers in May of 1907, **The Red Book Magazine** debuted in May 1903 as an action/adventure fiction magazine. With the introduction of **Blue Book Magazine** from **Monthly Story Magazine** in September of 1906, **The Red Book** changed focus somewhat to specialize in romantic adventure, providing a contrast with the action/adventure featured in **Blue Book.** Many **Blue Book** authors featured their more romantic adventure stories in **The Red Book** along with more romantic writers such as Agnes Morley Cleaveland, Hugh Poindexter, Rupert Hughes, Elinor Glyn and Hallie Erminie Rives. Adventure writers who tried their hand at romance in **Red Book** included Octavus Roy Cohen with "For Love of Sheila" in December of 1914 and George Allen England with "Love!" in August 1915. McCall's bought **Red Book** in October 1929 and, in January 1930, modified the name to **Redbook,** adding features of interest to women readers and beginning an evolutionary transition from a romantic fiction magazine to a women's magazine. Under editor Edwin Balmer, from 1929 to 1949, **Redbook** became more

literature oriented in its romantic fiction, publishing such authors as F. Scott Fitzgerald ("Six of One," February 1932), Sinclair Lewis (*Anne Vickers,* August-December 1932), and Lord Dunsany ("The Tale of the Diamond," January 1934.) Fiction was phased out, after Balmer left in 1949, under editors Wade Nichols, Robert Stein and Dawn Raffel, to become a women's interest magazine published currently by McCall's, with little or no fiction content.

Unremarkable issue pre-1949	**$15**	Unremarkable issue post-1949	**$5**
January 1906	**$25**	August 1911	**$30**
December 1914	**$35**	August 1915	**$25**
December 1916	**$30**	April 1917	**$40**
April-August 1919 (E.R. Burroughs serial, "Tarzan the Untamed")			
Single issue	**$25**	Complete run	**$175**
April 1920	**$36**	July 1924	**$35**
December 1927	**$25**	April 1928	**$30**
August-December 1932 (Anne Vickers serial)	**$175**	March 1933	**$25**

January 1934	$25

F. Scott Fitzgerald, original appearances: September 1925, January and February 1926, June 1926, February 1932, October 1934, June 1935, August 1935 and November 1941 **$150**

Ring (1922-present)

The death of Richard Kyle Fox in 1922 resulted in the decline of **The National Police Gazette's** (qv.) boxing coverage in the early 1900s, creating a void in boxing journalism. Yet boxing, with the arrival of Jack Dempsey as heavyweight champion, was rapidly gaining in popularity. In 1922, Nathaniel S. ("Nat") Fleischer stepped into this void, founding **The Ring.** Fleischer remained as editor and publisher for 50 years, during which the magazine earned recognition as the most authoritative voice in the sport, the self-titled "Bible of Boxing." Though not as influential as promoter/popularizer Fox, Fleischer's crusading editorials on issues such as corruption, the impact of television and fighter safety had a major impact on the sport. Although they didn't carry the weight of Fox's matchmaking and promoting of bouts, **The Ring's** rankings of fighters in all divisions became highly influential in matchmaking. After Fleischer's death, the magazine struggled to find a voice, and even ceased publication for a time in 1989. Early **Ring** magazines are sought after and certain bouts, as well as articles on specific boxers such as Gene Tunney and Max Baer, bring premiums.

Unremarkable single issue 1922-1929	$35	Unremarkable single issue 1930-1939	$20
Unremarkable single issue 1940-1949	$15	Unremarkable single issue 1950-1959	$10
Unremarkable single issue 1960 and later	$5	February 1922	$500
August 1930	$75	December 1930	$65
September 1931	$45	June 1933	$35
September 1933	$35	September 1934	$45
July 1938	$55	September 1938	$65
July 1939	$75	August 1941	$45
March 1943	$35	October 1947	$45
January 1949	$35	June 1950	$25
May 1953	$45		

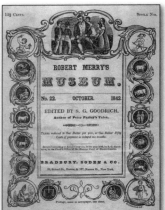

Robert Merry's Museum (1841-1872)

A children's monthly was founded in Boston in 1841 by Samuel G. Goodrich, who became "Robert Merry" of the **Museum**, an old peg-legged traveler and lover of children. The premise was Robert Merry would gather children around his knees and tell them stories and useful things, with "pictures to match." In its second year of publication, it moved to New York, where it was published for the next quarter century. **Robert Merry's Museum** had various publishers over its existence and Goodrich continued as editor until 1850, when he was appointed the American consul in Paris. The Rev. S.T. Allen succeeded Goodrich as editor, having been the publisher when Goodrich received his diplomatic appointment. The firm of "I.C. and J.N. Stearns, Publishers and Proprietors" took over in 1855 and continued to publish the **Museum** through 1867, when Stearns took over the newly founded National Temperance Society. The **Museum** declined after the Civil War, faced with new and vigorous competition from such new magazines as **Youth's Companion** (qv.) and **St. Nicholas** (qv.). Owned by Horace Fuller from 1867 through the final issue in 1872, the **Museum** was edited by Louisa Mae Alcott, but failed to sustain itself. The less didactic and newer children's magazines had caught the fancy of American children, and the older educationally and morally based presentation of the **Museum** couldn't effectively compete.

No complete collection of the **Museum's** 372 issues exists in the hands of any single library, and private collectors for more than a century have sought to bring together a single unified collection, which makes all issues important.

| Single issues | $60 | Bound volumes by publisher's number | $125 |

The Royal (1898-1939)

Publisher C. Arthur Pearson's magazine, **The Royal,** debuted in November 1898. Basically a fiction magazine in keeping with Pearson's roster of authors, **The Royal Magazine** is chiefly remembered and collected for its mystery stories featuring various detectives. Guy Boothby, Baroness Orczy, Victor Whitechurch, Sax Rohmer, Allen Upward, Rafael Sabatini and William Hope Hodgson all published in **The Royal.** The name was changed to **The New Royal Magazine** in December 1930. In June 1932, the

magazine changed gears, becoming a motion picture magazine as
The Royal Pictorial, changing its name to **Screen Pictorial** in July
1935, and finally shutting down with the issue of September 1939.
A few issues of the later movie incarnation are collectible, featuring
Dashiell Hammett and George Arliss.

Unremarkable issue	$10	Unremarkable six-month volume bound by Pearson	$35
Volumes:			
IX	$65	X	$55
XI	$60	XII	$100
XIV	$90		
Issues:			
November 1899	$45	May 1902	$70
November 1903	$25	December 1903	$25
April 1904	$60	May 1904	$20
October 1922	$20		
Royal Pictorial:		November 1934	$35

POE'S LAST POEM.

In the December number of our Magazine we announced that we had another poem of Mr. Poe's in hand, which we would publish in January. We supposed it to be his last, as we received it from him a short time before his decease. The sheet containing our announcement was scarcely dry from the press, before we saw the poem, *which we had bought and paid for*, going the rounds of the newspaper press, into which it had found its way through some agency that will perhaps be hereafter explained. It appeared first, we believe, in the New York Tribune. If we are not misinformed, two other Magazines are in the same predicament as ourselves. As the poem is one highly characteristic of the gifted and lamented author, and more particularly, as our copy of it differs in several places from that which has been already published, we have concluded to give it as already announced.

ANNABEL LEE.

A BALLAD.

BY EDGAR A. POE.

It was many and many a year ago,
In a kingdom by the sea,
That a maiden there lived whom you may know
By the name of Annabel Lee;
And this maiden she lived with no other thought
Than to love and be loved by me.

Sartain's Union Magazine (1849-1852)

John Sartain brought the art of mezzotint engraving, a technological advance in printmaking, from England to Philadelphia, where he emigrated with his family. He became an extremely successful artist with his engravings published in **Graham's Magazine, Godey's Lady's Book** and **Burton's Gentleman's Magazine.** Financially successful, he purchased the **Union Magazine** for $5,000 in 1848 along with William Sloanaker, the former business manager of **Graham's Magazine.** The name of the magazine was changed to **Sartain's Union Magazine of Literature and Art.**

Sartain's Union Magazine became a critical success, publishing Edgar Allan Poe's poem "The Bells" (November 1849) and Poe's essay "The Poetic Principle." John Sartain and Poe had previously worked together at **Graham's** and had become friends. In addition to Poe, **Sartain's** published important work by Henry Wadsworth Longfellow, James Russell Lowell, N.P. Willis, W. Gilmore Simms, the first English publication of "A Voyage in a Balloon" by Jules Verne (1852), and Catharine Maria Sedgwick's "Might Versus Right" and "Owasanook." The magazine also published the work of a little-known essayist named Henry David Thoreau with a series called "Ktaadn and the Maine Woods"(1848), "The Iron Horse" and "A Poet Buying a Farm" (1852). Unfortunately, the magazine was never a financial success and was forced to close down in 1852.

Single unremarkable issue	$45	January-December 1848 (Thoreau)	$400
January-June 1849 (Poe)	$150	July-December 1849 (Poe, "The Bells")	$250
January-June 1850 (Poe, "Annabel Lee")	$350	July-December 1850 (Poe)	$250
January-December 1851	$150	January-August 1852 (Jules Verne, Thoreau, "Walden")	$2,500

Saturday Evening Post (1821-1973)

"The **Saturday Evening Post** is the oldest Journal in America, having appeared regularly every week for the past 174 years, except for the short period when Philadelphia was in the hands of the British Army. The magazine was founded in 1728 and was edited and published by Benjamin Franklin, in whose day it was known as **The Pennsylvania Gazette.** In 1765, the publication passed into other hands, but its name continued until 1821 when it was changed to **The Saturday Evening Post** (Atkinson & Alexander, Aug. 4, 1821). The magazine was purchased in 1897 by The Curtis Publishing Company." (1902, from **The Saturday Evening Post** editorial page.) Cyrus Curtis, the owner of **The Ladies' Home Journal,** bought the **Post** from George R. Graham (**Graham's Magazine**) for $1,000. Graham had turned it into "A Family Newspaper, Neutral in Politics, Devoted to Morality, Pure Literature, Foreign and Domestic News, Agriculture, the Commercial Interests, Science, Art, and Amusement" with a circulation of 90,000.

The **Saturday Evening Post** was redesigned and, in January 1898, reappeared as a weekly publication. Curtis hired George Horace Lorimer as the editor and gave him total control. Lorimer shaped the **Post** into a magazine legend. In 1903, Lorimer paid $700 for the rights to serialize Jack London's *Call of the Wild* (June 20-July 18, 1903), illustrated by Charles Livingston Bull. Under Lorimer's direction, in 1908 the *Post* was selling more than 1 million copies a week and by 1913 had reached 2 million.

In March 1916, Lorimer met the young Norman Rockwell, thus embarking on Rockwell's long-term relationship with the magazine that lasted more than 45 years with 317 covers. In fact, there are books devoted solely to Rockwell's **Post** covers and their collectible prices. While Rockwell's wholesome images were closely aligned with the **Post's** ideals, other notable Lorimer **Post** cover artists were Harrison Fisher, J.C. Leyendecker, N.C. Wyeth, Philip Boileau, Penrhyn Stanlaws, Edward Penfield, Sarah Stilwell-Weber, Neysa McMein, John Knowles Hare, James McKell and John LaGatta. **Post** writers were a who's who of American and British fiction, contributing the "Uncle Remus" tales of Joel

Chandler Harris, Bret Harte, "The Proud Sheriff" by Eugene Manlove Rhodes, "Babylon Revisited" by F. Scott Fitzgerald, Agatha Christie's "Hercule Poirot" mysteries, "The Chase of the Golden Plate" by Jacques Futrelle, Albert Payson Terhune, P.G. Wodehouse, Earl Derr Biggers' "Charlie Chan," Ellis Parker Butler, Edith Wharton, Ring Lardner, William Faulkner, Irvin Cobb, Rex Stout, and the short story "Lassie" by Eric Knight, which evolved into a book and a literary icon. Circulation climbed to 3 million in 1937, and kept climbing throughout the war years until eventually it reached more than 6 million. However, the advent of television, the changing taste of American pop culture and legal problems brought about its demise.

Single issue unremarkable pre-1940s	$15	June 20-July 18, 1903 (Jack London, *Call of the Wild* complete)	$500
Sept. 19, 1903 (Joel Chandler Harris)	$25	Nov. 12, 19 and Dec. 3, 10, 17, 1904 (Florence Maybrick complete)	$150
Jan. 7, 1905 (Harrison Fisher cover)	$50	Sept, 29, 1906 (Jacques Futrelle)	$35
May 18, 1907 (Philip Goodwin)	$45	Sept. 26, 1908 (N.C. Wyeth cover)	$50
June 24, 1911 (Jack London, G.K. Chesterton)	$45	April 5, 1913 (Jack London, John R. Neill)	$45
June 21, 1913 (J.C. Leyendecker cover)	$85	Jan. 16, 1915 (Philip Boileau cover)	$40
May 1, 1915 (Rhodes, Mary Roberts Rinehart, Sarah Stil-Weber cover)	$40	May 20, 1916 (Rockwell's first cover)	$200
April 13, 1918 (Ellis Parker Butler)	$25	Nov. 13, 1920 (Octavus Roy Cohen, Neysa McMein cover)	$35
Oct. 29, 1921 (Ring Lardner)	$25	Jan. 28, 1922 (Terhune)	$35
June 21, 1930 (James McKell cover)	$25	February 1931 (Fitzgerald, "Babylon Revisited")	$45
June 18, 1932 (Earl Der Biggers, "Charlie Chan")	$35	Oct. 1, 1932 (Eugene Manlove Rhodes)	$35
Nov. 12, 1932 (Edith Wharton)	$25	Dec. 23, 1933 (P.G. Wodehouse, Leyendecker cover)	$65
Dec. 3, 1932 (William Faulkner)	$40	June 24, 1933 (F. Scott Fitzgerald, P.G. Wodehouse, Iverd cover)	$65
Feb. 3, 1934 (Penrhyn Stanlaws cover)	$40	June 22, 1935 (Rex Stout, Stribling, Iverd cover)	$50
May 15, 1937 (Agatha Christie, Leyendecker cover)	$65	July 4, 1936 (Leyendecker's Uncle Sam cover)	$125
April 23, 1938 (Rose Wilder Lane, Rockwell cover)	$75	Dec. 17, 1938 (Eric Knight, "Lassie," Rockwell cover)	$250

The Savoy (1896)

The Savoy was very much the stepchild of the **Yellow Book** (qv.). It hinged on three people, Leonard Smithers, a bookseller and fitful publisher; Arthur Symons, whose third book *London Nights,* published by Smithers, was the literary scandal of the season; and Aubrey Beardsley, recently dismissed in the Wilde flap at **Yellow Book.** Though it only lasted nine issues, two quarterly and seven monthly, all in 1896, **The Savoy** managed to publish a great many important pieces and no issue really seems to take precedence with collectors. Aside from the fact that every **Savoy** was an original Beardsley production, original poetry and short stories by W.B. Yeats, Ernest Dowson, Symonds and Beardsley are highly sought after, as are reviews of Neitzsche, Zola and Hardy's *Jude the Obscure* by Havelock Ellis. Symond's translation of Verlaine in the second issue, and his translation of Mallarme in the eighth; Yeats' essay on Blake spanning issues one, three and five; and Max Beerbohm's caricatures are all reasons **The Savoy** is a top ranked collectible. The magazine failed to draw an audience and, in the final issue, Symonds posited the whys of the failure of **The Savoy:** "...And then, worst of all, we assumed that there were very many people in the world who really cared for art, and really for art's sake. The more I consider it, the more I realize that this is not the case. Comparatively few people care for art at all, and most of these care for it because they mistake it for something else."

Complete set	$5,200	January 1896	$500
April 1896	$450	June 1896	$375
July 1896	$425	August 1896	$375
September 1896	$375	October 1896	$425
November 1896	$475	December 1896	$525

Scientific American (1845-present)

Scientific American claims to be the oldest continuously published publicly circulated magazine in the United States. It was founded in 1845 as a weekly broadsheet, subtitled "The Advocate of Industry and Enterprise, and Journal of Mechanical and Other Improvements," by Rufus Porter, who sold it to Orson Desaix Munn and Alfred Ely Beach after the 10th issue. The magazine founded the first branch of the U.S. Patent Agency in 1850 and added a Washington, D.C., branch in 1859. By 1900, more than 100,000 inventions had been patented using the technical help and legal advice of **Scientific American. Scientific American** chronicled major discoveries and inventions such as the Bessemer steel converter, the telephone and the incandescent light bulb. Thomas Edison, Samuel Morse and Elias Howe all contributed to the magazine under Munn & Company, which owned it for more than a century.

The magazine stayed ahead of the trends with articles on Marconi's experiments two decades before the advent of radio, photographs of the Wright Brothers' plane nearly two years before the successful Kitty Hawk flight, and Robert Goddard defending and explaining his work on developing a rocket capable of reaching "interplanetary distances" in 1921. In 1927, **Scientific American** reported on television. Gerard Piel, Dennis Flanagan and Donald Miller purchased **Scientific American** from Munn & Company in 1948. During the period of their ownership, several Nobel laureates published articles, and collectible issues featured such scientists as Albert Einstein, Francis Crick, Jonas Salk and Linus Pauling. The magazine was purchased by Verlagsgruppe Georg von Holtzbrinck, a German-based publishing group, in 1986 and continues to be published from New York.

Unremarkable Porter/Munn issues	$20	Unremarkable Piel/Flanagan issues	$15
Post-1986 issues	$5	June 1, 1889	$25
June 4, 1898	$40	Aug. 6, 1898	$50
Oct. 15, 1898	$50	April 20, 1901	$40
Jan. 9, 1904	$75	Dec. 15, 1906	$45
Dec. 4, 1908	$40	April 3, 1915	$35
June 17, 1916	$25	Feb. 16, 1918	$25

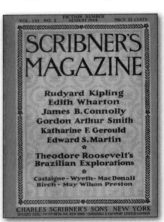

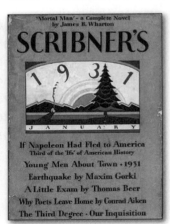

Scribner's (1887-1939)

First published in January 1887, it has been claimed that Charles Scribner's Sons spent more than $500,000 in setting up **Scribner's Magazine.** It was designed to compete with the successful **Atlantic Monthly** and **Harper's** magazines, as well as provide an additional outlet to advertise and review Scribner's books. The editor, Edward Burlingame, employed some of the best engravers in the country, making **Scribner's** an especially strong illustrative magazine. Primarily a literary journal, **Scribner's** occasionally published political material. This included the groundbreaking "How the Other Half Lives" (1889) and "The Poor in Great Cities" (1892) by Jacob A. Riis.

Scribner's was among the first American magazines to use full-color illustrations, which created a sensation in the magazine world when first introduced in 1900. **Scribner's Magazine** employed artists such as Howard Pyle, Howard Christy, Charles Marion Russell, Walter Everett, Maxfield Parrish and Frederic Remington in its heyday. Theodore Roosevelt had "African Game Trails" published in the magazine from October 1909 to September 1910, when the magazine reached its height of 215,000 subscribers. **Scribner's** employed writers such as Richard Harding Davis, Edith Wharton and John Galsworthy during World War I. From the American entrance into the war in 1917, each edition of **Scribner's** included four to six articles on the war. By 1930, circulation was down to 70,000 and the magazine had become a drag on the successful book publishing operations. **Scribner's** continued to produce the magazine through a final issue in May 1939.

Unremarkable single issue	$5	Unremarkable six-month volume	$20
Serials: Joel Chandler Harris "A Rainy Day with Uncle Remus," June-August 1881 Single issue	$55	Full run or volume	$225
Arthur Symonds, "The Waters of Venice," illustrated by Maxfield Parrish, January-June 1906 Single issue	$35	Full run or volume	$250
Ernest Hemingway, "A Farewell to Arms," May-October 1929 Single issue	$300	Full run or two volumes	$1,500
May 1887	$35	January 1889	$75
October 1895	$25	November 1913	$45
May 1920	$65	May 1930	$25
September 1930	$25	January 1931	$50
June 1931	$45	January 1932	$25
April 1933	$85	January 1938	$25

Smart Set (1900-1930)

The Smart Set arrived on March 10, 1900, with publisher Colonel William D'Alton Mann vowing its aim would "...simply and solely be to entertain 'smart' people." Subtitled "The Magazine of Cleverness," **Smart Set** aimed to be the master of the bon mot, the magazine most quoted in fashionable drawing rooms. It grew out of **Town Topics,** a society sheet that the Colonel had turned into one of the first "society gossip" weeklies. Under its first three editors, Arthur Grissom, Marvin Dana and Charles Harrison Towne, **The Smart Set** introduced Zona Gale, Henry Seidel Canby, Stewart Edward White, Frank Norris, Joaquin Miller and William Sydney Porter (O. Henry). In fact it was **Smart Set's** check for "The Lotos and the Bottle" that paid Porter's train ticket to New York from Pittsburgh.

In 1909, George Jean Nathan and H.L. Mencken joined the staff. John Adams Thayer purchased **The Smart Set** from Colonel Mann in 1911, turning over the managing editor's job to Norman Boyer, who really was just a "front" for Thayer himself. Thayer brought James Montgomery Flagg and Rose Cecil O'Neill on board. In 1913, Willard Huntington Wright, better known by his later pseudonym S.S. Van Dine, took the helm from Thayer and his surrogates and, with the help of Mencken and Nathan, set about transforming **Smart Set** into an irreverent, and often satirical literary magazine. Wright introduced D.H. Lawrence, George Moore, Yeats, Conrad, Robert Bridges and Strindberg to American audiences, and cultivated the homegrown talents of Albert Payson Terhune, Theodore Dreiser, Djuna Barnes, Ezra Pound, Sara Teasdale and Achmed Abdullah (Michael Romanoff). Wright only lasted a little more than a year before coming into conflict with Thayer.

The magazine drifted and Thayer sold it to paper magnate Eugene Crowe for bad debts at the end of 1914. Crowe turned it over to his publishing partner Eltinge Warner, who turned it over to Nathan and Mencken. Mencken and Nathan took over a nearly bankrupt magazine, printed on inferior paper. Without the wherewithal to pay top writers, the two editors invented pseudonyms and wrote many pieces themselves, as well as hunted for talented beginners. That hunt turned up Jim Tully, F. Scott Fitzgerald, Dashiell Hammett and Eugene O'Neill. By 1920, **Smart Set** was known as "the Aristocrat of Magazines." Talented newcomers drew established names despite the low pay: W. Somerset Maugham and James Branch Cabell, along with Theodore Dreiser and even Dorothy Parker, who made no secret of her dislike of Mencken, published in it. By 1923, **Smart Set** was a hot property again. At the beginning of 1924, **Smart Set** became the property of the Hearst magazine chain, while Mencken and Nathan moved on to the **The American Mercury** (qv.). Hearst tried three different incarnations in an attempt to revive **Smart Set,** but declining circulation and the fact that its stars went to Mencken and Nathan's **Mercury** doomed the magazine, which published its final issue June 15, 1930.

Unremarkable single issue	**$25**	September 1901	**$45**
May 1902	**$40**	January 1903	**$85**
August 1906	**$35**	June 1908	**$55**
May 1913	**$45**	August 1913 (Robinson Jeffers)	**$125**
September 1913 (Ezra Pound and D.H. Lawrence)	**$250**	November 1914	**$40**
March 1915	**$35**	May 1915	**$55**
May 1918	**$50**	November 1919 (F. Scott Fitzgerald)	**$175**
July 1923	**$35**	November 1923	**$35**

Southern Literary Messenger (1834-1864)

"Devoted to Every Department of Literature and the Fine Arts," **Southern Literary Messenger** was founded at Richmond, Va., by Thomas W. White. The magazine depended on Southern patriotism for its success, although it published Northern writers, too. After successfully publishing "Berenice," "Morella," and "Lionizing" in the **Messenger,** Edgar Allan Poe became the editor from July 1835 to January 1837. During Poe's tenure, circulation increased from 700 to 5,500. Poe also contributed his works, which included 83 reviews, six poems, four essays and three stories. Although White dismissed Poe as editor about Dec. 3, 1836, his official retirement was with the January issue. Poe remained a contributor until his death in 1849. His final contribution to the **Messenger,** "Annabel Lee," actually appeared a month after his death in the November 1849 issue.

Single unremarkable issue	$40	January 1835 (Poe possible)	$100
February 1835 (Poe possible)	$100	March 1835 (Poe)	$300
April 1835 (Poe)	$300	May 1835 (Poe)	$300
June 1835 (Poe)	$300	July 1835 (Poe)	$300
August 1835 (Poe)	$300	September 1835 (Poe)	$300
August 1836 (Poe)	$250	January 1837 (Poe, "Arthur Gordon Pym")	$350
February 1837 (Poe, "Arthur Gordon Pym")	$350	May 1837 (Poe)	$300
December 1844 (Poe)	$300	November 1849 (Poe, "Annabel Lee")	$350
May 1864 (Civil War)	$50		

St. Nicholas (1873-1943)

Designed for children, **St. Nicholas** magazine was published by Scribner's, debuting in November 1873. Mary Mapes Dodge was its editor until 1905, assisted by Frank Stockton from 1873 through 1876. William Fayal Clarke, from 1905-1927, was another long-term editor who shaped the magazine. **St. Nicholas** had a different focus from the older children's magazines, such as **Robert Merry's Museum** (qv.), and focused more on children's enjoyment than on didactic lessons.

The magazine was well produced under all three of its publishers: Scribner's, Century and American Educational Press/ Education Publishing, treating children with respect and not condescending to them. It published poems by Edna St. Vincent Millay and stories by Kipling, Ring Lardner and even a young William Faulkner. Rebecca Harding Davis, Sarah Orne Jewett, Frank Stockton, William Cullen Bryant, Rose Terry Cook, Bret Harte, Bayard Taylor and John Kendrich Bangs were among many normally adult-oriented authors publishing alongside Dodge, L. Frank Baum, Laura E. Richards, Louisa Mae Alcott, Carolyn

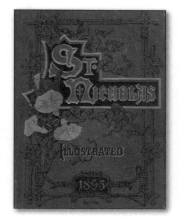

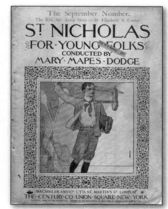

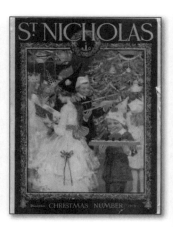

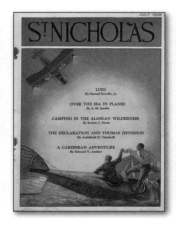

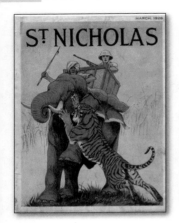
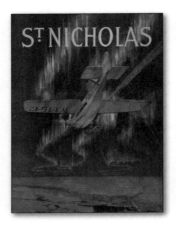
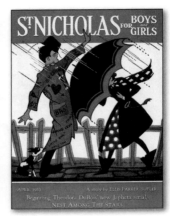

Wells and other classic children's writers. The illustrations by such
artists as W.W. Denslow, Harrison Cady, Gustave Dore, James
Montgomery Flagg, Maxfield Parrish, Howard Pyle and many
other top illustrators makes many issues of **St. Nicholas** exceptional
collectibles. **St. Nicholas** was published until paper shortages
resulting from World War II forced it to suspend publication with
the June issue of 1943.

Unremarkable issue pre-1930	**$15**	Unremarkable issue post-1930	**$7.50**
Bound in six-month books. Yearly volumes by publisher.			
Unremarkable six months	**$20**	Unremarkable yearly volume	**$35**
Serials:			
Louisa Mae Alcott, "Eight Cousins," 1875			
Issue	**$25**	Full run	**$300**
G.A. Henty, "The Sole Survivors," 1898-1899			
Issue	**$35**	Full run	**$425**
Jack London, "The Cruise of the Dazzler," 1902			
Issue	**$35**	Full run	**$325**
Issues containing Arthur Rackham	**$125**	July 1874	**$45**
March 1875	**$175**	May 1875	**$200**
January 1909	**$250**	February 1909	**$200**
November 1910	**$125**	April 1915	**$35**
October 1927	**$50**		

Story (1931-2000)

Story magazine was founded in 1931 by journalist and editor Whit Burnett, and his first wife, Martha Foley. The inaugural April/May 1931 issue of Story (167 copies) was printed on an old mimeograph machine in Vienna, Austria, and featured short stories by new authors. Story moved to New York City in 1933, where its success allowed the creation of The Story Press in 1936. By 1940, Story was over 20,000 circulation and had discovered such new authors as Joseph Heller, J.D. Salinger, Tennessee Williams and Richard Wright, as well as published the early work by Carson McCullers, William Saroyan and Ludwig Bemelmans. During the 1940s, Burnett, with his second wife, Hallie Southgate Burnett, continued to work with new authors through The Story Press and Story, publishing Norman Mailer, Truman Capote and John Knowles.

Through most of the 1950s, Story Press concentrated on books, suspending the magazine, which returned in 1960 and was suspended again in 1967 due to a lack of funds. A version of Story was published from 1989 to 2000, under the auspices of F+W Publications in Cincinnati, Ohio, and headed by publisher Richard Rosenthal and editor Lois Rosenthal. It reached a circulation of more than 40,000 subscribers at its height as a quarterly magazine, publishing Andrea Barrett, Barry Lopez, Joyce Carol Oates, Carol Shields, Junot Díaz, Elizabeth Graver and Abraham Rodriguez. Story ceased publication with a final Winter 2000 issue.

Unremarkable single issue	$15	June 1933	$30
December 1933	$25	January 1934	$25
May 1934	$75	November 1934	$60
April 1935	$25	April 1936	$25
June 1936	$25	July 1936	$25
August 1936	$250	August 1937	$35
March 1938	$25	May/June 1939	$25
September/October 1939	$50	January/February 1940	$25
March/April 1940 (First publication of J.D. Salinger)	$900	July/August 1941	$40
December/November 1942	$25	July/August 1943	$25
March/April 1945	$300	May/June 1945	$50
May/June 1963	$25		

Strand Magazine (1891-1950)

With the possible exception of Henry Luce's incarnation of **Life,** no middle class, general interest magazine has ever approached the success of George Newnes' **Strand. The Strand Magazine** mirrored the tastes, prejudices and intellectual limitations of the British middle class for half a century in the illustrated magazine that dethroned **Cornhill's** as Britain's magazine of fiction and **Macmillan's** as the king of journalism. From the first issue in January 1891, it was clear that **The Strand** was intended as entertainment. Newnes, a liberal and for a while a member of Parliament, was not a crusader in the pages of his magazine. He published only mild controversy and, instead, was content to mirror the conventions and poke subtle fun at the curiosities and eccentricities of his audience.

Newnes and his editor, H. Greenhough Smith, actively sought popular writers, shying away from the "literary." As Reginald Pound, editor from 1941-1946, put it: "...Pedestrian writers in a non-derogatory sense. Their feet planted squarely upon common ground...they remained content with the surer profits to be earned toiling on the lower slopes." Those "lower slopes" produced Arthur Conan Doyle's Sherlock Holmes and, with him, the popular acceptance of the modern mystery genre. Rudyard Kipling, Agatha Christie, W. Somerset Maugham, H.G. Wells, Anthony Hope, O. Henry, Dorothy L. Sayers, Aldous Huxley, Arnold Bennett, Grahame Greene, P.G. Wodehouse, H.C. McNeile (Sapper), Arthur Morrison and numerous other popular authors were published in **The Strand,** and several were introduced by it.

The Strand reveled in being in touch with the ordinary citizen, while **Macmillan's** featured didactic scientific articles and even a published argument between two of the age's greatest theologians. **The Strand** had popular writer Grant Allen explaining science as though to grade school children, and the theologians were pictured in light, entertaining "Illustrated Interviews." **The Strand** would last until 1950. Its demise was announced as if it were the death of a prominent figure on the BBC and echoed through the world's media as the extinction of a "British institution." Few magazines have ever had the influence of **The Strand,** on society, on illustration, on literature. And yet, the original premise was only to produce a magazine with "...a picture on every page." **The Strand** is generally collected, and original appearances of numerous articles, stories, serials and illustrations bring premium prices in the collector's market.

Unremarkable issue	**$20**	Unremarkable six-month volume bound by Newnes (Blue binding)	**$65**
Unremarkable six-month volume privately bound	**$35**	Volume One #1	**$55**
Volume One in Newnes' binding	**$100**	Volume One in private binding	**$75**

"The Adventures of Sherlock Holmes" First Series & Second Series, July 1891-June 1892

Single issues	**$50**	Complete run	**$650**
Volumes in Newnes' binding	**$300**	Volumes in private binding	**$150**

"The First Men in the Moon," December 1900-November 1901

Single issues	**$60**	Complete run	**$500**
Volumes in Newnes' binding	**$300**	Volumes in private binding	**$100**

"The Hound of the Baskervilles," July 1901-June 1902

Single issues	**$60**	Complete run	**$750**
Volumes in Newnes' binding	**$400**	Volumes in private binding	**$175**

Volumes or run containing "The First Men in the Moon" and "The Hound of the Baskervilles," December 1900-June 1902 **$1,500**

"The Return of Sherlock Holmes"

Single issues	**$50**	Complete run	**$650**
Volumes in Newnes' binding	**$350**	Volumes in private binding	**$125**

Issues containing Conan Doyle complete in issue **$45**

Issues containing Conan Doyle serials

Single issues	**$45**	Complete run	**$500**
Volumes in Newnes' binding	**$300**	Volumes in private binding	**$100**

October 1910 (E. Nesbit)	**$45**	April 1920 (P.G. Wodehouse)	**$90**
June 1920 (P.G. Wodehouse)	**$80**	July 1920 (P.G. Wodehouse)	**$90**
February 1921 (P.G. Wodehouse)	**$90**	July 1923 (P.G. Wodehouse)	**$75**
June 1930 (Edgar Wallace)	**$90**	February 1931 (W.S. Churchill)	**$100**
April 1931 (Sapper)	**$90**	December 1935 (P.G. Wodehouse)	**$100**
June 1937 (Margery Allingham)	**$45**	August 1937 (P.G. Wodehouse)	**$45**

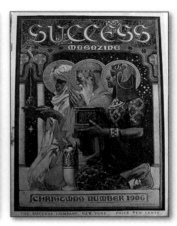

Success (1897-1924)

Founded by Orison Swett Marden in 1897, **Success** was
initially a non-fiction monthly featuring biographical sketches and
articles espousing the virtue of success. It featured contributions by
Theodore Dreiser, Booker T. Washington, Edward Everett Hale,
Mary A. Livermore and Julia Ward Howe in the early years of its
existence. After its first year, **Success** began to include fiction, such
as "The Magic Story" by Frederick Van Rensselaer Day. James H.
McGraw became its financial backer in 1900, and a major shift in
editorial viewpoint followed, with the magazine joining the popular
muckraking movement of the day. Merged with **The National Post**
in 1911, the merged magazine ceased publication five months later.
Revived by Marden in 1918, the magazine regained much of its
early success, only to end its second incarnation three years after
Marden's death in 1924. Several attempts to revive it produced a
few magazines with the title up to today.

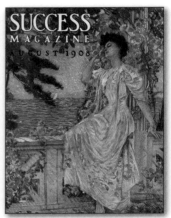

Unremarkable issue under Marden's editorship (either series)	**$75**	1898-1890 issue containing a Theodore Dreiser interview	**$175**
Feb. 4, 1899 (Ella Wheeler Wilcox interview)	**$225**	June 1900 (H. Rider Haggard)	**$200**
April 1908 (Herbert Dunton)	**$150**	December 1906	**$125**
Yearly volume	**$1,500**	Volume XII (1909)	**$2,000**

Sunday Magazine/Associated, Illustrated (1904-1918)

The **Sunday Magazine** was a weekly supplement published nationally and syndicated by two separate companies to various newspapers throughout the United States. They were usually about 20 pages of articles, fiction, poetry and serialized fiction with covers and interiors illustrated by important illustrators such as Joseph Clement Coll, James Montgomery Flagg, Rolf Armstrong, Philip Boileau, Earl Christy, J. Knowles Hare, Neysa McMein, Coles Phillips, Gene Pressler, Charles Livingston Bull, Haskell Coffin and Penrhyn Stanlaws.

Perhaps the most important of the syndicates was the **Associated Sunday Magazine** (it later became **Every Week,** a separate publication), which were carried in the *Boston Sunday Post, Buffalo Courier, Chicago Sunday Record-Herald, Denver Rocky Mountain News, Detroit News Tribune, Minneapolis Journal, New York Tribune, Philadelphia Press, Pittsburgh Sunday Post, St. Louis Republic* and *Washington Sunday Star.* The other important syndicate was the **Illustrated Sunday Magazine**, which appeared in the *Boston Sunday Herald, Buffalo Sunday Times, Cleveland*

Leader, Detroit Free Press, Louisville Courier-Journal, Milwaukee Sunday Sentinel, Minneapolis Tribune, New Orleans Daily Picayune, Philadelphia Record, Pittsburgh Gazette Times, Providence Sunday Tribune, Rochester Democrat and *Worcester Sunday Telegram.* In addition to the illustrators, important contributing writers included Kate M. Cleary (1905), Booker T. Washington, Arthur Conan Doyle's serializations of "Sir Nigel"(1906), the "Lost World"(1912) and the "Valley of Fear"(1914), Earl Derr Biggers' serialization of his first novel "Seven Keys To Baldpate"(1913), Jeffrey Farnol serialization "The Money Moon"(1911), L.M. Montgomery, C.N. and A.M. Williamson, John Kendrick Bangs and George Ade.

Although the paper quality of the Sunday Magazines was finer than the newspapers that carried them, they remain relatively scarce since they were discarded along with yesterday's papers.

Associated Sunday Magazine unremarkable single issue	**$10**
Associated Sunday Magazine Dec. 3, 1905-April 15, 1906, complete 20 issues (Doyle/Coll, "Sir Nigel")	**$750**
Associated Sunday Magazine (Doyle/Coll, "Sir Nigel") single issues	**$35**
Associated Sunday Magazine (Doyle/Coll, "Sir Nigel") Dec. 3, 1905, Jan. 14, Feb. 4, 1906 full color Coll covers each	**$50**
Associated Sunday Magazine March 26, 1905 (Kate Cleary)	**$30**
Associated Sunday Magazine April 16, 1905 (Kate Cleary)	**$30**
Associated Sunday Magazine May 21, 1905 (Kate Cleary)	**$30**
Associated Sunday Magazine June 25, 1905 (Booker T. Washington)	**$30**
Associated Sunday Magazine Aug. 20, 1905 (L.M. Montgomery, C.L. Bull cover)	**$25**
Associated Sunday Magazine June 30, 1907 (C.N.& A.M. Williamson)	**$25**
Associated Sunday Magazine March 22, 1908 (W.W. Denslow)	**$125**
Associated Sunday Magazine May 10, 1908 (Coll color cover)	**$50**
Associated Sunday Magazine March 20, 1910 (J.M. Flagg cover)	**$25**
Associated Sunday Magazine April 24, 1910 (Coll color cover)	**$50**

Associated Sunday Magazine Feb. 12, 1911 (Coll)	**$35**
Associated Sunday Magazine March 5, 1911 (Coll)	**$35**
Associated Sunday Magazine Oct. 1, 1911 (Jeffrey Farnol)	**$25**
Associated Sunday Magazine March 24, 1912-July 21, 1912 (complete 18 issues with full color March 24 Coll cover, Doyle/Coll, "Lost World")	**$2,000**
Associated Sunday Magazine 1912 single issues (Doyle/Coll, "Lost World")	**$100**
Associated Sunday Magazine March 24, 1912 (Coll, "Lost World" color cover)	**$150**
Associated Sunday Magazine Jan. 5, 1913 (Earl Der Biggers)	**$50**
Associated Sunday Magazine Sept. 6, 1914 (Coll/Doyle Tribute)	**$75**
Associated Sunday Magazine Sept. 13, 1914-Nov. 22, 1914 (Doyle, "Valley of Fear," Sherlock Holmes, complete)	**$1,500**
Associated Sunday Magazine single issue (Doyle, "Valley of Fear")	**$100**

Illustrated Sunday Magazine unremarkable single issue	**$7.50**
Illustrated Sunday Magazine Jan. 30, 1910 (Addison Saunders cover)	**$10**
Illustrated Sunday Magazine Dec. 11, 1910 (Earl Christy cover, Ellis Parker Butler)	**$15**
Illustrated Sunday Magazine April 9, 1911 (John Kendrick Bangs)	**$15**
Illustrated Sunday Magazine Nov. 26, 1911 (Earl Christy cover, John Kendrick Bangs)	**$15**
Illustrated Sunday Magazine Jan. 14, 1912 (Earl Christy cover, Elbert Hubbard)	**$15**
Illustrated Sunday Magazine Jan. 28, 1912 (Gelett Burgess)	**$10**
Illustrated Sunday Magazine July 21, 1912 (C.N. Williamson, Berton Braley)	**$15**

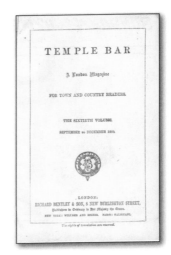

Temple Bar (1860-1906)

"A London Magazine for Town and Country Readers,"
Temple Bar was originally published by John Maxwell with
George Augustus Sala as the first editor (Anthony Trollope declined
the position in 1861). **Temple Bar** was initially an imitation
of **Cornhill Magazine.** In 1866, publisher Richard Bentley
combined **Bentley's Miscellany** with **Temple Bar** and appointed
his son, George Bentley, as editor. The audience of **Temple Bar**
was the middle-class Victorian reader. To that end, the periodical
featured literary essays, and current religious and scientific topics,
interspersed with entertaining stories and serialized novels.

The magazine attracted all the better known writers who
had contributed to **Bentley's Miscellany.** It presented the first
publication of "The American Senator" (May 1876-July 1877) by
Anthony Trollope and "The New Magdalen" (October 1872-July
1873). Other important writers who contributed to **Temple Bar**
included Bret Harte, Sheridan Le Fanu, Marie Corelli, Robert Louis
Stevenson, George Kingsley, Rhoda Broughton and Arthur Conan
Doyle with "Our Midnight Visitor" (February 1891). **Temple Bar's**
popularity declined with the death of George Bentley in 1895,
although Doyle was still a contributor, and Tolstoy, Turgenev and
Balzac were still being translated. Macmillan and Company bought
it in 1898 and struggled to keep it afloat until 1906.

Unremarkable four-month volumes **$15**			
Volume 1	**$165**	Volume 2	**$150**
Volume 3	**$120**	Volume 5	**$120**
Volume 11	**$200**	Volume 40	**$200**
Volume 65	**$50**	Volume 74	**$50**
Serial: Wilkie Collins, "The New Magdalen," October 1872-January 1874			
Single issue	**$45**	Complete run	**$900**

transition (1927-1950)

Created as a refuge for experimental writers by journalist, poet and linguist Eugene Jolas, his wife Maria and Elliot Paul, **transition** was, perhaps, the single most important journal of the modernist literary tradition. The object, from the beginning, was to create an outlet where diverse and innovative writers could express themselves and experiment in a "laboratory of the word" free from the restrictions of overly commercial publishing houses and conventional criticism. Finding the United States at the time far too restrictive while working at the **Double Dealer** (qv.), Jolas established **transition** in Paris in 1927 as a fitful quarterly.

transition was initially compounded of early modernist writers and rebellious American expatriate authors, such as James Joyce, William Carlos Williams, H.D., Alfred Kreymborg, Gertrude Stein, Kay Boyle, Samuel Beckett and Muriel Rukeyser, along with political writers, Negro voices from the Harlem Renaissance and various other artistic schools. This mix brought about a philosophical combination of irrational surrealism and language innovation, labeled "vertigralism." **transition** expanded into other art forms accepting a far greater variety of artistic genres including sculptors, civil rights activists, carvers, critics, and cartoonists. **transition** continued through the Spring issue of 1938 and is credited with establishing the avant-gardist tradition in new literary philosophies. Georges Duthuit revived it for six issues in 1948-1950.

Complete set of 27 Jolas issues	**$7,900**	transition 1	**$250**
transition 2	**$225**	transition 3	**$225**
transition 4	**$175**	transition 5	**$275**
transition 6	**$100**	transition 7	**$200**
transition 8	**$210**	transition 9	**$230**
transition 10	**$125**	transition 11	**$115**
transition 12	**$100**	transition 13	**$225**
transition 14	**$135**	transition 15	**$200**
transition 16	**$150**	transition 17	**$125**
transition 18	**$160**	transition 19	**$100**
transition 20	**$125**	transition 21	**$175**
transition 22	**$100**	transition 23	**$150**
transition 24	**$100**	transition 25	**$150**
transition 26 (Duchamps)	**$335**	transition 27	**$150**
Duthuit revival 1948-1950			**$30 each**

True (1937-1973)

True The Man's Magazine was the second generation of Captain Billy's Whiz Bang (qv.). It resulted from an expansion of Wilford Fawcett's magazine enterprises under his four sons. The Whiz Bang was transformed into Whiz Comics and featured Captain Marvel, a phenomenal success. The old Whiz Bang audience was served by the new True The Man's Magazine, debuting in 1937. True, like its predecessor, was slightly off-color and mildly disreputable, though it only vaguely hinted at the erotica that would dethrone it as the leading man's magazine in the 1960s with the rise of Playboy (qv.). Shunning nude photos, True featured pin-up art, notably the work of George Petty. Many True covers featured scantily clad ladies in distress with strategically ripped blouses. True featured articles on guns, the outdoors and other "manly" pursuits. It also pioneered coverage of the paranormal, outre and fortean phenomena usually mentioned in a blurb in newspapers and other magazines. True led the UFO coverage of the 1950s with articles by retired Marine Major and test pilot Donald Keyhoe. True ceased publication in 1973, unable to use suggestion and double entendre to compete with the overt eroticism of Playboy and the pornography of Penthouse.

Unremarkable single issue	$5	June 1946 (Petty)	$20
November 1946 (Petty)	$25	February 1947 (Keyhoe)	$20
September 1947 (Petty)	$20	January 1952 (Varga)	$30
March 1952 (Varga)	$35	May 1952 (Varga)	$30
August 1959 (Classic cars)	$15	February 1960 (Erroll Flynn)	$15
October 1961 (Shah of Iran)	$20	February 1963 (John Steinbeck)	$45
May 1968 (Colonel Sun)	$10	January-February 1969 (Anniversary issue)	$10

Truth (1881-1905)

Initially published as a news and gossip weekly, **Truth** became a humor magazine a la **Puck** and **Judge**, with brilliant color lithograph cartoons, under the editorship of Blakely Hall around 1891. **Truth** cartoons illustrated by artists such as Archie Gunn, A.B. Wensell, W. Granville-Smith, Thure de Thulstrup, Syd B. Griffin, George Luks and Hy Mayer, did not contain the controversial content that their competitors featured. Two famous comic artists that began their careers in **Truth** were Richard F. Outcault (The Yellow Kid), and the first woman cartoonist, Rose O'Neill (the Kewpies). In 1893, **Truth's** printer, the American Lithographic Company, gained controlling interest in the financially strapped publication. It changed the focus of the magazine to a more serious and artistic bent and, in 1899, it became a monthly featuring exquisitely printed color covers and chromolithos on heavy coated stock. The content included biographies of artists like C.C. Curran by writers such as Theodore Dreiser, famous residences in Newport, fashion news, fiction by Henry James, Stephen Crane and other quality authors, and a children's page. It was considered one of the most beautiful publications in America, with great Art Nouveau covers by William de Leftwich Dodge, Alphonse Mucha, Leyendecker and others. Eventually, financial problems of the American Lithographic Company made it impossible to produce such an extravagant publication and it was forced to close.

June 30, 1894	$30	Dec. 22, 1894	$30
June 22, 1895	$30	Jan. 11, 1896	$30
February 1899 (Dreiser)	$65	April 1899	$45
September 1899 (Dreiser)	$65	June 1900	$45
July 1900	$45		

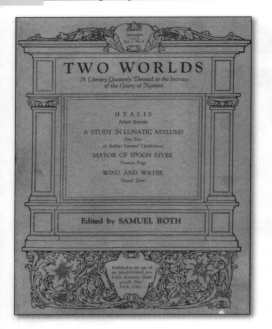 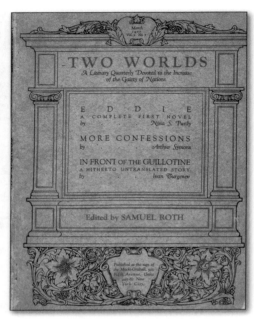

Two Worlds/Casanova Jr.'s Tales/American Aphrodite/Beau Book

Samuel Roth's magazines, all erotic and/or pornographic, were published between his prison terms and all had repercussions in the legal arena. **Two Worlds**' unauthorized publication of banned books such as *Ulysses* by James Joyce created a sensation and the eventual court cases that resulted in Roth's imprisonment paved the way for the publication of such books as Henry Miller's *Tropics* in the United States. Roth's magazines pushed at the envelope of obscenity statutes constantly and are an important part of any collection of banned and censored material.

Two Worlds

Single issue of Volume One (September 1925-June 1926)	**$75**	Single issue of Volumes 2 and 3 (September 1926-December 1927)	**$50**
Complete run of nine issues	**$975**	Volume One	**$150**
Complete run of *Finnegan's Wake* (September 1925-September 1926)	**$750**	Complete run of *Ulysses* (December 1925-March 1927)	**$450**
Bound volumes (three issued, all signed by Roth)	**$350**	Bound volumes (each)	**$100**

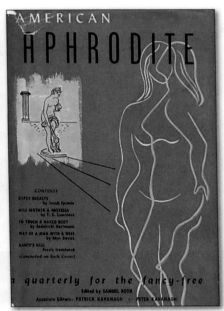

Casanova Jr.

April 1926	$40	July 1926	$40
October 1926	$40	January 1927	$40
April 1927	$35	July 1927	$35
October 1927	$37		

American Aphrodite

Volumes One and Two single issues	$30	Succeeding volumes, single issues	$7

Beau Book

Complete run October 1926-October 1927 (numbered)	$250	Complete run October 1926-October 1927 (unnumbered)	$75
Single issue (numbered)	$25	Single issue (unnumbered)	$10

Vanity Fair (1914-present)

Vanity Fair was to be about "the things people talk about at parties: the arts, sports, humor and so forth," according to its editor Frank Crowninshield. He told his readers that, merely by virtue of being his readers, they belonged to a privileged group. "That we are trying to appeal to Americans of some little sophistication, we not only admit but boast of, but not that pseudo-sophistication bred of money alone, but rather the sophistication which is the natural and happy result of wide travel, some little knowledge of the world, and a pleasing familiarity with the five arts and the four languages," he wrote in an early issue. The magazine was launched by Conde Nast in 1914, under the purchased name of a British literary journal.

Crowninshield was an avid avant gardist and, through **Vanity Fair,** he introduced Americans to Picasso, Rouault, Matisse, Van Gogh and Gaugin. It was a magazine of social culture and good living, according to Crowninshield, "an immense number of things which society, money and position bring in their train: painting, tapestries, rare books, smart dresses, dances, gardens, country houses, correct cuisine and pretty women." Crowninshield's vision resulted in the photography of Edward Steichen, notably of celebrities, and beginning the careers of Dorothy Parker and Robert Benchley. It introduced America to avant garde and future pop culture in e.e. cummings, Man Ray, Gertrude Stein, Walter Winchell, Noël Coward, Edmund Wilson, P.G. Wodehouse, Alexander Woollcott and Cecil Beaton. In reality, a "little" literary/art magazine, overblown in the hands of a major publisher, it was a victim of the Depression, publishing its last issue in December 1936. Revived in 1984, as a clone of Helen Gurley Brown's version of **Cosmopolitan,** it remains in publication.

Unremarkable single issue of revival	**$5**	Unremarkable single issue of original	**$25**
Unremarkable single issue containing Steichen Celebrity Portrait	**$30**	Unremarkable single issue 1917-1920 containing Robert Benchley and/or Dorothy Parker	**$45**
Unremarkable single issue (1915-1934 with John Held Jr. cover or illustration)	**$65**	June 1922 (First Man Ray Paris Portrait)	**$150**
Unremarkable single issue containing Man Ray Portrait	**$85**	July 1923 (Gertrude Stein)	**$65**
Unremarkable single issue (after 1926 containing e.e. cummings)	**$55**	Unremarkable single issue containing Picasso or Matisse	**$50**
Unremarkable single issue (1925-1934 with Miguel Covarrubias cover)	**$55**	October 1933 (Walt Disney)	**$35**
July 1934 (Ernest Hemingway)	**$50**	January 1935 (Uncle Sam)	**$55**
June 1935 (Marlene Dietrich)	**$35**	August 1935 (Adolf Hitler)	**$40**
October 1935 (The Lindberghs)	**$45**		

Vogue (1892-present)

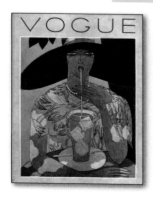

Vogue magazine was founded by Arthur Turnure and Harry McVickar in 1892. It was a fashion magazine similar to **Harper's Bazar,** with simple dress-making patterns that women could purchase by mail. **Vogue's** most influential editor, Edna Woolman Chase, however, featured a hand-cut pattern designed by Rosa Payne in 1905 that created an unheard of demand for original designer **Vogue** patterns. In fact, after the purchase of the magazine by Conde Nast, **Vogue Patterns** grew so large that it eventually became a separate entity. The combination of Mrs. Chase and Conde Nast made **Vogue** an unparalleled influence in the international world of high fashion.

In 1914, World War I halted the Paris couture business. New York City, where **Vogue** was headquartered, became the new fashion center. By 1920, the **Vogue Patterns** business had become so extensive that the patterns no longer appeared in **Vogue** magazine, but were featured instead in their own publication. **Vogue** covered the couture collections of young Parisian designers like Coco Chanel and Jean Patou, who had become the rage with American women. In addition, to fashion coverage, Mrs. Chase featured Art Deco style cover art by Helen Dryden, George Plank, F.X. Leyendecker and George Lepape. Typical **Vogue** features were "Motoring into 1917," "A French Actress and Her Paris Home," "Where The Bahamas Sun Themselves" and "Eloping With Father's Choice." Mrs. Chase, through her artistic and literary choices, set the tone for the magazine's style that exists today.

Single unremarkable issue pre-1950s	**$20**	July 1893	**$35**
September 1899	**$35**	Aug. 1, 1916 (George Plank, Erte)	**$150**
March 15, 1917 (George Lepape)	**$125**	Nov. 15, 1917 (George Plank, Dorothy Parker)	**$150**
March 15, 1918 (Helen Dryden)	**$125**	April 1, 1918 (George Plank Peacock cover)	**$250**
May 15, 1918 (Helen Dryden)	**$125**	Nov. 15, 1918 (George Lepape)	**$125**
Feb 1, 1919 (Messerole cover)	**$125**	June 1, 1920 (Helen Dryden)	**$125**
July 15, 1923 (Bradley Walker Tomlin cover)	**$100**	Jan. 15, 1924 (George Plank cover)	**$125**
Jan. 1, 1925 (George Lepape cover)	**$175**	Dec. 14, 1938	**$30**

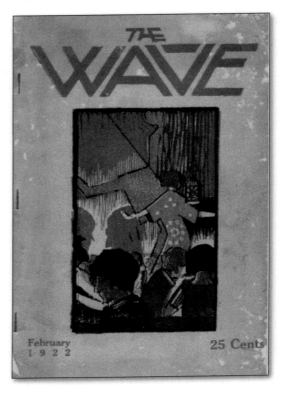

The Wave (1922-1923)

Published somewhat irregularly by Steen Hinrichsen in Chicago in 1922 and 1923, **The Wave** was a little literary magazine edited by Vincent Starrett. There are seven issues of **The Wave**, which was billed as a monthly; the final issue dated September 1923. The magazine reflected Starrett's enthusiasm for Welch author Arthur Machen with three issues including: *The Marriage of Panurge* (January 1922); an excerpt from *The Secret Glory* (February 1922) and *The Art of Dickens* (Christmas 1922). Issue Six in June 1923 was stopped by the post office due to a naked silhouette on the rear cover, and a second printing with a bathing suit covering the silhouette was issued. An extremely scarce collectible, **The Wave** is rarely available and is pricey when a copy, even in fair condition, reaches the market. Tape-repaired copies are sold for more than $100.

Number One, January 1922	**$450**	Number Two, February 1922	**$375**
Number Three, December (Christmas) 1922	**$375**	Number Four, February 1923	**$325**
Number Five, April 1923	**$325**	Number Six A, June 1923 (With naked silhouette)	**$500**
Number Six B, June 1923 (With silhouette in bathing suit)	**$400**	Number Seven, September 1923	**$350**

Windsor (1895-1939)

The Windsor Magazine, "An Illustrated Monthly for Men and Women," was a **Strand**-like publication geared to the Victorian middle class. British royalty was a prime topic, with photos and articles. Obviously, the magazine's use of the name **Windsor** and its cover design of Windsor Castle were part of this marketing concept. While Arthur Conan Doyle did contribute articles and fiction to the **Windsor,** (in fact, his first Sherlock Holmes story, "A Study In Scarlet," was reprinted as a Christmas Supplement in 1895), Holmes via Doyle belonged to **The Strand** audience.

What the **Windsor** did offer to mystery fans, however, was "The Rivals of Sherlock Holmes." Arthur Morrison's "Chronicles of Martin Hewitt, Investigator" presented **The Windsor** audience with a low-key Sherlock Holmes, minus Dr. Watson. More importantly, Morrison's other unique invention, Horace Dorrington, (1897) was an East End scoundrel who became a respected but deeply corrupt private detective. On the side of evil, Guy Boothby presented his "Dr Nikola" stories in **The Windsor**, "Dr. Nikola" being the sinister predecessor to Sax Rohmer's "Dr. Fu Manchu." Other writers who contributed to the success of **The Windsor** included Marie Corelli, H. Rider Haggard (Haggard's "Ayesha, The Return of She" was serialized in **The Windsor** in 1905), Grant Allen, Hall Caine, Rudyard Kipling and Jack London. The illustrations that accompanied **The Windsor** stories

were by artists like Cecil Aldin, Warwick Goble, Louis Wain, Penrhyn Stanlaws and the early work of G.E. Studdy. **The Windsor** definitely was capable of holding its own next to **The Strand.**

Single unremarkable issue **$15**	January-June 1895 (Louis Wain, Arthur Morrison, Le Queux) **$25**
June-November 1897 (Jubilee issue, "Dorrington") **$35**	December 1898-May 1899 (Doyle, Harte) **$50**
December 1900-May 1901 (Haggard, Boothby) **$40**	June-November 1901 (Churchill, Kipling) **$25**
December 1901-May 1902 (Richard Marsh, Pett- Ridge, Kipling) **$25**	June 1903-November 1903 (Baroness Orczy) **$25**
December 1903-May 1904 (Jack London, Ellis Parker Butler) **$45**	June 1904-November 1904 (Jack London, Haggard) **$45**
December 1904-May 1905 (Haggard, "Ayesha") **$100**	June 1905-November 1905 (Haggard, "Ayesha") **$100**
June-November 1908 (P.G. Wodehouse, Jack London) **$65**	December 1908-May 1909 (G.E. Studdy, J.S. Fletcher) **$50**
December 1909-May 1909 (Haggard, "Nile") **$50**	June-November 1912 (William Hope Hodgson, Collies) **$50**

Woman's Home Companion (1911-1957)

Woman's Home Companion was Crowell's women's magazine, a lesser entry in the women's magazine arena until the editorship was given to Gertrude Battles Lane in 1911 and full responsibility given to her in 1912. Under Lane's editorship, the magazine was consistently first or second in circulation among women's magazines through her death in 1941. She introduced the famous "Kewpies" and Dottie Darling by Rose O'Neill, both extremely popular at the time and collectible now.

While leaning toward feminist causes, she published Sinclair Lewis, P.G. Wodehouse, Ellis Parker Butler, Heywood Broun, Dubose Heyward, Carl Sandburg and F. Scott Fitzgerald among articles and stories by women writers such as: Sophie Kerr, Edna Ferber, Mary Wilkins-Freeman, Ellen Glasgow, Elinor Wiley, Marjorie Bowen, Kathleen Norris, Dorothy Canfield, Zona Gale, Edna St. Vincent Millay and Pearl S. Buck. It was a mark of her editorship that she published Katharine Dos Passos, in preference to John, and Eleanor, in preference to Franklin, Roosevelt. The magazine never recovered from the shortages of World War II or the death of Lane, and lingered through declining readership through a final issue in January 1957.

Unremarkable Lane and pre-Lane issues	**$15**	Unremarkable post-Lane issues	**$7.50**
December 1912 (Rose O'Neill, Kewpies)	**$25**	January 1921 (Neysa McMein)	**$45**
December 1925 (F. Scott Fitzgerald)	**$125**	September 1925 (F. Scott Fitzgerald)	**$65**
November 1925 (F. Scott Fitzgerald)	**$75**	May 1927 (F. Scott Fitzgerald)	**$75**
December 1928 (Edna St. Vincent Millay)	**$55**	December 1945 (Steinbeck's "Pearl")	**$75**
February 1951 (Noel Coward)	**$25**	January 1956 (Shirley Jackson)	**$25**

Yank (1942-1945)

Yank, which first appeared on June 17, 1942, was the most widely read and most popular magazine in the history of the U.S. Army. Twenty-three editions were published during World War II, before the last issue in December 1945. With printing presses in Honolulu, Cairo, Tokyo, Okinawa, Rome, Trinidad, Saipan and other places, **Yank's** weekly circulation was 2.6 million, with a readership of nearly 10 million. The magazine was staffed entirely by enlisted soldiers, and employed artists and writers in its New York headquarters and at the front.

Volume One #1 ("Salute")	**$75**	Volume Three #50 June 1, 1945 ("Victory")	**$20**
British editions	**$10**	Unremarkable issues	**$5**
Complete run 1941-1945	**$500**		